C-460 CAREER EXAMINATION SERIES

This is your
PASSBOOK for...

Machinist

Test Preparation Study Guide
Questions & Answers

NATIONAL LEARNING CORPORATION®

COPYRIGHT NOTICE

This book is SOLELY intended for, is sold ONLY to, and its use is RESTRICTED to individual, bona fide applicants or candidates who qualify by virtue of having seriously filed applications for appropriate license, certificate, professional and/or promotional advancement, higher school matriculation, scholarship, or other legitimate requirements of education and/or governmental authorities.

This book is NOT intended for use, class instruction, tutoring, training, duplication, copying, reprinting, excerption, or adaptation, etc., by:

1) Other publishers
2) Proprietors and/or Instructors of "Coaching" and/or Preparatory Courses
3) Personnel and/or Training Divisions of commercial, industrial, and governmental organizations
4) Schools, colleges, or universities and/or their departments and staffs, including teachers and other personnel
5) Testing Agencies or Bureaus
6) Study groups which seek by the purchase of a single volume to copy and/or duplicate and/or adapt this material for use by the group as a whole without having purchased individual volumes for each of the members of the group
7) Et al.

Such persons would be in violation of appropriate Federal and State statutes.

PROVISION OF LICENSING AGREEMENTS – Recognized educational, commercial, industrial, and governmental institutions and organizations, and others legitimately engaged in educational pursuits, including training, testing, and measurement activities, may address request for a licensing agreement to the copyright owners, who will determine whether, and under what conditions, including fees and charges, the materials in this book may be used them. In other words, a licensing facility exists for the legitimate use of the material in this book on other than an individual basis. However, it is asseverated and affirmed here that the material in this book CANNOT be used without the receipt of the express permission of such a licensing agreement from the Publishers. Inquiries re licensing should be addressed to the company, attention rights and permissions department.

All rights reserved, including the right of reproduction in whole or in part, in any form or by any means, electronic or mechanical, including photocopying, recording, or by any information storage and retrieval system, without permission in writing from the Publisher.

Copyright © 2025 by

National Learning Corporation

212 Michael Drive, Syosset, NY 11791
(516) 921-8888 • www.passbooks.com
E-mail: info@passbooks.com

PASSBOOK® SERIES

THE *PASSBOOK® SERIES* has been created to prepare applicants and candidates for the ultimate academic battlefield – the examination room.

At some time in our lives, each and every one of us may be required to take an examination – for validation, matriculation, admission, qualification, registration, certification, or licensure.

Based on the assumption that every applicant or candidate has met the basic formal educational standards, has taken the required number of courses, and read the necessary texts, the *PASSBOOK® SERIES* furnishes the one special preparation which may assure passing with confidence, instead of failing with insecurity. Examination questions – together with answers – are furnished as the basic vehicle for study so that the mysteries of the examination and its compounding difficulties may be eliminated or diminished by a sure method.

This book is meant to help you pass your examination provided that you qualify and are serious in your objective.

The entire field is reviewed through the huge store of content information which is succinctly presented through a provocative and challenging approach – the question-and-answer method.

A climate of success is established by furnishing the correct answers at the end of each test.

You soon learn to recognize types of questions, forms of questions, and patterns of questioning. You may even begin to anticipate expected outcomes.

You perceive that many questions are repeated or adapted so that you can gain acute insights, which may enable you to score many sure points.

You learn how to confront new questions, or types of questions, and to attack them confidently and work out the correct answers.

You note objectives and emphases, and recognize pitfalls and dangers, so that you may make positive educational adjustments.

Moreover, you are kept fully informed in relation to new concepts, methods, practices, and directions in the field.

You discover that you are actually taking the examination all the time: you are preparing for the examination by "taking" an examination, not by reading extraneous and/or supererogatory textbooks.

In short, this PASSBOOK®, used directedly, should be an important factor in helping you to pass your test.

MACHINIST

DUTIES AND RESPONSIBILITIES

Under supervision, Machinists do bench, general shop and outside machinist's work. They set up and operate machine tools, such as engine lathes, milling machines, drill presses, planers and grinders; use tools and instruments required for machinist's work; do outside machinist's work in the inspection, overhaul and repair of all types of main and auxiliary stationary power plant, marine propulsion, water and disposal works equipment; maintain, repair, test, overhaul and replace all types of building systems equipment such as fans, blowers, exhausters, pumps and compressors; fabricate obsolete parts from existing parts or sketches; direct subordinates in the performance of various maintenance and/or repair tasks; prepare reports and requisitions; and maintain records and inventories of supplies and materials.

Responsible for troubleshooting, maintaining, repairing and installing mechanical components and subcomponents of cranes, conveyors, automated guided vehicles, HVAC systems, turntables, transfer tables, car wash machines, diesel locomotives, engines and other heavy equipment/machines; cleaning of tools, equipment and parts with wire brushes, torches and cleaning solvents; inspection of various equipment types for structural damage, integrity and wear according to policy/regulations; grinding, boring, cutting, bending, sizing, shaping, slotting, milling, planning, sanding, fabricating and filing of various machine and engine parts; operating grinders, borers, drills, sanders, lathes and milling machinery; use of various hand and power tools and measuring instruments, such as micrometers, calipers and J&M gauges; reads and interprets schematics, blueprints, shop drawings, technical manuals and other written documentation in the completion of assigned tasks; inspects various engine fluids (such as oil, water, governor fluid) for viscosity and presence. Will be required to become qualified to troubleshoot, repair and test all air brake equipment and its subcomponents. Must be familiar with basic machine shop mathematics, indexing and operation of various shop machinery. May operate a motor vehicle or equipment in the performance of assigned duties; and perform related work.

SCOPE OF THE EXAMINATION

The written multiple-choice test may include questions on operation and maintenance of all machine shop equipment; hand tools and machine shop practices; machinery components; measuring devices and instruments; metals and heat treatment; reading comprehension and plan reading; related machine shop mathematics; safety; supervision and reports; and other related areas.

HOW TO TAKE A TEST

I. YOU MUST PASS AN EXAMINATION

A. *WHAT EVERY CANDIDATE SHOULD KNOW*

Examination applicants often ask us for help in preparing for the written test. What can I study in advance? What kinds of questions will be asked? How will the test be given? How will the papers be graded?

As an applicant for a civil service examination, you may be wondering about some of these things. Our purpose here is to suggest effective methods of advance study and to describe civil service examinations.

Your chances for success on this examination can be increased if you know how to prepare. Those "pre-examination jitters" can be reduced if you know what to expect. You can even experience an adventure in good citizenship if you know why civil service exams are given.

B. *WHY ARE CIVIL SERVICE EXAMINATIONS GIVEN?*

Civil service examinations are important to you in two ways. As a citizen, you want public jobs filled by employees who know how to do their work. As a job seeker, you want a fair chance to compete for that job on an equal footing with other candidates. The best-known means of accomplishing this two-fold goal is the competitive examination.

Exams are widely publicized throughout the nation. They may be administered for jobs in federal, state, city, municipal, town or village governments or agencies.

Any citizen may apply, with some limitations, such as the age or residence of applicants. Your experience and education may be reviewed to see whether you meet the requirements for the particular examination. When these requirements exist, they are reasonable and applied consistently to all applicants. Thus, a competitive examination may cause you some uneasiness now, but it is your privilege and safeguard.

C. *HOW ARE CIVIL SERVICE EXAMS DEVELOPED?*

Examinations are carefully written by trained technicians who are specialists in the field known as "psychological measurement," in consultation with recognized authorities in the field of work that the test will cover. These experts recommend the subject matter areas or skills to be tested; only those knowledges or skills important to your success on the job are included. The most reliable books and source materials available are used as references. Together, the experts and technicians judge the difficulty level of the questions.

Test technicians know how to phrase questions so that the problem is clearly stated. Their ethics do not permit "trick" or "catch" questions. Questions may have been tried out on sample groups, or subjected to statistical analysis, to determine their usefulness.

Written tests are often used in combination with performance tests, ratings of training and experience, and oral interviews. All of these measures combine to form the best-known means of finding the right person for the right job.

II. HOW TO PASS THE WRITTEN TEST

A. NATURE OF THE EXAMINATION

To prepare intelligently for civil service examinations, you should know how they differ from school examinations you have taken. In school you were assigned certain definite pages to read or subjects to cover. The examination questions were quite detailed and usually emphasized memory. Civil service exams, on the other hand, try to discover your present ability to perform the duties of a position, plus your potentiality to learn these duties. In other words, a civil service exam attempts to predict how successful you will be. Questions cover such a broad area that they cannot be as minute and detailed as school exam questions.

In the public service similar kinds of work, or positions, are grouped together in one "class." This process is known as *position-classification*. All the positions in a class are paid according to the salary range for that class. One class title covers all of these positions, and they are all tested by the same examination.

B. FOUR BASIC STEPS

1) Study the announcement

How, then, can you know what subjects to study? Our best answer is: "Learn as much as possible about the class of positions for which you've applied." The exam will test the knowledge, skills and abilities needed to do the work.

Your most valuable source of information about the position you want is the official exam announcement. This announcement lists the training and experience qualifications. Check these standards and apply only if you come reasonably close to meeting them.

The brief description of the position in the examination announcement offers some clues to the subjects which will be tested. Think about the job itself. Review the duties in your mind. Can you perform them, or are there some in which you are rusty? Fill in the blank spots in your preparation.

Many jurisdictions preview the written test in the exam announcement by including a section called "Knowledge and Abilities Required," "Scope of the Examination," or some similar heading. Here you will find out specifically what fields will be tested.

2) Review your own background

Once you learn in general what the position is all about, and what you need to know to do the work, ask yourself which subjects you already know fairly well and which need improvement. You may wonder whether to concentrate on improving your strong areas or on building some background in your fields of weakness. When the announcement has specified "some knowledge" or "considerable knowledge," or has used adjectives like "beginning principles of..." or "advanced ... methods," you can get a clue as to the number and difficulty of questions to be asked in any given field. More questions, and hence broader coverage, would be included for those subjects which are more important in the work. Now weigh your strengths and weaknesses against the job requirements and prepare accordingly.

3) Determine the level of the position

Another way to tell how intensively you should prepare is to understand the level of the job for which you are applying. Is it the entering level? In other words, is this the position in which beginners in a field of work are hired? Or is it an intermediate or advanced level? Sometimes this is indicated by such words as "Junior" or "Senior" in the class title. Other jurisdictions use Roman numerals to designate the level – Clerk I, Clerk II, for example. The word "Supervisor" sometimes appears in the title. If the level is not indicated by the title, check the description of duties. Will you be working under very close supervision, or will you have responsibility for independent decisions in this work?

4) Choose appropriate study materials

Now that you know the subjects to be examined and the relative amount of each subject to be covered, you can choose suitable study materials. For beginning level jobs, or even advanced ones, if you have a pronounced weakness in some aspect of your training, read a modern, standard textbook in that field. Be sure it is up to date and has general coverage. Such books are normally available at your library, and the librarian will be glad to help you locate one. For entry-level positions, questions of appropriate difficulty are chosen – neither highly advanced questions, nor those too simple. Such questions require careful thought but not advanced training.

If the position for which you are applying is technical or advanced, you will read more advanced, specialized material. If you are already familiar with the basic principles of your field, elementary textbooks would waste your time. Concentrate on advanced textbooks and technical periodicals. Think through the concepts and review difficult problems in your field.

These are all general sources. You can get more ideas on your own initiative, following these leads. For example, training manuals and publications of the government agency which employs workers in your field can be useful, particularly for technical and professional positions. A letter or visit to the government department involved may result in more specific study suggestions, and certainly will provide you with a more definite idea of the exact nature of the position you are seeking.

III. KINDS OF TESTS

Tests are used for purposes other than measuring knowledge and ability to perform specified duties. For some positions, it is equally important to test ability to make adjustments to new situations or to profit from training. In others, basic mental abilities not dependent on information are essential. Questions which test these things may not appear as pertinent to the duties of the position as those which test for knowledge and information. Yet they are often highly important parts of a fair examination. For very general questions, it is almost impossible to help you direct your study efforts. What we can do is to point out some of the more common of these general abilities needed in public service positions and describe some typical questions.

1) General information

Broad, general information has been found useful for predicting job success in some kinds of work. This is tested in a variety of ways, from vocabulary lists to questions about current events. Basic background in some field of work, such as sociology or economics, may be sampled in a group of questions. Often these are principles which have become familiar to most persons through exposure rather than through formal training. It is difficult to advise you how to study for these questions; being alert to the world around you is our best suggestion.

2) Verbal ability

An example of an ability needed in many positions is verbal or language ability. Verbal ability is, in brief, the ability to use and understand words. Vocabulary and grammar tests are typical measures of this ability. Reading comprehension or paragraph interpretation questions are common in many kinds of civil service tests. You are given a paragraph of written material and asked to find its central meaning.

3) Numerical ability

Number skills can be tested by the familiar arithmetic problem, by checking paired lists of numbers to see which are alike and which are different, or by interpreting charts and graphs. In the latter test, a graph may be printed in the test booklet which you are asked to use as the basis for answering questions.

4) Observation

A popular test for law-enforcement positions is the observation test. A picture is shown to you for several minutes, then taken away. Questions about the picture test your ability to observe both details and larger elements.

5) Following directions

In many positions in the public service, the employee must be able to carry out written instructions dependably and accurately. You may be given a chart with several columns, each column listing a variety of information. The questions require you to carry out directions involving the information given in the chart.

6) Skills and aptitudes

Performance tests effectively measure some manual skills and aptitudes. When the skill is one in which you are trained, such as typing or shorthand, you can practice. These tests are often very much like those given in business school or high school courses. For many of the other skills and aptitudes, however, no short-time preparation can be made. Skills and abilities natural to you or that you have developed throughout your lifetime are being tested.

Many of the general questions just described provide all the data needed to answer the questions and ask you to use your reasoning ability to find the answers. Your best preparation for these tests, as well as for tests of facts and ideas, is to be at your physical and mental best. You, no doubt, have your own methods of getting into an exam-taking mood and keeping "in shape." The next section lists some ideas on this subject.

IV. KINDS OF QUESTIONS

Only rarely is the "essay" question, which you answer in narrative form, used in civil service tests. Civil service tests are usually of the short-answer type. Full instructions for answering these questions will be given to you at the examination. But in case this is your first experience with short-answer questions and separate answer sheets, here is what you need to know:

1) Multiple-choice Questions

Most popular of the short-answer questions is the "multiple choice" or "best answer" question. It can be used, for example, to test for factual knowledge, ability to solve problems or judgment in meeting situations found at work.

A multiple-choice question is normally one of three types—
- It can begin with an incomplete statement followed by several possible endings. You are to find the one ending which *best* completes the statement, although some of the others may not be entirely wrong.
- It can also be a complete statement in the form of a question which is answered by choosing one of the statements listed.

- It can be in the form of a problem – again you select the best answer.

Here is an example of a multiple-choice question with a discussion which should give you some clues as to the method for choosing the right answer:

When an employee has a complaint about his assignment, the action which will *best* help him overcome his difficulty is to
- A. discuss his difficulty with his coworkers
- B. take the problem to the head of the organization
- C. take the problem to the person who gave him the assignment
- D. say nothing to anyone about his complaint

In answering this question, you should study each of the choices to find which is best. Consider choice "A" – Certainly an employee may discuss his complaint with fellow employees, but no change or improvement can result, and the complaint remains unresolved. Choice "B" is a poor choice since the head of the organization probably does not know what assignment you have been given, and taking your problem to him is known as "going over the head" of the supervisor. The supervisor, or person who made the assignment, is the person who can clarify it or correct any injustice. Choice "C" is, therefore, correct. To say nothing, as in choice "D," is unwise. Supervisors have and interest in knowing the problems employees are facing, and the employee is seeking a solution to his problem.

2) True/False Questions

The "true/false" or "right/wrong" form of question is sometimes used. Here a complete statement is given. Your job is to decide whether the statement is right or wrong.

SAMPLE: A roaming cell-phone call to a nearby city costs less than a non-roaming call to a distant city.

This statement is wrong, or false, since roaming calls are more expensive.

This is not a complete list of all possible question forms, although most of the others are variations of these common types. You will always get complete directions for answering questions. Be sure you understand *how* to mark your answers – ask questions until you do.

V. RECORDING YOUR ANSWERS

Computer terminals are used more and more today for many different kinds of exams.

For an examination with very few applicants, you may be told to record your answers in the test booklet itself. Separate answer sheets are much more common. If this separate answer sheet is to be scored by machine – and this is often the case – it is highly important that you mark your answers correctly in order to get credit.

An electronic scoring machine is often used in civil service offices because of the speed with which papers can be scored. Machine-scored answer sheets must be marked with a pencil, which will be given to you. This pencil has a high graphite content which responds to the electronic scoring machine. As a matter of fact, stray dots may register as answers, so do not let your pencil rest on the answer sheet while you are pondering the correct answer. Also, if your pencil lead breaks or is otherwise defective, ask for another.

Since the answer sheet will be dropped in a slot in the scoring machine, be careful not to bend the corners or get the paper crumpled.

The answer sheet normally has five vertical columns of numbers, with 30 numbers to a column. These numbers correspond to the question numbers in your test booklet. After each number, going across the page are four or five pairs of dotted lines. These short dotted lines have small letters or numbers above them. The first two pairs may also have a "T" or "F" above the letters. This indicates that the first two pairs only are to be used if the questions are of the true-false type. If the questions are multiple choice, disregard the "T" and "F" and pay attention only to the small letters or numbers.

Answer your questions in the manner of the sample that follows:

32. The largest city in the United States is
    A. Washington, D.C.
    B. New York City
    C. Chicago
    D. Detroit
    E. San Francisco

1) Choose the answer you think is best. (New York City is the largest, so "B" is correct.)
2) Find the row of dotted lines numbered the same as the question you are answering. (Find row number 32)
3) Find the pair of dotted lines corresponding to the answer. (Find the pair of lines under the mark "B.")
4) Make a solid black mark between the dotted lines.

VI. BEFORE THE TEST

Common sense will help you find procedures to follow to get ready for an examination. Too many of us, however, overlook these sensible measures. Indeed, nervousness and fatigue have been found to be the most serious reasons why applicants fail to do their best on civil service tests. Here is a list of reminders:

- Begin your preparation early – Don't wait until the last minute to go scurrying around for books and materials or to find out what the position is all about.
- Prepare continuously – An hour a night for a week is better than an all-night cram session. This has been definitely established. What is more, a night a week for a month will return better dividends than crowding your study into a shorter period of time.
- Locate the place of the exam – You have been sent a notice telling you when and where to report for the examination. If the location is in a different town or otherwise unfamiliar to you, it would be well to inquire the best route and learn something about the building.
- Relax the night before the test – Allow your mind to rest. Do not study at all that night. Plan some mild recreation or diversion; then go to bed early and get a good night's sleep.
- Get up early enough to make a leisurely trip to the place for the test – This way unforeseen events, traffic snarls, unfamiliar buildings, etc. will not upset you.
- Dress comfortably – A written test is not a fashion show. You will be known by number and not by name, so wear something comfortable.

- Leave excess paraphernalia at home – Shopping bags and odd bundles will get in your way. You need bring only the items mentioned in the official notice you received; usually everything you need is provided. Do not bring reference books to the exam. They will only confuse those last minutes and be taken away from you when in the test room.
- Arrive somewhat ahead of time – If because of transportation schedules you must get there very early, bring a newspaper or magazine to take your mind off yourself while waiting.
- Locate the examination room – When you have found the proper room, you will be directed to the seat or part of the room where you will sit. Sometimes you are given a sheet of instructions to read while you are waiting. Do not fill out any forms until you are told to do so; just read them and be prepared.
- Relax and prepare to listen to the instructions
- If you have any physical problem that may keep you from doing your best, be sure to tell the test administrator. If you are sick or in poor health, you really cannot do your best on the exam. You can come back and take the test some other time.

VII. AT THE TEST

The day of the test is here and you have the test booklet in your hand. The temptation to get going is very strong. Caution! There is more to success than knowing the right answers. You must know how to identify your papers and understand variations in the type of short-answer question used in this particular examination. Follow these suggestions for maximum results from your efforts:

1) Cooperate with the monitor

The test administrator has a duty to create a situation in which you can be as much at ease as possible. He will give instructions, tell you when to begin, check to see that you are marking your answer sheet correctly, and so on. He is not there to guard you, although he will see that your competitors do not take unfair advantage. He wants to help you do your best.

2) Listen to all instructions

Don't jump the gun! Wait until you understand all directions. In most civil service tests you get more time than you need to answer the questions. So don't be in a hurry. Read each word of instructions until you clearly understand the meaning. Study the examples, listen to all announcements and follow directions. Ask questions if you do not understand what to do.

3) Identify your papers

Civil service exams are usually identified by number only. You will be assigned a number; you must not put your name on your test papers. Be sure to copy your number correctly. Since more than one exam may be given, copy your exact examination title.

4) Plan your time

Unless you are told that a test is a "speed" or "rate of work" test, speed itself is usually not important. Time enough to answer all the questions will be provided, but this does not mean that you have all day. An overall time limit has been set. Divide the total time (in minutes) by the number of questions to determine the approximate time you have for each question.

5) Do not linger over difficult questions

If you come across a difficult question, mark it with a paper clip (useful to have along) and come back to it when you have been through the booklet. One caution if you do this – be sure to skip a number on your answer sheet as well. Check often to be sure that you have not lost your place and that you are marking in the row numbered the same as the question you are answering.

6) Read the questions

Be sure you know what the question asks! Many capable people are unsuccessful because they failed to *read* the questions correctly.

7) Answer all questions

Unless you have been instructed that a penalty will be deducted for incorrect answers, it is better to guess than to omit a question.

8) Speed tests

It is often better NOT to guess on speed tests. It has been found that on timed tests people are tempted to spend the last few seconds before time is called in marking answers at random – without even reading them – in the hope of picking up a few extra points. To discourage this practice, the instructions may warn you that your score will be "corrected" for guessing. That is, a penalty will be applied. The incorrect answers will be deducted from the correct ones, or some other penalty formula will be used.

9) Review your answers

If you finish before time is called, go back to the questions you guessed or omitted to give them further thought. Review other answers if you have time.

10) Return your test materials

If you are ready to leave before others have finished or time is called, take ALL your materials to the monitor and leave quietly. Never take any test material with you. The monitor can discover whose papers are not complete, and taking a test booklet may be grounds for disqualification.

VIII. EXAMINATION TECHNIQUES

1) Read the general instructions carefully. These are usually printed on the first page of the exam booklet. As a rule, these instructions refer to the timing of the examination; the fact that you should not start work until the signal and must stop work at a signal, etc. If there are any *special* instructions, such as a choice of questions to be answered, make sure that you note this instruction carefully.

2) When you are ready to start work on the examination, that is as soon as the signal has been given, read the instructions to each question booklet, underline any key words or phrases, such as *least, best, outline, describe* and the like. In this way you will tend to answer as requested rather than discover on reviewing your paper that you *listed without describing*, that you selected the *worst* choice rather than the *best* choice, etc.

3) If the examination is of the objective or multiple-choice type – that is, each question will also give a series of possible answers: A, B, C or D, and you are called upon to select the best answer and write the letter next to that answer on your answer paper – it is advisable to start answering each question in turn. There may be anywhere from 50 to 100 such questions in the three or four hours allotted and you can see how much time would be taken if you read through all the questions before beginning to answer any. Furthermore, if you come across a question or group of questions which you know would be difficult to answer, it would undoubtedly affect your handling of all the other questions.

4) If the examination is of the essay type and contains but a few questions, it is a moot point as to whether you should read all the questions before starting to answer any one. Of course, if you are given a choice – say five out of seven and the like – then it is essential to read all the questions so you can eliminate the two that are most difficult. If, however, you are asked to answer all the questions, there may be danger in trying to answer the easiest one first because you may find that you will spend too much time on it. The best technique is to answer the first question, then proceed to the second, etc.

5) Time your answers. Before the exam begins, write down the time it started, then add the time allowed for the examination and write down the time it must be completed, then divide the time available somewhat as follows:
    - If 3-1/2 hours are allowed, that would be 210 minutes. If you have 80 objective-type questions, that would be an average of 2-1/2 minutes per question. Allow yourself no more than 2 minutes per question, or a total of 160 minutes, which will permit about 50 minutes to review.
    - If for the time allotment of 210 minutes there are 7 essay questions to answer, that would average about 30 minutes a question. Give yourself only 25 minutes per question so that you have about 35 minutes to review.

6) The most important instruction is to *read each question* and make sure you know what is wanted. The second most important instruction is to *time yourself properly* so that you answer every question. The third most important instruction is to *answer every question*. Guess if you have to but include something for each question. Remember that you will receive no credit for a blank and will probably receive some credit if you write something in answer to an essay question. If you guess a letter – say "B" for a multiple-choice question – you may have guessed right. If you leave a blank as an answer to a multiple-choice question, the examiners may respect your feelings but it will not add a point to your score. Some exams may penalize you for wrong answers, so in such cases *only*, you may not want to guess unless you have some basis for your answer.

7) Suggestions
    a. Objective-type questions
        1. Examine the question booklet for proper sequence of pages and questions
        2. Read all instructions carefully
        3. Skip any question which seems too difficult; return to it after all other questions have been answered
        4. Apportion your time properly; do not spend too much time on any single question or group of questions

5. Note and underline key words – *all, most, fewest, least, best, worst, same, opposite*, etc.
6. Pay particular attention to negatives
7. Note unusual option, e.g., unduly long, short, complex, different or similar in content to the body of the question
8. Observe the use of "hedging" words – *probably, may, most likely*, etc.
9. Make sure that your answer is put next to the same number as the question
10. Do not second-guess unless you have good reason to believe the second answer is definitely more correct
11. Cross out original answer if you decide another answer is more accurate; do not erase until you are ready to hand your paper in
12. Answer all questions; guess unless instructed otherwise
13. Leave time for review

b. Essay questions
  1. Read each question carefully
  2. Determine exactly what is wanted. Underline key words or phrases.
  3. Decide on outline or paragraph answer
  4. Include many different points and elements unless asked to develop any one or two points or elements
  5. Show impartiality by giving pros and cons unless directed to select one side only
  6. Make and write down any assumptions you find necessary to answer the questions
  7. Watch your English, grammar, punctuation and choice of words
  8. Time your answers; don't crowd material

8) Answering the essay question

Most essay questions can be answered by framing the specific response around several key words or ideas. Here are a few such key words or ideas:

M's: manpower, materials, methods, money, management
P's: purpose, program, policy, plan, procedure, practice, problems, pitfalls, personnel, public relations

  a. Six basic steps in handling problems:
    1. Preliminary plan and background development
    2. Collect information, data and facts
    3. Analyze and interpret information, data and facts
    4. Analyze and develop solutions as well as make recommendations
    5. Prepare report and sell recommendations
    6. Install recommendations and follow up effectiveness

  b. Pitfalls to avoid
    1. *Taking things for granted* – A statement of the situation does not necessarily imply that each of the elements is necessarily true; for example, a complaint may be invalid and biased so that all that can be taken for granted is that a complaint has been registered

2. *Considering only one side of a situation* – Wherever possible, indicate several alternatives and then point out the reasons you selected the best one
3. *Failing to indicate follow up* – Whenever your answer indicates action on your part, make certain that you will take proper follow-up action to see how successful your recommendations, procedures or actions turn out to be
4. *Taking too long in answering any single question* – Remember to time your answers properly

IX. AFTER THE TEST

Scoring procedures differ in detail among civil service jurisdictions although the general principles are the same. Whether the papers are hand-scored or graded by machine we have described, they are nearly always graded by number. That is, the person who marks the paper knows only the number – never the name – of the applicant. Not until all the papers have been graded will they be matched with names. If other tests, such as training and experience or oral interview ratings have been given, scores will be combined. Different parts of the examination usually have different weights. For example, the written test might count 60 percent of the final grade, and a rating of training and experience 40 percent. In many jurisdictions, veterans will have a certain number of points added to their grades.

After the final grade has been determined, the names are placed in grade order and an eligible list is established. There are various methods for resolving ties between those who get the same final grade – probably the most common is to place first the name of the person whose application was received first. Job offers are made from the eligible list in the order the names appear on it. You will be notified of your grade and your rank as soon as all these computations have been made. This will be done as rapidly as possible.

People who are found to meet the requirements in the announcement are called "eligibles." Their names are put on a list of eligible candidates. An eligible's chances of getting a job depend on how high he stands on this list and how fast agencies are filling jobs from the list.

When a job is to be filled from a list of eligibles, the agency asks for the names of people on the list of eligibles for that job. When the civil service commission receives this request, it sends to the agency the names of the three people highest on this list. Or, if the job to be filled has specialized requirements, the office sends the agency the names of the top three persons who meet these requirements from the general list.

The appointing officer makes a choice from among the three people whose names were sent to him. If the selected person accepts the appointment, the names of the others are put back on the list to be considered for future openings.

That is the rule in hiring from all kinds of eligible lists, whether they are for typist, carpenter, chemist, or something else. For every vacancy, the appointing officer has his choice of any one of the top three eligibles on the list. This explains why the person whose name is on top of the list sometimes does not get an appointment when some of the persons lower on the list do. If the appointing officer chooses the second or third eligible, the No. 1 eligible does not get a job at once, but stays on the list until he is appointed or the list is terminated.

X. HOW TO PASS THE INTERVIEW TEST

The examination for which you applied requires an oral interview test. You have already taken the written test and you are now being called for the interview test – the final part of the formal examination.

You may think that it is not possible to prepare for an interview test and that there are no procedures to follow during an interview. Our purpose is to point out some things you can do in advance that will help you and some good rules to follow and pitfalls to avoid while you are being interviewed.

What is an interview supposed to test?

The written examination is designed to test the technical knowledge and competence of the candidate; the oral is designed to evaluate intangible qualities, not readily measured otherwise, and to establish a list showing the relative fitness of each candidate – as measured against his competitors – for the position sought. Scoring is not on the basis of "right" and "wrong," but on a sliding scale of values ranging from "not passable" to "outstanding." As a matter of fact, it is possible to achieve a relatively low score without a single "incorrect" answer because of evident weakness in the qualities being measured.

Occasionally, an examination may consist entirely of an oral test – either an individual or a group oral. In such cases, information is sought concerning the technical knowledges and abilities of the candidate, since there has been no written examination for this purpose. More commonly, however, an oral test is used to supplement a written examination.

Who conducts interviews?

The composition of oral boards varies among different jurisdictions. In nearly all, a representative of the personnel department serves as chairman. One of the members of the board may be a representative of the department in which the candidate would work. In some cases, "outside experts" are used, and, frequently, a businessman or some other representative of the general public is asked to serve. Labor and management or other special groups may be represented. The aim is to secure the services of experts in the appropriate field.

However the board is composed, it is a good idea (and not at all improper or unethical) to ascertain in advance of the interview who the members are and what groups they represent. When you are introduced to them, you will have some idea of their backgrounds and interests, and at least you will not stutter and stammer over their names.

What should be done before the interview?

While knowledge about the board members is useful and takes some of the surprise element out of the interview, there is other preparation which is more substantive. It *is* possible to prepare for an oral interview – in several ways:

1) Keep a copy of your application and review it carefully before the interview

This may be the only document before the oral board, and the starting point of the interview. Know what education and experience you have listed there, and the sequence and dates of all of it. Sometimes the board will ask you to review the highlights of your experience for them; you should not have to hem and haw doing it.

2) Study the class specification and the examination announcement

Usually, the oral board has one or both of these to guide them. The qualities, characteristics or knowledges required by the position sought are stated in these documents. They offer valuable clues as to the nature of the oral interview. For example, if the job involves supervisory responsibilities, the announcement will usually indicate that knowledge of modern supervisory methods and the qualifications of the candidate as a supervisor will be tested. If so, you can expect such questions, frequently in the form of a hypothetical situation which you are expected to solve. NEVER go into an oral without knowledge of the duties and responsibilities of the job you seek.

3) Think through each qualification required

Try to visualize the kind of questions you would ask if you were a board member. How well could you answer them? Try especially to appraise your own knowledge and background in each area, *measured against the job sought*, and identify any areas in which you are weak. Be critical and realistic – do not flatter yourself.

4) Do some general reading in areas in which you feel you may be weak

For example, if the job involves supervision and your past experience has NOT, some general reading in supervisory methods and practices, particularly in the field of human relations, might be useful. Do NOT study agency procedures or detailed manuals. The oral board will be testing your understanding and capacity, not your memory.

5) Get a good night's sleep and watch your general health and mental attitude

You will want a clear head at the interview. Take care of a cold or any other minor ailment, and of course, no hangovers.

What should be done on the day of the interview?

Now comes the day of the interview itself. Give yourself plenty of time to get there. Plan to arrive somewhat ahead of the scheduled time, particularly if your appointment is in the fore part of the day. If a previous candidate fails to appear, the board might be ready for you a bit early. By early afternoon an oral board is almost invariably behind schedule if there are many candidates, and you may have to wait. Take along a book or magazine to read, or your application to review, but leave any extraneous material in the waiting room when you go in for your interview. In any event, relax and compose yourself.

The matter of dress is important. The board is forming impressions about you – from your experience, your manners, your attitude, and your appearance. Give your personal appearance careful attention. Dress your best, but not your flashiest. Choose conservative, appropriate clothing, and be sure it is immaculate. This is a business interview, and your appearance should indicate that you regard it as such. Besides, being well groomed and properly dressed will help boost your confidence.

Sooner or later, someone will call your name and escort you into the interview room. *This is it.* From here on you are on your own. It is too late for any more preparation. But remember, you asked for this opportunity to prove your fitness, and you are here because your request was granted.

What happens when you go in?

The usual sequence of events will be as follows: The clerk (who is often the board stenographer) will introduce you to the chairman of the oral board, who will introduce you to the other members of the board. Acknowledge the introductions before you sit down. Do not be surprised if you find a microphone facing you or a stenotypist sitting by. Oral interviews are usually recorded in the event of an appeal or other review.

Usually the chairman of the board will open the interview by reviewing the highlights of your education and work experience from your application – primarily for the benefit of the other members of the board, as well as to get the material into the record. Do not interrupt or comment unless there is an error or significant misinterpretation; if that is the case, do not hesitate. But do not quibble about insignificant matters. Also, he will usually ask you some question about your education, experience or your present job – partly to get you to start talking and to establish the interviewing "rapport." He may start the actual questioning, or turn it over to one of the other members. Frequently, each member undertakes the questioning on a particular area, one in which he is perhaps most competent, so you can expect each member to participate in the examination. Because time is limited, you may also expect some rather abrupt switches in the direction the questioning takes, so do not be upset by it. Normally, a board member will not pursue a single line of questioning unless he discovers a particular strength or weakness.

After each member has participated, the chairman will usually ask whether any member has any further questions, then will ask you if you have anything you wish to add. Unless you are expecting this question, it may floor you. Worse, it may start you off on an extended, extemporaneous speech. The board is not usually seeking more information. The question is principally to offer you a last opportunity to present further qualifications or to indicate that you have nothing to add. So, if you feel that a significant qualification or characteristic has been overlooked, it is proper to point it out in a sentence or so. Do not compliment the board on the thoroughness of their examination – they have been sketchy, and you know it. If you wish, merely say, "No thank you, I have nothing further to add." This is a point where you can "talk yourself out" of a good impression or fail to present an important bit of information. Remember, *you close the interview yourself.*

The chairman will then say, "That is all, Mr. _____, thank you." Do not be startled; the interview is over, and quicker than you think. Thank him, gather your belongings and take your leave. Save your sigh of relief for the other side of the door.

How to put your best foot forward

Throughout this entire process, you may feel that the board individually and collectively is trying to pierce your defenses, seek out your hidden weaknesses and embarrass and confuse you. Actually, this is not true. They are obliged to make an appraisal of your qualifications for the job you are seeking, and they want to see you in your best light. Remember, they must interview all candidates and a non-cooperative candidate may become a failure in spite of their best efforts to bring out his qualifications. Here are 15 suggestions that will help you:

1) Be natural – Keep your attitude confident, not cocky

If you are not confident that you can do the job, do not expect the board to be. Do not apologize for your weaknesses, try to bring out your strong points. The board is interested in a positive, not negative, presentation. Cockiness will antagonize any board member and make him wonder if you are covering up a weakness by a false show of strength.

2) Get comfortable, but don't lounge or sprawl

Sit erectly but not stiffly. A careless posture may lead the board to conclude that you are careless in other things, or at least that you are not impressed by the importance of the occasion. Either conclusion is natural, even if incorrect. Do not fuss with your clothing, a pencil or an ashtray. Your hands may occasionally be useful to emphasize a point; do not let them become a point of distraction.

3) Do not wisecrack or make small talk

This is a serious situation, and your attitude should show that you consider it as such. Further, the time of the board is limited – they do not want to waste it, and neither should you.

4) Do not exaggerate your experience or abilities
In the first place, from information in the application or other interviews and sources, the board may know more about you than you think. Secondly, you probably will not get away with it. An experienced board is rather adept at spotting such a situation, so do not take the chance.

5) If you know a board member, do not make a point of it, yet do not hide it
Certainly you are not fooling him, and probably not the other members of the board. Do not try to take advantage of your acquaintanceship – it will probably do you little good.

6) Do not dominate the interview
Let the board do that. They will give you the clues – do not assume that you have to do all the talking. Realize that the board has a number of questions to ask you, and do not try to take up all the interview time by showing off your extensive knowledge of the answer to the first one.

7) Be attentive
You only have 20 minutes or so, and you should keep your attention at its sharpest throughout. When a member is addressing a problem or question to you, give him your undivided attention. Address your reply principally to him, but do not exclude the other board members.

8) Do not interrupt
A board member may be stating a problem for you to analyze. He will ask you a question when the time comes. Let him state the problem, and wait for the question.

9) Make sure you understand the question
Do not try to answer until you are sure what the question is. If it is not clear, restate it in your own words or ask the board member to clarify it for you. However, do not haggle about minor elements.

10) Reply promptly but not hastily
A common entry on oral board rating sheets is "candidate responded readily," or "candidate hesitated in replies." Respond as promptly and quickly as you can, but do not jump to a hasty, ill-considered answer.

11) Do not be peremptory in your answers
A brief answer is proper – but do not fire your answer back. That is a losing game from your point of view. The board member can probably ask questions much faster than you can answer them.

12) Do not try to create the answer you think the board member wants
He is interested in what kind of mind you have and how it works – not in playing games. Furthermore, he can usually spot this practice and will actually grade you down on it.

13) Do not switch sides in your reply merely to agree with a board member
Frequently, a member will take a contrary position merely to draw you out and to see if you are willing and able to defend your point of view. Do not start a debate, yet do not surrender a good position. If a position is worth taking, it is worth defending.

14) Do not be afraid to admit an error in judgment if you are shown to be wrong

The board knows that you are forced to reply without any opportunity for careful consideration. Your answer may be demonstrably wrong. If so, admit it and get on with the interview.

15) Do not dwell at length on your present job

The opening question may relate to your present assignment. Answer the question but do not go into an extended discussion. You are being examined for a *new* job, not your present one. As a matter of fact, try to phrase ALL your answers in terms of the job for which you are being examined.

Basis of Rating

Probably you will forget most of these "do's" and "don'ts" when you walk into the oral interview room. Even remembering them all will not ensure you a passing grade. Perhaps you did not have the qualifications in the first place. But remembering them will help you to put your best foot forward, without treading on the toes of the board members.

Rumor and popular opinion to the contrary notwithstanding, an oral board wants you to make the best appearance possible. They know you are under pressure – but they also want to see how you respond to it as a guide to what your reaction would be under the pressures of the job you seek. They will be influenced by the degree of poise you display, the personal traits you show and the manner in which you respond.

ABOUT THIS BOOK

This book contains tests divided into Examination Sections. Go through each test, answering every question in the margin. We have also attached a sample answer sheet at the back of the book that can be removed and used. At the end of each test look at the answer key and check your answers. On the ones you got wrong, look at the right answer choice and learn. Do not fill in the answers first. Do not memorize the questions and answers, but understand the answer and principles involved. On your test, the questions will likely be different from the samples. Questions are changed and new ones added. If you understand these past questions you should have success with any changes that arise. Tests may consist of several types of questions. We have additional books on each subject should more study be advisable or necessary for you. Finally, the more you study, the better prepared you will be. This book is intended to be the last thing you study before you walk into the examination room. Prior study of relevant texts is also recommended. NLC publishes some of these in our Fundamental Series. Knowledge and good sense are important factors in passing your exam. Good luck also helps. So now study this Passbook, absorb the material contained within and take that knowledge into the examination. Then do your best to pass that exam.

EXAMINATION SECTION

EXAMINATION SECTION
TEST 1

DIRECTIONS: Each question or incomplete statement is followed by several suggested answers or completions. Select the one that BEST answers the question or completes the statement. *PRINT THE LETTER OF THE CORRECT ANSWER IN THE SPACE AT THE RIGHT.*

1. Screw stock is USUALLY an alloy of copper, 1.____
   A. zinc, and nickel
   B. zinc, and tin
   C. zinc, and lead
   D. and zinc

2. The MOST desirable alloy steel for use in automobile springs is 2.____
   A. chromium-molybdenum
   B. silicon-manganese
   C. chromium-nickel
   D. manganese-molybdenum

3. An alloy of approximately 2/3 nickel and 1/3 copper (with small amounts of iron, manganese, and silicon) is COMMONLY referred to as 3.____
   A. Muntz metal
   B. Inconel
   C. Nickel silver
   D. Monel

4. When using the *thread dial* in the cutting of a thread on a lathe, it is NOT proper to close the split nut at any 4.____
   A. un-numbered line on the dial for a 5 1/4 per inch thread
   B. odd-numbered line on the dial for a 10 1/2 per inch thread
   C. line on the dial for a 6 per inch thread
   D. numbered line on the dial for a 7 per inch thread

5. On a modern lathe, the *constant surface speed control* separately controls the speed of the 5.____
   A. cross feed
   B. lead screw
   C. spindle
   D. feed rod

6. In a finish grinding operation on cast iron, the surface speed of the work should be MOST NEARLY _____ feet/min. 6.____
   A. 60   B. 110   C. 150   D. 200

7. The size of a standard hardened and ground lathe material is USUALLY marked 7.____
   A. on the large end
   B. on both ends
   C. on the small end
   D. near the middle

8. A half-center used in facing work looks MOST NEARLY like 8.____

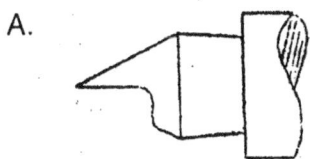

A.   B.

1

C. 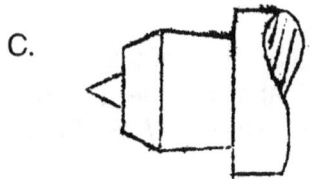   D.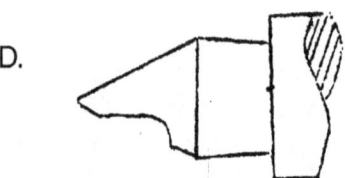

9. Assume that a cross-feed screw on a special lathe has 10 threads per inch and the scale on the cross-feed screw is divided up into 50 equal divisions.
   If it is desired to take a second cut on a stock which will reduce the stock diameter by 012", the feed should be moved in MOST NEARLY _____ divisions.

   A. 12   B. 6   C. 3   D. 1 1/2

10. For a very fine polishing on a lathe, it is MOST desirable to use a _____ spindle speed, _____ cloth, and a _____ pressure on the work.

    A. high; oiled crocus; heavy
    B. medium; oiled crocus; light
    C. low; fine oiled emery; light
    D. low; fine dry emery; very light

11. On a lathe, when extreme accuracy for centering a moderately heavy piece of work is needed, it is MOST desirable to use a _____ chuck.

    A. drill
    B. two-jaw
    C. three-jaw self-centering universal
    D. four-jaw independent

12. Of the following, the piece of equipment NOT generally used in lathe work is a(n)

    A. angle plate   B. boring bar
    C. swage block   D. gang mandrel

13. The MOST NEARLY CORRECT of the following statements about *lapping* is that it is a process in which a surface is abraded by rubbing

    A. dry with a harder material
    B. dry with a softer material
    C. with a softer material charged with fine abrasive particles in a vehicle such as grease
    D. with a harder material charged with fine abrasive particles in a vehicle such as oil

14. In connection with centerless external grinding, the statement which is MOST NEARLY CORRECT is that the

    A. grinding wheels are approximately of the same size
    B. grinding wheels revolve at the same speed
    C. shafts of the grinding wheels are not parallel
    D. grinding wheels run in opposite directions

15. Assume that a grinding wheel is marked *C14-N12-S23* by the manufacturer. This marking MOST likely indicates

   A. the manufacturer's inventory control number
   B. a vitrified bond silicon carbide wheel with fine grain size
   C. a silicate bonded aluminum oxide wheel with coarse grain size
   D. a silicate bonded silicon carbide wheel with coarse grain size

16. If, in the three-wire-method of measuring pitch diameters of screw threads, the actual micrometer reading over the wires is greater than the properly calculated reading, it is likely that the

   A. wires used are oversized
   B. thread needs further cutting
   C. thread is satisfactory
   D. thread is cut too deep

17. To produce a true flat on an iron surface, it is BEST to use a

   A. planer
   B. shaper
   C. scraper
   D. milling machine

18. In lay-out work, the LEAST useful means for making scribed lines on steel more distinct is the use of

   A. bluing
   B. copper sulphate
   C. dilute acetic acid
   D. colored lacquer

19. The GREAT advantage of electron beam machining is that

   A. it can be used on massive work since it removes material slowly
   B. it can be used on miniaturized work since it removes material slowly
   C. the equipment needed costs much less than the equipment needed for electrical discharge machining
   D. a steady beam can be used to drill holes, up to 1/2 inch in diameter, instantaneously in metal thicknesses up to 12 inches

20. One disadvantage of electrical discharge machining is that this method CANNOT be used when

   A. it is desired to remove material at a slow rate
   B. the material to be machined is an electrical conductor
   C. the material to be machined has a Brinell of over 400
   D. a surface finish of less than 500 microinches is required

21. When a thread is to be used to transmit a maximum amount of power with minimum friction, it is MOST desirable to cut a(n) _____ thread.

   A. American National
   B. American National Acme
   C. 29 degree worm
   D. square

22. A safety lathe dog differs from an ordinary lathe dog in that the former has

   A. two diametral tails for positive drive
   B. a tail of soft metal which shears under dangerous load
   C. a large headed setscrew for secure clamping
   D. a headless setscrew that does not protrude

23. Location of the center at the end of a piece of round stock is MOST easily accomplished by using

    A. a surface gage
    B. spring calipers
    C. dividers
    D. a center head

24. A *combination set* has a

    A. scale, square head, universal bevel, and a radius gage
    B. scale, bevel protractor, center head, and square head
    C. level, bevel protractor, radius gage, and center head
    D. scale, universal bevel, radius gage, and square head

25. A telescoping gage is USUALLY used for making

    A. measurements of long lengths
    B. measurements of large external diameters
    C. measurements with a comparator
    D. internal measurements

26. The recommended number of teeth per inch on a hacksaw blade that is to be used for cutting thin sheet metal and thin tubing is MOST NEARLY

    A. 32   B. 24   C. 18   D. 14

27. Among the common types of files that are used in machine shops, the file that has two *safe* edges is known as a _____ file.

    A. pillar   B. mill   C. hand   D. flat

28. Trammel points CANNOT be used

    A. as inside calipers
    B. for scribing arcs from holes
    C. as a surface gage
    D. for scribing arcs from punch marks

29. A wiggler indicator is used PRIMARILY for

    A. measuring frequency of vibration
    B. indicating gear backlash
    C. centering work in machine tools
    D. determinations of surface finish

30. Toolmakers' buttons are USUALLY used for

    A. plugging inaccurately drilled holes
    B. laying out holes accurately
    C. gaging hole sizes
    D. checking shallow hole depths

31. Among the following gages, the one which is used to check a specific profile of an object is called a _____ gage.

    A. *go* ring
    B. radius
    C. drill and wire
    D. *not go* plug

32. For average work, the proper cutting speed to use in a small power hacksaw should be MOST NEARLY _____ to _____ strokes per minute.

   A. 10; 20   B. 30; 40   C. 50; 60   D. 80; 100

33. A sine bar is a tool that may be used for accurate

   A. boring
   B. centering of round stock
   C. torque measurement
   D. angle measurement

34. Assume that there were 50 threads per inch on a micrometer spindle (instead of the usual 40), and the thimble was graduated in 20 divisions (instead of the usual 25).
   With 50 divisions on the barrel (instead of the usual 40), the setting shown at the right on such a micrometer would indicate a reading of
   A. .078"
   B. .093"
   C. .096"
   D. .098"

35. With a setting as shown above in the sketch showing part of a 3" - 4" inside micrometer, the dimension being measured is MOST NEARLY

   A. 3.989"   B. 3.890"   C. 3.611"   D. 3.389"

36. A micrometer graduated to read to .0001" USUALLY has

   A. no vernier scale
   B. a vernier scale on the anvil
   C. a vernier scale on the barrel
   D. a vernier scale on the thimble

37. A profilometer is an instrument which may be used for

   A. tracing outlines on shop drawings
   B. measuring surface roughness
   C. controlling movement of the shaper toolslide
   D. measuring the areas of irregular figures

38. Assume that a tapered shank having a 0.600 inch per foot taper goes into a taper gage too far by 0.200 inch.
From this it can CORRECTLY be said that the diameter of the taper is too small by

    A. 0.005"   B. 0.010"   C. 0.015"   D. 0.020"

39. With reference to the measurement of hardness, a *Brale* is a

    A. hardened steel ball 1 centimeter in diameter
    B. Moh's scale of hardness of 3
    C. hardened steel ball 1 1/16 inch in diameter
    D. diamond cone

40. A Brinell number of 400 corresponds MOST NEARLY to a

    A. Rockwell C of 42
    B. Rockwell B of 84
    C. Sclerescope number of 21
    D. tensile strength of 84,000 psi

41. With reference to milling, the statement which is MOST NEARLY CORRECT is:

    A. Heavy down milling cuts can be made safely on any milling machine
    B. Down milling results in poorest metal finishes
    C. Down milling does not require as firm a clamping of work as in up milling
    D. With hard surfaced materials, down milling gives greater productivity per sharpening

42. Assume that on a milling machine fitted with a dividing head, 24 evenly spaced cuts are to be taken around the circumference of a work piece.
With a 40 to 1 gear ratio and a 36 hole index circle, the number of holes to be indexed with plain indexing after each cut is MOST NEARLY

    A. 20   B. 40   C. 60   D. 80

43. To be able to take two cuts on a piece of work in a milling machine so that the cuts are 30 minutes of arc apart, the minimum number of holes for plain indexing on an index circle fitted with a 40 to 1 gear ratio, should be MOST NEARLY

    A. 8   B. 12   C. 18   D. 36

44. The designation *righthand cutter* is the proper designation to use when referring to an _____ cutter that rotates _____ when viewed from the front end of the _____.

    A. end-mill; counterclockwise; spindle
    B. end-mill; clockwise; spindle
    C. arbor-type; clockwise; arbor
    D. arbor-type; counterclockwise; arbor

45. Assume that a jobbing shop is to submit a price for a contract involving 300 pieces of work. Assume that material costs 25 cents per piece, labor costs $3.75 an hour, and a lathe operator can complete 5 pieces in an hour.
If overhead is 40% of material and labor costs and the profit is 10% of all costs, the submitted price for the entire job will be MOST NEARLY

   A. $315.12   B. $438.90   C. $450.00   D. $462.00

46. The following formula is used in connection with the three-wire method of measuring pitch diameters of screw threads: $G = \dfrac{0.57735}{N}$, where G = wire size and N = number of threads per inch.
According to this formula, the proper size of wire for a 1" - 8NC thread is MOST NEARLY

   A. .0722"   B. .7217"   C. .0072"   D. .0074"

47. A millimeter is 1/25.4 of an inch and there are 10 millimeters to a centimeter.
If a piece of stock measures 127 centimeters long, the length of the stock, in feet and inches, would be MOST NEARLY _____ ft. _____ inch(es).

   A. 2; 1   B. 4; 2   C. 8; 4   D. 41; 8

48. The MAIN purpose of the tang on a taper shank drill is to

   A. supply the negative action required to drive the drill
   B. serve as a holder when the drill is being sharpened
   C. provide the means for removing the drill by use of a drift
   D. relieve the stress on the drill in heavy use

49. The statement concerning drills which is MOST NEARLY CORRECT is:

   A. Taper shanks are available only on drills where the diameter is 1/2" or larger
   B. Straight shank drills are available in sizes up to 3" diameter
   C. Taper shanks are available for drills of all sizes
   D. Straight shank drills are available in sizes up to 1/2" diameter

50. Assume that the number of teeth on each gear of a compound gear train is shown above.
If the 60 tooth gear makes 60 clockwise revolutions per minute, the 20 tooth gear will MOST likely make _____ rpm.

   A. 480   B. 720   C. 960   D. 1200

KEY (CORRECT ANSWERS)

1. C	11. D	21. D	31. B	41. C
2. B	12. C	22. D	32. C	42. C
3. D	13. C	23. D	33. D	43. C
4. A	14. C	24. B	34. A	44. A
5. C	15. D	25. D	35. D	45. D
6. A	16. B	26. A	36. C	46. A
7. A	17. C	27. A	37. B	47. B
8. D	18. C	28. C	38. B	48. C
9. C	19. B	29. C	39. D	49. D
10. A	20. D	30. B	40. A	50. C

TEST 2

DIRECTIONS: Each question or incomplete statement is followed by several suggested answers or completions. Select the one that BEST answers the question or completes the statement. *PRINT THE LETTER OF THE CORRECT ANSWER IN THE SPACE AT THE RIGHT.*

1. With reference to twist drills, the statement MOST NEARLY CORRECT is: 1._____

   A. When a high speed drill is being ground dry, it should be dipped in water to cool it
   B. To cut properly, one cutting lip should be ground longer than the other
   C. The lip clearance should be approximately 12 degrees
   D. The angle that the lips form with the centerline of the drill should be 69 degrees

2. When drilling a hole in 1020 steel with a 3/4" HSS drill, the MOST desirable drill speed and feed would be MOST NEARLY _____ rpm and _____ ipr. 2._____

   A. 600; .003   B. 900; .010   C. 1200; .020   D. 1500; .025

3. Assume that a lathe has a spindle speed of 144 revolutions per minute while 12 threads per inch are to be cut along the entire 6" length of a 2" diameter piece of stock. The MINIMUM time required to complete the first cut is MOST NEARLY 3._____

   A. 1 minute   B. 45 seconds   C. 30 seconds   D. 15 seconds

4. A cam to give a lift of 2" is to be made by drilling an off-center hole in a 3" diameter circular disk so that the disk can be mounted on a shaft. The hole should be located 4._____

   A. 1/2" off center   B. 1" off center
   C. on the circumference   D. the job is impossible

5. The hole diameter for a shaft in a journal bearing has a dimension of $3.408"^{+.002}_{-.003}$ and the shaft dimension is $3.404"^{+.000}_{-.001}$. The limits of the clearance for the shaft in the bearing are MOST NEARLY _____ max. _____ min. 5._____

   A. .009"; .001"   B. .008"; .001"   C. .007"; .002"   D. .007"; .001"

6.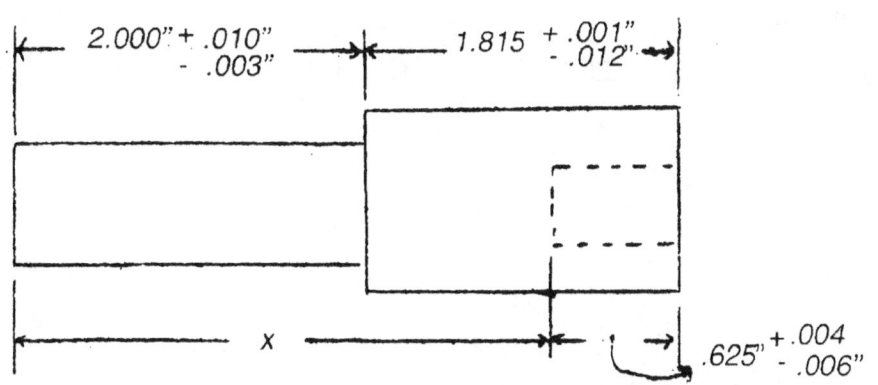

   According to the above sketch which indicates a work piece to be manufactured as per indicated dimensions and tolerances, the MAXIMUM dimension for X is MOST NEARLY 6._____

   A. 3.250"   B. 3.254"   C. 3.267"   D. 3.276"

7.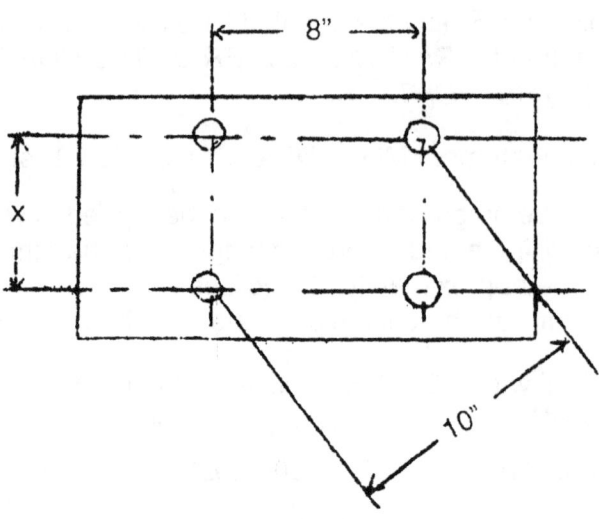

According to the above sketch (assume that it is desired to drill four holes in a plate), the dimension X is MOST NEARLY

A. 5.62"   B. 5.81"   C. 6.00"   D. 6.25"

8. Assume that the following Webber blocks are made available to you: .1003, .1004, .1007, .1009, .100, .105, .107, .112, .115, .128, .130, .146, .250, .450, 1.000.
Of the above blocks, the SMALLEST number of blocks you could use to establish the dimension of 1.3427" is _____ blocks.

A. 4   B. 5   C. 6   D. 8

9.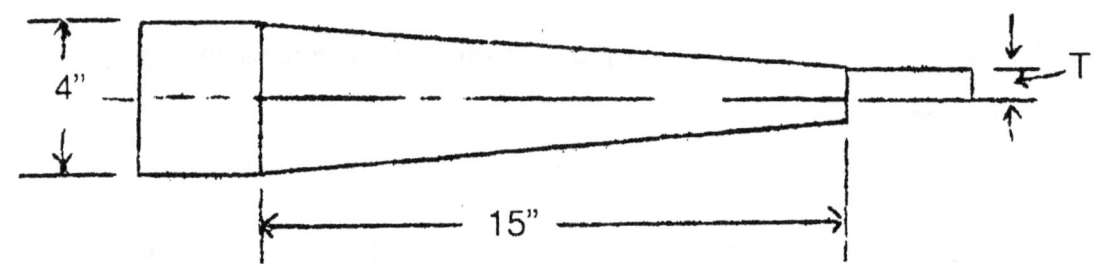

Assuming that the taper in the above drawing is one inch per foot, the dimension T will be MOST NEARLY

A. .750"   B. 1.250"   C. 1.375"   D. 1.438"

10.

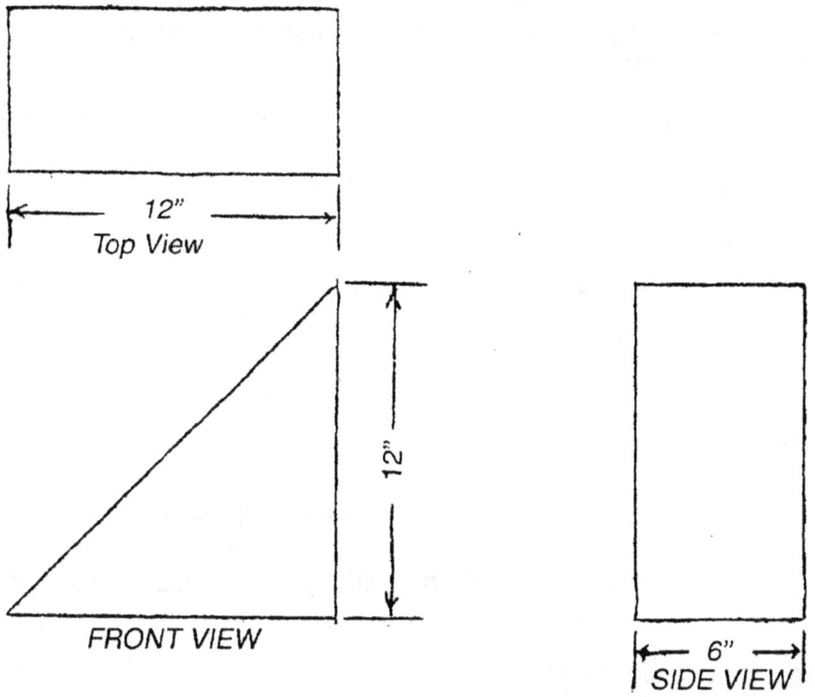

[Figure: Three views of a triangular prism. Top View: 12" wide rectangle. Front View: right triangle with 12" height. Side View: rectangle 6" wide.]

If steel weighs 480 lbs. per cu.ft., the weight of the above object will be MOST NEARLY (assume that the object pictured in the following three views is solid and made of steel) _____ lbs.

A. 70 B. 120 C. 146 D. 224

11. In comparing mechanically and hydraulically driven shapers, the statement MOST NEARLY CORRECT is:

 A. Quicker return strokes can be obtained by mechanical drives
 B. Hydraulic drives are less complicated and cheaper than mechanical drives
 C. With hydraulic drives, cutting stroke velocities are more uniform than with mechanical drives
 D. A shaper with hydraulic drive is more easily overloaded

12. In using a shaper to machine a 2" x 6" x 1" rectangular block, the PREFERRED order of machining the surfaces, where the 2" x 6" surfaces are the top and bottom and the 1" x 6" surfaces are the sides, is

 A. 1-side, 2-top, 3-bottom, 4-side 2
 B. 1-top, 2-bottom, 3-side 1, 4-side 2
 C. 1-top, 2-side, 3-side 2, 4-bottom
 D. 1-side 1, 2-side 2, 3-top, 4-bottom

13. With reference to formed tooth milling cutters, it can CORRECTLY be said that

 A. the cutters do not have any relief
 B. such cutters can be used only for milling simple contours
 C. when the faces of the teeth are sharpened, the contour of the cutting edge is unchanged
 D. they cannot be used in gang milling

14. Assume that specifications call for tightening a nut with a torque of 900 inch pounds. To accomplish this, the tangential force applied to the end of an 18 inch wrench would have to be MOST NEARLY _____ lbs.

    A. 50 B. 75 C. 112.5 D. 150

15. It is desired to connect two pipe fittings as shown below:

    This could be accomplished by using a length of pipe threaded on both sides in addition to a

    A. coupling and a straight cross
    B. nipple, a 90° elbow, and a union
    C. nipple, a 90° street elbow, and a union
    D. nipple, a coupling, and a union

16. In requisitioning sheets of very coarse abrasive cloth, the requested grit size should be MOST NEARLY

    A. 36 B. 80 C. 180 D. 320

17. Fullers, flatters, and swages are tools USUALLY used in

    A. casting (foundry work)   B. forging
    C. plumbing   D. welding

18. With reference to files, the statement MOST NEARLY CORRECT is:

    A. A new file should be broken in by using it first on brass or bronze
    B. Files should be oiled when filing cast iron
    C. The body and tang of a file are both very brittle
    D. Rubbing chalk between the teeth of a file will cause pinning

19. An N-16 thread, as designated in the American National Thread System, indicates that the thread has a

    A. 1/16" crest   B. 16" lead
    C. half angle of 16°   D. 1/16" pitch

20. The electrolytic process in which the thickness of the protective layer of aluminum oxide on aluminum is increased is called

    A. metalizing   B. electroplating
    C. anodizing   D. parkerizing

21. Ferrous castings are USUALLY repaired by the process known as 21._____

    A. brass soldering   B. dip brazing
    C. braze welding   D. resistance brazing

22. Soldering with a soldering iron requires the use of a flux on the parts to be joined. 22._____
    The material used LEAST frequently as a flux is

    A. sal ammoniac   B. zinc chloride
    C. rosin   D. none of the above

23. The LEAST desirable method of removing a broken tap from a hole is to try to 23._____

    A. use a tap *extractor*
    B. jar the tap loose with a punch
    C. break the tap into small pieces
    D. drill the tap out

24. In order to relieve stresses and to induce softness in steels, the MOST effective heat 24._____
    treatment that can be used is called

    A. annealing   B. carburizing
    C. quenching   D. nitriding

25. When quenching is resorted to in the heat treatment of steel, it is UNDESIRABLE to use 25._____

    A. volatile oils   B. sodium hydroxide
    C. potassium hydroxide   D. brine

26. The compound MOST frequently used in casehardening is 26._____

    A. potassium hydroxide   B. potassium cyanide
    C. sodium sulphate   D. cryolite

27. The terms *standard, ratchet, offset,* and *clutch head* USUALLY refer to 27._____

    A. box wrenches   B. screwdrivers
    C. pipe wrenches   D. spanners

28. For the purpose of filing a slot or keyway, it would be DESIRABLE to use a _____ file. 28._____

    A. pillar   B. flat   C. mill   D. taper

Questions 29-30.

DIRECTIONS: Questions 29 and 30 are to be answered in accordance with the paragraph below.

When one is making the selection of grinding wheel specifications, the first variable factor to consider is the wheel speed, which influences the grade and the bond of the wheel. It is recommended that the grade should be determined in this way: the higher the wheel speed with relation to work speed, the softer the wheel should be. When, for any reason, the wheel speed is reduced, then it may be expected that the wheel will wear faster, but this can be overcome by choosing a wheel of a harder grade, assuming that the grade was correct for the initial speed.

29. It can be said that the MOST important piece of information in the above paragraph is:

    A. The higher the relative wheel speed, the softer should be the wheel
    B. Wheel speed is a variable factor
    C. At low speeds, wheels wear rapidly
    D. When a wheel slows down, it should be replaced by a harder grade

30. According to the above paragraph, NO indication is made that

    A. there are other factors to be considered besides speed
    B. hard wheels at low speed wear faster than soft wheels at high speed
    C. the lower the speed, the harder should be the grade
    D. the selection of the bond of the wheel is affected by speed

31. The carriage or saddle on an engine lathe is BEST described as the

    A. movable part which slides over the ways between the headstock and tailstock
    B. movable casting located opposite the headstock on the ways
    C. object that directly supports the cutting tool
    D. two heavy metal sides located lengthwise which ways or V's formed upon them

32. In setting up a milling machine for *rapid or direct* method of indexing, it is necessary to

    A. connect the index plate to the spindle by means of a gear train
    B. disengage the worm and gear
    C. index by means of the index plate and index crank
    D. change the size of gear on the worm

33. The gears BEST suited to transmit motion between shafts whose center lines intersect are _____ gears.

    A. spur B. bevel C. helical D. spiral

34. Coolants made of soluble oils or emulsions should NOT be used for machining

    A. bronze   B. aluminum
    C. magnesium   D. alloy steels

35. When using high-speed tool bits, ordinary machine steel is generally turned on a lathe at a speed, in feet per minute, of MOST NEARLY

    A. 30 to 45   B. 50 to 75
    C. 90 to 150   D. 175 to 225

36. The speed of the cutting stroke, for planing steel castings, roughing, and finishing, in feet per minute, is MOST NEARLY

    A. 30 to 40   B. 50 to 75
    C. 100 to 150   D. 160 to 200

37. Planing speeds are lower than cutting speeds for turning MAINLY because in planing

    A. higher speeds would require special coolants
    B. it is not practicable to use an ample supply of cutting fluid
    C. special tool bits would be required for the higher speeds than those for turning
    D. the table moves in only one direction

38. A 1/2" diameter screw, 13 threads per inch, American Coarse Thread Series, right hand, and loose fit is USUALLY specified on a drawing as

    A. 1/2" - 13NC - 4 - RH   B. 1/2" - 13NC - 3 - LH
    C. 1/2" - 13NC - 2   D. 1/2" - 13NC - 1

39. An arbor is a device for

    A. holding parts to be machined
    B. holding and driving cutting tools
    C. holding parts on a magnetic grinder
    D. enlarging small holes in thin metals

40. Five graduations on the barrel of a micrometer caliper indicates an opening of MOST NEARLY

    A. .005"   B. .025"   C. .125"   D. .135"

41. Seventeen graduations on the barrel of a micrometer caliper and nineteen graduations on the thimble indicates an opening of MOST NEARLY

    A. .545"   B. .444"   C. .394"   D. .339"

42. Increasing the speed of the shaper after completing the roughing cuts results in

    A. chattering
    B. a better finish
    C. increasing internal stresses
    D. warpage

43. A device used for supporting irregular shaped objects in a steady rest of a lathe is called a

    A. hold down   B. cube or box parallel
    C. parallel   D. cat head

44. In producing a large number of small screws, studs or bolts on a lathe, the PROPER chuck to use for this type of work is the _____ chuck.

    A. independent   B. universal
    C. draw-in   D. combination

45. The proper side rake angle of a cutting tool for turning soft brass is MOST NEARLY

    A. 6   B. 20   C. 30   D. 35

46. *The machinist is machining a bearing housing of <u>conventional</u> design.*
    In the above statement, the word *conventional* means MOST NEARLY

    A. complicated   B. superior
    C. new   D. common

47. When turning a piece of <u>tenacious</u> metal on a lathe, a lubricant is used to prevent excessive friction by conducting the heat away.
In the above statement, the word *tenacious* means MOST NEARLY

 A. annealed   B. soft   C. tough   D. coarse

47.____

48. In a particular shop, a machinist is assigned to the task of <u>coordinating</u> various machining operations.
In the above statement, the word *coordinating* means MOST NEARLY

 A. repairing   B. replacing
 C. testing   D. scheduling

48.____

49. The machinist made an <u>insignificant</u> error.
In the above statement, the word *insignificant* means MOST NEARLY

 A. serious   B. accidental
 C. minor   D. hidden

49.____

50. Some machinists have the faculty of knowing when there is work to be done and do not have to be stimulated into doing it.
These machinists may be said to possess

 A. neatness   B. individuality
 C. obedience   D. initiative

50.____

KEY (CORRECT ANSWERS)

1. C	11. C	21. C	31. A	41. B
2. A	12. C	22. A	32. B	42. B
3. C	13. C	23. D	33. B	43. D
4. B	14. A	24. A	34. C	44. C
5. D	15. C	25. A	35. C	45. A
6. C	16. A	26. B	36. A	46. D
7. C	17. B	27. B	37. B	47. C
8. A	18. A	28. A	38. D	48. D
9. C	19. D	29. A	39. B	49. C
10. B	20. C	30. B	40. C	50. D

EXAMINATION SECTION
TEST 1

DIRECTIONS: Each question or incomplete statement is followed by several suggested answers or completions. Select the one that BEST answers the question or completes the statement. *PRINT THE LETTER OF THE CORRECT ANSWER IN THE SPACE AT THE RIGHT.*

Questions 1-4.

DIRECTIONS: Questions 1 through 4, inclusive, are to be answered in accordance with the lathe tool bit shown below.

 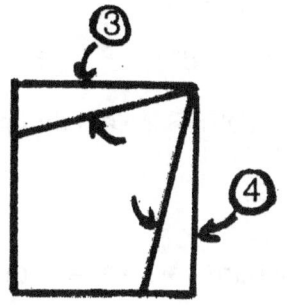

1. The front clearance angle is indicated by the angle labeled

   A. 1　　B. 2　　C. 3　　D. 4

2. The top rake angle is indicated by the angle labeled

   A. 1　　B. 2　　C. 3　　D. 4

3. The side clearance angle is indicated by the angle labeled

   A. 1　　B. 2　　C. 3　　D. 4

4. The side rake angle is indicated by the angle labeled

   A. 1　　B. 2　　C. 3　　D. 4

5. When threading internal holes, tap breakage will MOST likely be greater when

   A. tap drills used are too small in diameter
   B. the taper tap is used first
   C. using tap drills for American Standard Coarse-thread series
   D. using tap drills for American Standard Fine-thread Series

6. The PRIMARY reason for a twist drill *splitting up the center* is that the

   A. cutting edges were ground at different angles
   B. lips were ground at different lengths
   C. lip clearance angle was too great
   D. lip clearance angle was insufficient

17

7. The appropriate lip angle clearance of a twist drill is MOST NEARLY

   A. 1 to 3°   B. 7 to 10°   C. 14 to 17°   D. 19 to 22°

8. Tap drill diameter = O.D. of screw - $\dfrac{1}{\text{threads/in.}}$

   Using the formula given above, the tap drill diameter required for a 7/16 x 20 screw is MOST NEARLY

   A. 0.25"   B. 0.39"   C. 0.45"   D. 0.47"

9. When draw-filing is used on a piece of work, the type of finish produced on the work is MOST NEARLY

   A. rippled   B. coarse   C. smooth   D. knurled

10. The PROPER file a machinist should use for finishing ordinary flat surfaces is the _____ file.

    A. Pillar   B. Warding   C. Hooktooth   D. Hand

11. An all hard saw blade should be used in a hacksaw frame when sawing

    A. tool steel
    B. channel iron
    C. aluminum
    D. thin wall copper tubing

12. In the operation of a drill press, the SAFEST way to brush chips away from a moving drill is to use

    A. gloves
    B. an oil can
    C. cotton waste
    D. a wooden rod

13. The length, in inches, of a leather belt required to go around two 12" diameter pulleys 6'0" on centers is MOST NEARLY

    A. 199.5"   B. 181.7"   C. 175.3"   D. 162.4"

14. Assume that the drill speed for drilling iron is 100 feet per minute.
    To obtain this speed, a 1" diameter drill must rotate at approximately _____ r.p.m.

    A. 300   B. 380   C. 600   D. 1000

15. With reference to a *Plain Vertical Spindle Drilling Machine*, the spindle generally

    A. can be moved up and down
    B. can only be moved down
    C. is stationary and the table adjustable
    D. can be inclined for angular work

16. The surface gage is generally NOT used for

    A. laying out
    B. leveling and lining up work
    C. checking angles and tapers
    D. locating centers on rough work

17. A round nose chisel is BEST suited for chipping 17.____

    A. flat surfaces   B. V-shaped grooves
    C. filleted corners   D. flat bottom grooves

18. Of the following SAE steel grade designations, the one which designates a molybdenum steel is SAE 18.____

    A. 4027   B. 3140   C. 2330   D. 1117

19. Of the following SAE steel grade designations, the one which designates a carbon steel is SAE 19.____

    A. 1020   B. 4042   C. 5150   D. 8622

20. Grinding machine wheels should be inspected for flaws 20.____

    A. while they are in motion
    B. at the end of each working day
    C. prior to starting the machine
    D. only after being dressed

21. Cast iron is ordinarily machined 21.____

    A. with a soluble oil
    B. with 60 second mineral oil
    C. dry
    D. with mineral oil with 10% fat

22. *Unilateral tolerance,* as related to a basic dimension, on drawings, means that the total tolerance is 22.____

    A. in two directions
    B. in one direction
    C. allowed for rough finish
    D. allowed for fine finish

23. The classification of fit for rotating parts, such as connecting rod bearings to crankshafts, is USUALLY called a _____ fit. 23.____

    A. push   B. driving   C. running   D. shrinkage

24. A process involving first heating and then cooling of metal to induce softening is BEST known as 24.____

    A. annealing   B. case hardening
    C. quenching   D. nitriding

Questions 25-28.

DIRECTIONS: Questions 25 through 28, inclusive, are to be answered in accordance with the sketch shown below.

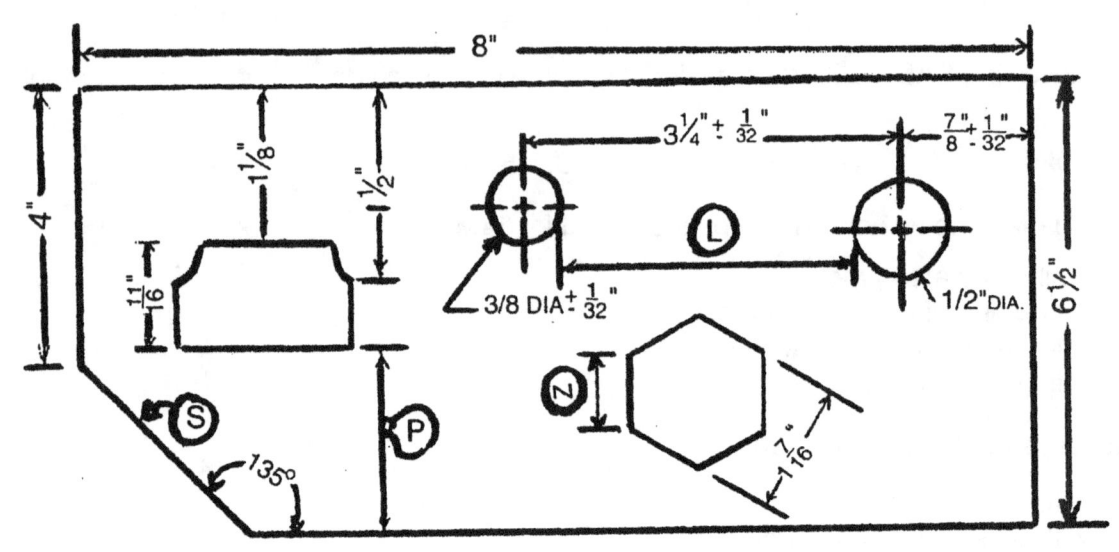

NOT TO SCALE

25. The maximum length of dimension L in the above sketch is MOST NEARLY

 A. 2 59/64"   B. 2 55/64"   C. 2 37/64"   D. 2 31/64"

26. The length of dimension N on the regular hexagon in the above sketch is MOST NEARLY

 A. 23/32"   B. 21/32"   C. 19/32"   D. 17/32"

27. The length of dimension S in the above sketch is MOST NEARLY

 A. 5"   B. 4 3/32"   C. 3 5/16"   D. 3 17/32"

28. The length of dimension P in the above sketch is MOST NEARLY

 A. 4 3/16"   B. 4 3/8"   C. 4 11/16"   D. 4 15/16"

29. Assume that a gear and pinion have a ratio of 3 to 1. If the gear is rotating at 300 revolutions per minute, the speed of the pinion, in revolutions per minute, is MOST NEARLY

 A. 100   B. 300   C. 900   D. 1800

30. A 2" square rod, 6" in length, is machined to a 2" diameter round rod, same length. The amount of material to be removed, in cubic inches, is MOST NEARLY

 A. 5   B. 7   C. 9   D. 10

31. The object of tempering or drawing steel is to reduce the

 A. softness   B. brittleness
 C. ductility   D. strength

32. When grinding a piece of metal, you note that the sparks given off show several interrupted, dotted, brownish-red spark lines with ball-shaped end sparks of dark blood-red color. Some of these burst into small red stars of a few rays, slightly lighter in color. In this case, the material being ground is MOST likely

    A. chrome steel
    B. high speed steel
    C. carbon steel
    D. iron

33. A left-hand tool holder is USUALLY used for

    A. facing toward a live center and for turning close to the chuck
    B. turning material with a large diameter and for facing toward a dead center
    C. producing a knurled finish
    D. producing threads of a fine finish with close limits

34. A 12" diameter pulley revolving at 1000 revolutions per minute is belted to a 24" diameter pulley revolving at 500 revolutions per minute.
    The belt speed, in feet per minute, is MOST NEARLY

    A. 1570   B. 3150   C. 6280   D. 7000

35. If steel weighs 0.28 pounds per cubic inch, then the weight, in pounds, of a 2" square steel bar 120" long is MOST NEARLY

    A. 115   B. 125   C. 135   D. 155

36. In the sketch shown at the right, the diameter A is equal to
    A. 1 9/16"
    B. 1 3/4"
    C. 1 7/8"
    D. 1 15/16"

    (TAPER PER FOOT = .75", height 1 1/2", length 6")

37. The addendum of a spur gear is BEST described as the

    A. number of teeth for each inch of pitch diameter
    B. portion of the tooth between the pitch circle and the root circle
    C. distance from the center of a tooth to the center of the next consecutive tooth
    D. portion of the tooth which projects above or outside of the pitch circle

38. The kind of flux used in soldering copper and brass is

    A. stearin
    B. zinc chloride
    C. sal ammoniac
    D. muriatic acid

39. The addition of zinc to solder will

    A. remove the oxide in soldering
    B. cause the latter to flow more freely
    C. lower the melting point
    D. cause the latter to flow sluggishly

40. In order to protect yourself from injury when starting a grinding machine, it is ADVISABLE to stand

    A. on one side of the machine and push the starting button
    B. in front of the machine and push the starting button
    C. in front of the machine, adjust the tool rest, and push the starting button
    D. on one side of the machine, press the work against the wheel, and then push the starting button

41. When operating a drill press in a machine shop, the operator should

    A. wear gloves at all times
    B. stop the moving chuck by hand
    C. unlock the chuck with hammer blows
    D. wear snug-fitting clothing

42. If a motor bearing on a large electric motor becomes dangerously hot while driving a boring mill, the BEST thing to do is

    A. cool it quickly by squirting with cold water
    B. oil or grease the bearing freely and increase speed of motor
    C. stop the motor and check for oil and grease
    D. run the motor slowly under load until the bearing cools off

43. *It is not the revolutions that destroy machinery, but the friction.*
    In the above statement, the word *friction* means MOST NEARLY

    A. rotation   B. speed
    C. evolution   D. resistance

44. When steel is heated, the color which indicates the HIGHEST temperature is

    A. white   B. red   C. orange   D. yellow

45. Of the following instruments, the one which is usually used to measure tapers on round stock is called a

    A. ring gage   B. sine bar
    C. vernier caliper   D. hermaphrodite caliper

46. The gauge number of a wire USUALLY indicates its

    A. weight   B. quality   C. strength   D. diameter

47. Assume a lathe has a lead screw of 12 threads per inch and a compound gearing with a ratio of 2 to 1.
    In order to cut 52 threads per inch, it is necessary to use 52 teeth on the lead screw gear and a stud gear of _____ teeth.

    A. 12   B. 24   C. 36   D. 48

48. Assume a lathe has a lead screw of 7 threads per inch and it is necessary to cut a thread of 18 threads per inch.
    If the gear on the lead screw has 72 teeth, then the gear on the stud must have _____ teeth.

    A. 12   B. 22   C. 28   D. 32

49. The number of threads per inch on a 1/2" screw, having American Coarse Threads, is MOST NEARLY

    A. 13 B. 15 C. 17 D. 19

50. The front clearance angle of a lathe cutting tool is MOST NEARLY

    A. 0 to 7° B. 8 to 15° C. 17 to 25° D. 27 to 30°

KEY (CORRECT ANSWERS)

1. B	11. A	21. C	31. B	41. D
2. A	12. D	22. B	32. B	42. C
3. D	13. B	23. C	33. B	43. D
4. C	14. B	24. A	34. B	44. A
5. A	15. A	25. B	35. C	45. B
6. D	16. C	26. A	36. C	46. D
7. B	17. C	27. D	37. D	47. B
8. B	18. A	28. C	38. B	48. C
9. C	19. A	29. C	39. D	49. A
10. D	20. C	30. A	40. A	50. B

TEST 2

DIRECTIONS: Each question or incomplete statement is followed by several suggested answers or completions. Select the one that BEST answers the question or completes the statement. *PRINT THE LETTER OF THE CORRECT ANSWER IN THE SPACE AT THE RIGHT.*

1. The MAJOR thread diameter of a number 12 machine screw is MOST NEARLY   1.____

   A. .164"   B. .175"   C. .190"   D. .216"

2. For general machine shop work, the proper tap drill number to use for a 6/32 machine screw is MOST NEARLY   2.____

   A. 40   B. 33   C. 25   D. 21

3. The MAIN difference between a plain and a universal shaper can BEST be explained by the difference in the   3.____

   A. type of table each has
   B. material being machined
   C. automatic feed of the tool bit
   D. setting of the stroke of the ram for length and position

4. The Brinell test, as used in general machine shop work, is a test to determine metal   4.____

   A. roughness   B. temperature
   C. hardness   D. melting point

5. The process used in producing non-circular holes or internal slots and keyways on a production basis is USUALLY called   5.____

   A. tapering   B. broaching
   C. milling   D. reaming

6. The length of stroke on a planer is USUALLY regulated by   6.____

   A. adjustable dogs or stops on the sides of the platen
   B. the horizontal cross-rail above the platen
   C. the footstock
   D. adjusting the saddle

7. To make certain that a reamer follows a bored hole accurately, one should use a   7.____

   A. drill pad   B. taper reamer
   C. floating reamer driver   D. cherry reamer

8. When a considerable amount of machining is being done on a long shaft, it may be necessary to adjust the tailstock of a lathe a number of times because of the   8.____

   A. wear on the tailstock center
   B. expansion of the shaft
   C. pressure on the face plate
   D. flexibility of the shaft

9. Of the following, the device that is USUALLY used to measure the run-out of a shaft is a   9.____

   A. tachometer
   B. try bar
   C. gage block
   D. dial indicator

10. A screw pitch gauge is USUALLY used to determine the   10.____

    A. depth of a thread
    B. angle of the pitch of a screw
    C. width of the base of a thread
    D. number of threads per inch

11. In turning or facing an irregular piece of work on a lathe, the able machinist would MOST likely use a(n) _____ chuck.   11.____

    A. universal
    B. utility
    C. joint
    D. independent

12. High spots on a surface plate which has been in use for some time are BEST removed by means of a   12.____

    A. scraper
    B. router
    C. sander
    D. grinding wheel

13. The process in which an iron-base alloy is heated above the critical temperature or transformation range and then allowed to cool in still air or room temperature is called   13.____

    A. normalizing
    B. hardening
    C. tempering
    D. spheroidizing

14. A cold chisel is USUALLY used for chipping   14.____

    A. filleted corners and concave surfaces
    B. grooves and narrow slots
    C. V-shape grooves in cast iron
    D. flat surfaces or cutting through thin metal

15. A particular material is shown on a drawing as SAE 4042. This material is MOST likely a _____ steel.   15.____

    A. molybdenum
    B. nickel
    C. manganese
    D. chromium

16. Which one of the following types of threads is MOST suitable for thrust purposes involving high stresses in one direction only? _____ thread.   16.____

    A. Brown & Sharpe Worm
    B. Acme
    C. Buttress
    D. Sharp V

17. The instrument USUALLY used to scribe a circle 30" in diameter is called a(n)   17.____

    A. divider
    B. trabbel
    C. toolmakers' button
    D. hermaphrodite caliper

18. The number of threads per inch on the spindle of a micrometer is USUALLY   18.____

    A. 20
    B. 30
    C. 40
    D. 25

25

19. The tool used for checking concentricity on lathe work is USUALLY called a(n)

    A. outside caliper B. inside caliper
    C. dial indicator   D. plug gage

20. The tool BEST used for scribing a horizontal line at a given height is called a _____ gage.

    A. planer   B. scale   C. surface   D. sine

21. The grinding of a large number of small parts on a centerless grinder can be expedited by the use of _____ feeds.

    A. hopper   B. miller   C. straight   D. cross

22. Which one of the following statements is MOST NEARLY CORRECT concerning abrasive grinding wheels?

    A. Mounting flanges should be recessed at least 1/16 of an inch.
    B. Grinding on the flat sides of straight wheels is a good practice.
    C. Small wheels do not require a hood.
    D. Emery is not a natural abrasive.

23. Regarding a milling cutter, that portion which is just behind the cutting edge of a milling cutter tooth is called the

    A. secondary relief   B. face
    C. land   D. primary relief

24. In order to prevent milling cutters from dragging on the work, the PRIMARY relief angle or clearance is USUALLY ground from _____ to _____ degrees.

    A. 2; 3   B. 5; 6   C. 8; 10   D. 12; 15

25. The type of milling machine that has a work table which can be swiveled in a horizontal plane is USUALLY called _____ milling machine.

    A. universal   B. plain
    C. special   D. planer type

26. To obtain a surface speed of 4400 feet per minute, a 6 inch drive pulley will have to revolve at an R.P.M. of MOST NEARLY

    A. 1800   B. 3200   C. 2200   D. 2800

27. The smallest diameter of a circular steel plate from which a 1.25" square can be cut is MOST NEARLY

    A. 1.76"   B. 1.86"   C. 1.67"   D. 1.96"

28. $M = D + 3G - \dfrac{1.5155}{N}$, where M = measurement over wires, D = .750, G = .05774, and N = 10.
    Given the above formula and data, select the micrometer reading over 3 wires for a 3/4 N.C. thread.

    A. .7717   B. .7728   C. .7731   D. .7749

29. A gear with 85 teeth is driven by a pinion having 32 teeth. What is the speed of the gear, in R.P.M., if the pinion revolves at 475 R.P.M.?

    A. 179   B. 189   C. 299   D. 1250

30. In facing a gear blank on a lathe, the compound rest is swiveled at an angle of 30 from the face of the work and the tool fed in with the compound feed screw.
    In this particular case, for every thousandth the tool is advanced with the compound feed screw, the thickness of the work is reduced by

    A. .001"   B. .002"   C. .0005"   D. .00075"

31. The 18-8 stainless steel is often referred to as a steel having about 18 percent

    A. nickel   B. tungsten   C. chromium   D. manganese

32. The term used to express the axial movement of a lathe tool for each revolution of the work piece is called the

    A. cutting speed
    B. cutting rate
    C. cutting power
    D. cutting feed

33. The cutting fluid or coolant to use when machining tough metals such as stainless steel is the

    A. high sulphur oils
    B. emulsified oil mixtures
    C. low sulphur oils
    D. conventional soluble oils

34. To find the right size of packing (square sectional type) to install in a stuffing box, the able machinist would MOST likely measure _____ and then divide by 2.

    A. the stuffing box bore and subtract rod diameter,
    B. the stuffing box bore and add rod diameter,
    C. outside diameter of gland and add rod diameter,
    D. inside diameter of gland and add outside diameter

35. The rigidity of arbors which are used for milling machine cutters is USUALLY increased by _____ the arbor.

    A. increasing the length of
    B. heat treating
    C. increasing the diameter of
    D. case hardening

36. In reference to a radial drill, the statement MOST NEARLY CORRECT is:

    A. The work is moved towards the drill-spindle head when drilling
    B. Only roughing-in work is done with the radial drill
    C. Better work can be done with this machine if manual feed is used rather than automatic feed
    D. There are usually 30 to 40 spindle speeds obtainable on an ordinary radial drill

37. Monel is an alloy consisting MAINLY of

    A. nickel and copper
    B. chromium and nickel
    C. iron and nickel
    D. nickel and German silver

38. Which one of the following wire gage systems is used for non-ferrous metals?

    A. Brown & Sharpe   B. Washburn & Moen
    C. U.S. Standard Gage   D. Birmingham Wire Gage

39. In reference to a vertical boring mill, the statement MOST NEARLY CORRECT is:

    A. Two heads can be adjusted to cut simultaneously at different diameters
    B. The work must be clamped to the table in a vertical position
    C. The engine lathe and vertical boring mill have very little in common
    D. It is usually very difficult to clamp and *true* a large job for *turning* on a vertical boring mill

40. In a reciprocating water pump, the packing ring that takes the GREATEST wear is usually located

    A. next to the gland
    B. next to the cylinder
    C. in the middle of the stuffing box
    D. 3/4 of the way in towards the cylinder

41.

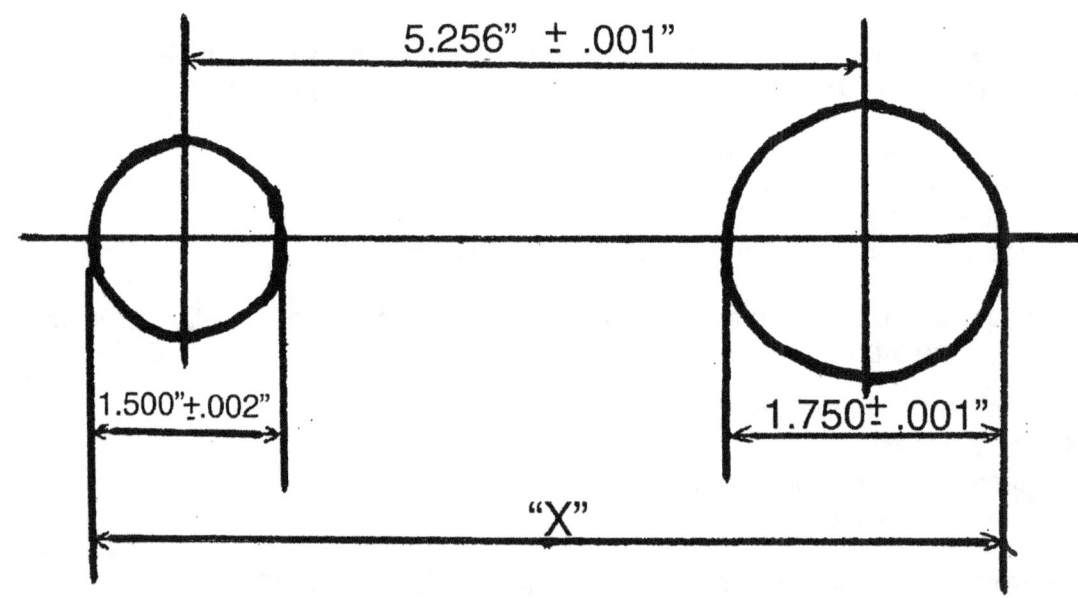

In the diagram shown on the preceding page, the maximum dimension for X is MOST NEARLY

A. 6.8810"   B. 6.8829"   C. 6.8835"   D. 6.8837"

42. Which one of the above cross-sectional symbols USUALLY represents brass material on a shop drawing?

   A. 1 B. 2 C. 3 D. 4

43. The expression *drawing a drill* is often referred to when

   A. rehardening a drill
   B. drilling a large hole through a pilot hole
   C. a drill *runs off* the center-punch mark and must be brought back to the center
   D. drilling brass and the drill *hogs* into the metal

44. The cutting speed of milling cutters depends MAINLY on the

   A. kind of material being cut
   B. diameter of the cutter
   C. coolant used
   D. time allowed for the job

45. Which one of the following items is NOT commonly used in conjunction with lathe work?

   A. Boring bar holder   B. Clamp dog
   C. Step block   D. Expanding mandrel

46. The peripheral or surface speed, in feet per minute, of a grinding wheel is USUALLY somewhere between

   A. 2000 and 3000   B. 3500 and 4000
   C. 5000 and 6000   D. 6500 and 7000

47. In order to cut a gear having 18 teeth on a milling machine, by means of plain or simple indexing, the able machinist would rotate the index-crank _____ times for each tooth.

   A. 2 2/9   B. 3 2/9   C. 4 2/9   D. 1 2/9

48. The following is a list of Johansson blocks available to you to establish the dimension of 1.2721": .1001, .1009, .1004, .149, .147, .123, .800, .124, .900, .1002.
   The FEWEST number of these blocks which you could use to establish this dimension of 1.2721" is _____ blocks.

   A. 3   B. 4   C. 5   D. 6

49. In general, when sawing a piece of mild steel with a hacksaw, the machinist should

   A. use a coarse blade for thin work
   B. draw the blade loosely in the frame
   C. draw the blade extremely tight in the frame
   D. use a pressure of 20 lbs. per inch of contact area of the teeth

50. Which one of the following attachments is NOT usually used on a milling machine? 50.____
    _____ attachment.

    A. High speed
    B. Rack-milling
    C. Vertical spindle
    D. Stepdown

KEY (CORRECT ANSWERS)

1. D	11. D	21. A	31. C	41. C
2. B	12. A	22. A	32. D	42. C
3. A	13. A	23. C	33. A	43. C
4. C	14. D	24. B	34. A	44. A
5. B	15. A	25. A	35. C	45. C
6. A	16. C	26. D	36. D	46. C
7. C	17. B	27. A	37. A	47. A
8. B	18. C	28. A	38. A	48. B
9. D	19. C	29. A	39. A	49. D
10. D	20. C	30. C	40. A	50. D

EXAMINATION SECTION
TEST 1

DIRECTIONS: Each question or incomplete statement is followed by several suggested answers or completions. Select the one that BEST answers the question or completes the statement. *PRINT THE LETTER OF THE CORRECT ANSWER IN THE SPACE AT THE RIGHT.*

1. When using differential indexing on a milling machine, the index-plate is USUALLY rotated by gearing connected with the

    A. radial arm
    B. dividing-head spindle
    C. universal
    D. foot stock

    1._____

2. A piece of round stock is 8 inches long. A taper of 3/4 inch per foot is required on the stock. The lathe tail-stock center should be set over from the centerline position _____ inch.

    A. 3/16   B. 1/4   C. 5/16   D. 3/8

    2._____

3. In repairing a particular pump, it was necessary for a machinist to make four studs from a steel bar. Assuming the length of each stud measures 2 3/16", 1 11/32", 2 1/4", and 1 7/8", and 1/8" waste is allowed for each cut taken and 1/32" is allowed for facing each end, then the length of rod needed is MOST NEARLY

    A. 8 7/16"   B. 8 9/32"   C. 7 31/32"   D. 8 3/32"

    3._____

4. Which one of the following statements concerning a lathe is MOST NEARLY CORRECT?
   The

    A. threading mechanism should be used for general feeding
    B. live center is usually hard, and the dead center soft
    C. axis of the main spindle determines the centerline of the lathe
    D. tailstock slide has no short transverse adjustment

    4._____

5. The part of a lathe that contains the gears and clutches for transmitting motion from the feed rod to the carriage is called the

    A. saddle
    B. apron
    C. headstock
    D. cross slide

    5._____

6. Regarding planers, the statement MOST NEARLY CORRECT is:

    A. Hardness of material is the most important factor in planing cast iron and ordinary steels
    B. A deep cut with a light feed is better than a light cut and heavy feed
    C. As depth of cut is increased, the work speed should be increased
    D. By using carbide tools, it is advantageous to increase the feed

    6._____

7. When grinding crankpins, it is necessary to hold the main crankshaft in an offset position so that the axis of the crankpin to be ground will coincide with the axis of rotation or centerline of the grinding machine.
   In this particular case, the amount of offset is equal to _____ throw of the crank.

    7._____

A. 1/4 the   B. 1/2 the   C. 3/4 the   D. the full

Questions 8-9.

DIRECTIONS: Questions 8 and 9 are based on the following passage.

The wheels used for internal grinding should generally be softer than those used for other grinding operations, because the contact area between the wheel and work is comparatively large. A soft wheel that will cut with little pressure should be used to prevent springing the spindle. The grade of the wheel depends upon the character of the work and the stiffness of the machine, and, where a large variety of work is being ground, it may not be practicable to have an assortment of wheels adapted to all conditions. By adjusting the speed, however, a wheel not exactly suited to the work in hand can often be used. If the wheel wears too rapidly, it should be run faster, and, if it tends to glaze, the speed should be diminished.

8. On the basis of the above passage, it may BEST be said that

   A. the type and grade of wheel are independent of the sturdiness of the machine
   B. by increasing the wheel speed, parts can easily be internally ground
   C. wheels used for outside grinding usually have a smaller contact area between the wheel and work
   D. to carry on hand an assortment of wheels for all conceivable internal grinding jobs is economical

9. On the basis of the above passage, it may BEST be said that

   A. in general, if a wheel wears too rapidly, the speed should be decreased
   B. by decreasing the wheel speed, a wheel not quite appropriate for the job may sometimes be used
   C. where a large variety of work is being ground, the grade of wheel depends on the diameter of the wheel
   D. if a wheel tends to glaze, it should run faster

10. A three-inch diameter steel bar two feet long weighs MOST NEARLY (assume steel weighs 480 lbs./cu.ft.) _____ lbs.

    A. 48   B. 58   C. 68   D. 78

11. Which one of the following statements concerning the numbering system used with Morse standard taper shanks is MOST NEARLY CORRECT?

    A. The taper per inch does not always increase with each larger taper number.
    B. The tapers are numbered from 1 to 7, inclusive.
    C. The taper per foot is 1/12 that of the taper per inch.
    D. Morse tapers are not generally used on the shanks of twist drills.

12. The micrometer equipped with a vernier scale USUALLY has an accuracy of

    A. .001"   B. .0001"   C. .00001"   D. .00002"

13. A cracked malleable iron casting can BEST be repaired by welding or brazing it with rods made of

    A. cast iron   B. steel
    C. bronze   D. white metal

14. The flexible couplings of a pumping unit (centrifugal pump and motor) are BEST aligned with the use of a _____ and feeler gage.   14.____

    A. straight edge B. dial indicator
    C. tachometer D. ram

15. To get the best performance from a steel twist drill, which is to be used on heat treated steels or drop forgings such as automobile connecting rods, the cutting edges of the drill should be ground so that the angle, in degrees, included between the two lips is MOST NEARLY   15.____

    A. 60 B. 90 C. 118 D. 125

16. Stay bolts are usually installed to prevent flexing of boiler heads. These stay bolts   16.____

    A. are welded to the heads
    B. have a fusible plug at one end
    C. are made of non-ferrous material
    D. are usually threaded rods

17. The cutting stroke speed of a shaper ram, in feet per minute, having a stroke of 8 inches and making 54 strokes per minute, is MOST NEARLY   17.____

    A. 40 B. 80 C. 50 D. 60

18. A device used to take up slack in cables and tie rods is called a   18.____

    A. turnbuckle B. clevis
    C. collar screw D. wing nut

19. A lathe with a lead number of 8 has a 24 tooth gear on the stud and a 48 tooth gear on the screw. This lathe is geared to cut _____ threads per inch.   19.____

    A. 16 B. 4 C. 32 D. 8

20. The diametral pitch of a gear usually indicates the   20.____

    A. size of the tooth
    B. type of tooth
    C. number of teeth per inch of circular pitch
    D. number of teeth per inch of root circle

21. Draw filing can BEST be done to get a smooth finish with the use of a _____ cut file.   21.____

    A. double B. second C. single D. cross

22. A *drift* is a tool used to   22.____

    A. drive taper pins and cotter pins
    B. align holes for bolts and rivets
    C. mark layout lines with small indentations
    D. drilling stone or concrete

23. A *pawl* is a device which is USUALLY found on a   23.____

    A. lathe B. shaper
    C. drill press D. hand grinder

24. The American Standard Taper Pipe Thread is made with a taper of ____ per foot.

    A. 1/4"   B. 3/8"   C. 1/2"   D. 3/4"

25. The distance a screw thread advances axially in one turn is called

    A. pitch   B. lead
    C. angle of thread D. crest

26. $P = K \times f \times d$ with K for cast iron = 132,000, f = feed/rev. and d = depth of cut.
    Using the chip pressure formula above, the chip pressure, in pounds, on a single-pointed tool, when machining cast iron using a feed of .012" per revolution and taking a cut 1/4" deep, would be MOST NEARLY

    A. 130   B. 390   C. 330   D. 30

27. The size of a thread on a bolt could be determined by using a _____ gage.

    A. snap   B. screw pitch
    C. *go*   D. ring

28. A cold chisel is a very dangerous tool when

    A. the cutting edge is too sharp
    B. used with a ball peen hammer
    C. used with a bronze-faced hammer
    D. the head is mushroomed

29. A pair of bevel gears with the same number of teeth and with shafts at right angles to each other is called a _____ gear.

    A. spiral bevel   B. spur
    C. parallel   D. miter

30. The MAIN object of *drawing* the temper in a piece of steel is to reduce its

    A. strength   B. malleability
    C. ductility   D. brittleness

31. The tap drill for a 10/24 American National Coarse Thread is MOST NEARLY No.

    A. 36   B. 33   C. 26   D. 21

32. If a pulley rotates at 175 R.P.M. and is belt-driven by a 12" diameter pulley which rotates at 275 R.P.M., then the diameter of the driven pulley is MOST NEARLY

    A. 15"   B. 19"   C. 16"   D. 23"

33. A snap gage is USUALLY used in connection with

    A. holes   B. threads
    C. sine bars D. outside diameters

34. In the formation of gear teeth, one of the systems in general use today is the *Involute System*.
    The pressure angle for this particular system is USUALLY

    A. 12.5°   B. 13.5°   C. 20.0°   D. 14.5°

35. _____ steels are USUALLY case hardened.

    A. High speed
    B. Cold rolled
    C. Alloy
    D. Chromium

36. In negative rake cutting on a lathe, the *back rake* surface of the tool

    A. is held 90° to the movement of the work
    B. points in the direction of work movement
    C. points opposite to the work movement
    D. causes material to be sheared from the work

37. When turning rough forgings or steel castings on a lathe using a sintered carbide tool, the tool should be ground with a

    A. zero back rake
    B. positive back rake
    C. negative back rake
    D. negative side rake of 15° to 20°

38. If a supervisor states that a particular type of breakdown on an automotive engine is *general*, he means it is MOST NEARLY

    A. timely
    B. unimportant
    C. obvious
    D. prevalent

39. The type of machine used for milling irregular slots, contours, etc. on parts of machines or instruments is called a

    A. Brinell
    B. Rockwell
    C. Pantograph
    D. Scleroscope

40. The part of a truck that allows one rear wheel to rotate faster than its mate when going around a corner is called the

    A. transmission
    B. universal
    C. differential
    D. crankshaft

41. A hacksaw blade with 14 teeth per inch is BEST used for sawing

    A. structural steel
    B. aluminum (#20 B. & S. gauge sheets)
    C. brass (#22 B. & S. gauge sheets)
    D. high speed steel

42. The lead of a screw that has a double thread is MOST NEARLY _____ the pitch.

    A. one-half
    B. one-quarter
    C. twice
    D. four times

43. To finish the bottoms of narrow slots, the file BEST used is the

    A. taper   B. square   C. vixen   D. flat

44. The thread that has a 45° thread angle is COMMONLY known as the

    A. Acme
    B. Square
    C. Buttress
    D. Brown & Sharpe Worm

45. To get a smooth finish, draw filing can BEST be done by a machinist with the use of a _____ cut file.

    A. double B. second C. single D. cross

46. The amount of material USUALLY left for finishing when filing on a lathe is MOST NEARLY

    A. .001" B. .004" C. .005" D. .007"

47. V-blocks and clamps are USUALLY used to hold _____ stock.

    A. square B. flat C. brass D. round

48. Of the following, when a fast cutting file is required, the able machinist should use a

    A. single cut bastard
    B. single cut smooth
    C. double cut bastard
    D. double cut smooth

49. The chisel used for chipping filleted corners and concave surfaces is a

    A. round point
    B. flat
    C. diamond point
    D. cape

50. The hand tap used to start a thread is called a _____ tap.

    A. plug
    B. taper
    C. bottoming
    D. drive

KEY (CORRECT ANSWERS)

1. B	11. A	21. C	31. C	41. A
2. B	12. B	22. B	32. B	42. C
3. B	13. C	23. B	33. D	43. B
4. C	14. A	24. D	34. D	44. C
5. B	15. D	25. B	35. B	45. C
6. B	16. D	26. B	36. B	46. A
7. D	17. A	27. B	37. C	47. D
8. C	18. A	28. D	38. D	48. C
9. B	19. A	29. D	39. C	49. A
10. A	20. A	30. D	40. C	50. B

TEST 2

DIRECTIONS: Each question or incomplete statement is followed by several suggested answers or completions. Select the one that BEST answers the question or completes the statement. *PRINT THE LETTER OF THE CORRECT ANSWER IN THE SPACE AT THE RIGHT.*

1. High spots on a surface plate which has been in use for some time are BEST removed by means of a   1._____
   - A. router
   - B. sander
   - C. grinding wheel
   - D. scraper

2. The CORRECT lip clearance angle to grind on a drill is GENERALLY   2._____
   - A. 8°
   - B. 12°
   - C. 18°
   - D. 22°

3. The APPROXIMATE drill speed, in feet per minute, for drilling cast iron is   3._____
   - A. 50
   - B. 150
   - C. 200
   - D. 250

4. For drilling in steel, the angle that the lips or cutting edges should make with the axis of the drill is MOST NEARLY   4._____
   - A. 39°
   - B. 49°
   - C. 59°
   - D. 72°

5. The number of threads per inch for a screw with a pitch of .375 inches is   5._____
   - A. 2 1/3
   - B. 2 1/4
   - C. 2 2/3
   - D. 2 1/3

6. The MAJOR thread diameter of a number 10 machine screw is   6._____
   - A. .164"
   - B. .175"
   - C. .190"
   - D. .215"

7. The tap drill size required for an 8-32 thread is number   7._____
   - A. 40
   - B. 35
   - C. 21
   - D. 29

8. The number of threads per inch of a 3/8" screw, standard American National Coarse Threads, is MOST NEARLY   8._____
   - A. 12
   - B. 14
   - C. 16
   - D. 18

9. To remove a drill from the sleeve or socket on a drill press, one would use a   9._____
   - A. drift punch
   - B. drill rod
   - C. drill drift
   - D. chuck key

10. A cape chisel is USUALLY used for chipping   10._____
    - A. grooves and slots in metal surfaces
    - B. corners and concave surfaces
    - C. flat surfaces or cutting through thin metal
    - D. V-shape grooves on soft metals

11. An expanding mandrel is used for
    A. holding and driving cutting tools
    B. enlarging small holes
    C. extracting broken screws
    D. holding work to be machined

12. The distance from the outside diameter of a spur gear to the pitch circle of the gear is called the
    A. dedendum
    B. total depth
    C. addendum
    D. working depth

13. The type of gearing that eliminates the use of thrust bearings on the shafts is called _____ gearing.
    A. spur
    B. bevel
    C. herringbone
    D. spiral

14. The vernier scale on a one inch micrometer is located on the
    A. frame
    B. spindle
    C. thimble
    D. sleeve

15. A thread micrometer is used on threads for measuring _____ diameter.
    A. minor
    B. major
    C. pitch
    D. shoulder

16. A sine bar is used to measure
    A. hole diameters
    B. pitch diameters
    C. tapers
    D. out of round surfaces

17. Which one of the following is generally used for setting a surface gauge?
    A. Gage blocks
    B. Planer gauge
    C. Inside caliper
    D. Combination square

18. A center gauge is used to check
    A. diameters of holes
    B. threads
    C. lines on rough work
    D. tapers

19. The tool used to locate the centers on the end of a round piece of stock for turning on a lathe is called
    A. hermaphrodite calipers
    B. outside calipers
    C. inside calipers
    D. dividers

20.

SKETCH "A"
1" Micrometer

In the above sketch A, the reading shown is
    A. .327
    B. .323
    C. .343
    D. .348

21. In the above sketch, B, the reading shown is

    A. .498   B. .462   C. .502   D. .505

SKETCH "B"

1" Micrometer

22. A vernier protractor is used in a machine shop to measure

    A. angles   B. threads   C. fillets   D. radii

23. Which one of the following would the able machinist use to check a piece of work in a lathe for concentricity?

    A. Vernier calipers   B. Snap gage
    C. Dial indicator   D. Plug gage

24. A brazed joint is generally made with the use of a _____ solder.

    A. copper soldering iron and soft
    B. copper soldering iron and hard
    C. torch and hard
    D. torch and soft

25. Which one of the following statements relative to the care of grinding wheels is CORRECT?

    A. Wheels should be stored in a damp place.
    B. Wheels should be mounted without flanges.
    C. In mounting wheels on spindles, the wheel nuts should be screwed on very tightly.
    D. Wheels should be equipped with blotting paper gaskets on each side.

26. Which one of the following is NOT a safe practice in a machine shop?

    A. Wearing short sleeve shirts
    B. Wearing goggles for grinding operations
    C. Stopping a machine for another operator in case of an accident
    D. Slowing down moving machine parts with one's hands after the power has been shut off

27. In grinding a piece of steel, one observes long club-shaped sparks, smooth light lines, light yellow in color, and no small stars.
The steel is MOST likely _____ steel.

    A. high carbon   B. low carbon
    C. chrome   D. high speed

Questions 28-32.

DIRECTIONS: Column I below lists words commonly used in a machine shop, and Column II gives definitions for these words. For each word listed in Column I, write in the space at the right the letter in front of its definition in Column II.

COLUMN I

28. Back lash
29. Allowance
30. End Mill
31. Clearance
32. Chatter

COLUMN II

A. Used for cutting slots and edges of work
B. Used for cutting convex grooves
C. Difference in dimensions of mating parts
D. Space allowed to prevent interference
E. Vibration of tool or work
F. Lost motion in movable parts
G. Amount of variation permitted on dimensions of a machined part

33. A machinist who makes a significant error makes one which is MOST NEARLY
   A. important
   B. accidental
   C. meaningless
   D. doubtful

34. A machinist who is given explicit directions is given directions which are MOST NEARLY
   A. forceful
   B. erroneous
   C. confusing
   D. definite

35. A machinist who is zealous in his work is one who is MOST NEARLY
   A. enthusiastic
   B. envious
   C. courteous
   D. patient

36. A machinist who is working on a job which is to be expedited is working on one which is to be MOST NEARLY
   A. supervised
   B. hastened
   C. carefully done
   D. dismantled

37. The MAIN purpose of a cutting fluid is to
   A. improve the finish
   B. remove the generated heat
   C. wash away the chips
   D. prevent rust

38. The procedure to follow in the lubrication of the machinery in a machine shop is to lubricate
   A. when you have time
   B. at regular intervals
   C. when necessary
   D. while the machinery is running

39. A steel plate is to be case hardened. This plate would MOST likely be of _____ steel. 39.____

    A. low carbon B. high carbon
    C. vanadium alloy D. high speed

40. Hardened steels are sometimes reheated to relieve the internal strain and to increase the toughness. 40.____
    This process is called

    A. quenching B. carburizing
    C. tempering D. annealing

41. If the base of a right triangle is 9" and the altitude is 12", the length of the third side will be 41.____

    A. 13" B. 14" C. 15" D. 16"

42. If a steel bar 1" in diameter and 12' long weighs 32 lbs., then the weight of a piece of this bar 5'9" long is MOST NEARLY _____ lbs. 42.____

    A. 15.33 B. 15.26 C. 16.33 D. 15.06

43. The diameter of a circle whose circumference is 12" is MOST NEARLY 43.____

    A. 3.82" B. 3.72" C. 3.62" D. 3.52"

44. A dimension of 39/64 inches converted to decimals is MOST NEARLY 44.____

    A. .600" B. .609" C. .607" D. .611"

45. A gear blank casting weighs 24 lbs. If the machined gear weighs 16.8 lbs. when finished, the percent of the blank which is wasted is 45.____

    A. 20 B. 30 C. 40 D. 70

46. The outside diameter of a 10 diametral pitch gear having 50 teeth is MOST NEARLY 46.____

    A. 5.2" B. 5.4" C. 10" D. 5"

47. A 9" pulley revolving at 950 R.P.M. is belted to a 20" pulley. 47.____
    The R.P.M. of the 20" pulley is MOST NEARLY

    A. 2100 B. 2000 C. 450 D. 427

48. 48.____

    In the above sketch, the taper, per foot, is equal to

    A. 3/8" B. 1 7/8" C. 2 3/8" D. 2 1/4"

49. A grinding wheel 6" in diameter rotates at 3200 R.P.M. The surface speed, in feet per minute, is MOST NEARLY

    A. 4500   B. 5500   C. 5000   D. 6000

50.

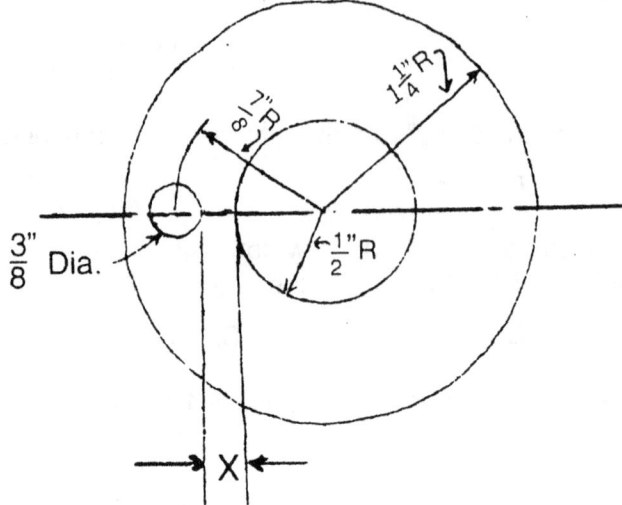

In the above sketch, the distance X is equal to

    A. 1/8"   B. 3/16"   C. 1/4"   D. 5/16"

KEY (CORRECT ANSWERS)

1. D	11. D	21. C	31. D	41. C
2. B	12. C	22. A	32. E	42. A
3. A	13. C	23. C	33. A	43. A
4. C	14. D	24. C	34. D	44. B
5. C	15. C	25. D	35. A	45. B
6. C	16. C	26. D	36. B	46. A
7. D	17. D	27. B	37. B	47. D
8. C	18. B	28. F	38. B	48. D
9. C	19. A	29. C	39. A	49. C
10. A	20. D	30. A	40. C	50. B

EXAMINATION SECTION
TEST 1

DIRECTIONS: Each question or incomplete statement is followed by several suggested answers or completions. Select the one that BEST answers the question or completes the statement. *PRINT THE LETTER OF THE CORRECT ANSWER IN THE SPACE AT THE RIGHT.*

1. Backlash in gears which mesh together
   A. tends to reduce noise
   B. decreases with wear
   C. is the *play* when gears are reversed
   D. reduces the need for lubrication

2. A tapered shaft six inches long has end diameters of 2 inches and 1 1/2 inches. The rod has a taper per foot of _____ inch(es).
   A. 1 1/2   B. 1   C. 3/4 of an   D. 1/2 of an

3. If a 1 1/2 inch circular shaft is required to be machined to a tolerance of plus or minus three thousandths of an inch, a circular shaft will have to be scrapped if it has a diameter of _____ inches.
   A. 1.496   B. 1.497   C. 1.502   D. 1.506

4. The area of a circular plate will be reduced by 5% if a sector removed from it has an angle of _____ degrees.
   A. 18   B. 24   C. 32   D. 60

5. If a 4 1/16 inch shaft wears six thousandths of an inch, the new diameter will be _____ inches.
   A. 4.0031   B. 4.0565   C. 4.0578   D. 4.0605

6. A pinion with 12 teeth engages a gear rack having 6 teeth per inch. When the rack has moved two inches, the pinion will have made _____ revolution(s).
   A. 1/4 of a   B. 1/2 of a   C. 1   D. 2

7. The gases MOST commonly used together in the torch cutting of steel are oxygen and
   A. nitrogen   B. hydrogen   C. acetylene   D. methane

8. The MOST important precaution which should be taken if a number of men are in a small enclosure constantly using carbon tetrachloride for cleaning parts is to
   A. have plenty of fire extinguishers around because of the inflammability of the liquid
   B. make certain the enclosure has adequate ventilation
   C. have the men wear rubber gloves because this liquid is corrosive
   D. make certain the men wear safety goggles

9. A material used for lining bearings in order to reduce friction is
   A. babbitt   B. cast iron
   C. carbon steel   D. malleable iron

10. One of your men tells you that a small electric hand drill he has been using has burned out. On inspecting the drill, you notice the man was using a 3/4" drill bit having a 1/4" shank to fit the drill.
In this case, you should tell him

   A. that he should have used a 3/4" drill with a 3/4" shank in this drill
   B. that the failure was probably due to pressing too lightly on the drill while drilling
   C. that failure under these conditions is sometimes due to overloading the drill by excessive pressure while drilling
   D. nothing, but allow him to proceed with the job using a similar drill in good condition

11. The designation 18-4-1 as it refers to steel is indicative of a type of _____ steel.

   A. low carbon   B. corrosion resistant
   C. high speed tool   D. forging quality

12. The sum of 1 1/2, 2 1/32, 4 3/16, and 1 7/8 is MOST NEARLY

   A. 9.593   B. 9.625   C. 9.687   D. 10.593

13. The cone angle of the countersinking tool for flat head machine screws is MOST NEARLY

   A. 60°   B. 82°   C. 90°   D. 118°

14. It is GENERALLY preferred that, for cutting brittle materials such as gray cast iron or magnesium, the cone angle on a drill should be

   A. less than 85°   B. between 90° and 118°
   C. between 118° and 135°   D. between 135° and 180°

15. In order to hold a round workpiece securely to a work bed of a milling machine, it is PREFERABLE to mount the workpiece _____ to the table.

   A. on an angle plate bolted
   B. in a three-jaw check bolted
   C. in V-blocks clamped
   D. on a rotary attachment bolted

16. The designation 51-1/2 A 18-2 on a milling machine arbor indicates an arbor of

   A. #50 taper, 1 1/2 inches diameter, style A, 18 inches length, and a No. 2 bearing
   B. #51 1/2 taper, style A, 18 1/8 inches length
   C. #51 1/2 taper, style A, 18 1/4 inches length with a pilot support
   D. #18 taper, 2 inches diameter, style A, 51 1/2 inches long

17. A plate 10 inches long is to have four 3/4 inch diameter holes drilled on 2 1/4 inch centers. In connection with this plate, answer the following problem:
The two end holes are to have equal distances from the ends of the plate.
The distance from the end of the plate to the center of the first hole should be _____ inches.

   A. 1 1/2   B. 1 5/8   C. 1 3/4   D. 2

18. A typical application of a *follower rest* on a lathe is to support

    A. a short workpiece for internal threading
    B. the pilot bearing of a style *C* arbor
    C. the taper attachment with the small end toward the tailstock
    D. a long workpiece and prevent it from springing away from the tool

19. Of the following, the MAJOR advantage of an expansion reamer is that

    A. holes can be progressively enlarged
    B. one tool can be used for either hand or machine reaming
    C. it can be easily adjusted to act as either a rose chucking or finishing reamer
    D. it can be quickly adjusted to an exact size

20. *Loading and galling* in a drilling operation is USUALLY caused by using

    A. drills with cutting lips with unequal angles
    B. drills with improper web thinning
    C. drills with cutting lips of unequal length
    D. wrong type of drill or inadequate cutting fluid application

21. To determine hardness of a material over a very minute area, such as a microhardness test, one would employ the

    A. Moh's hardness scale
    B. Vichers hardness test
    C. Tukon tester
    D. Durometer

22. The device used to determine the hardness of a metal by measuring the resistance it offers to the penetration of a steel ball under pressure is

    A. Brinell
    B. Rockwell
    C. Scleroscope
    D. Brush surface analyzer

23. A heat treatment applied to steel that consists of heating the steel slightly above its critical range and cooling very slowly under controlled conditions is called

    A. normalizing
    B. case hardening
    C. annealing
    D. tempering

24. A fixed gage for measuring external dimensions having one gaging surface fixed while the opposite surface may be adjusted over a small range and locked in any desired position is called a

    A. snap gage
    B. ring gage
    C. air gage
    D. comparator

25. The height of a surface gage is usually set by using a(n)

    A. sine bar
    B. angle plate
    C. protractor
    D. combination square

26. The one of the following that is NOT generally used to lubricate cutting tools is

    A. mineral oil
    B. soda water
    C. kerosene
    D. lard oil

27. The standard marking system 32A50-J5VBE on a grinding wheel indicates MOST NEARLY that the wheel

   A. has a medium grain size
   B. is silicate bonded
   C. has a fine grain size
   D. abrasive is corundum

28. When dressing a grinding wheel, the MOST commonly used type of wheel dresser is the

   A. mechanical dresser
   B. abrasive wheel
   C. abrasive stick
   D. silver point

29. Allowance fit between plain cylindrical parts is BEST described by which one of the following?

   A. Total permissible variation of size
   B. Applicable maximum and minimum size
   C. Limits of size prescribed for clearance only
   D. Minimum clearance or maximum interference between mating parts

30. The one of the following that is USUALLY responsible for damaging milling cutters is

   A. high speeds
   B. coarse feeds
   C. dull cutters
   D. poor rigidity of the workpiece

31. The one of the following features that distinguishes a universal milling machine from a plain milling machine is

   A. cutting tool
   B. power feeds
   C. less selection of feeds
   D. swivel table

32. For the rapid index plate of a Brown and Sharpe index head on milling machines, the number of equally placed holes is

   A. 16   B. 20   C. 24   D. 30

33. The diametral pitch of a spur gear with 40 teeth and a pitch diameter of 4.0 inches is

   A. 5   B. 10   C. 20   D. 40

34. In a centerless grinder, the axial movement of the workpiece for through-feed grinding is accomplished by the

   A. end feed
   B. work rest guide
   C. regulating wheel
   D. taper of the grinding wheel

35. In the honing of an internal cylinder, the USUAL method of tool control is to

   A. combine a rapid rotation with an oscillatory motion
   B. gradually force the stones against the wall by hydraulic pressure
   C. move the head radially while rotating the tool slowly
   D. combine a slow rotation with an oscillatory axial motion

36. A 2" in diameter shaft is making 67 RPM in a lathe. The cutting speed is MOST NEARLY _____ fpm.

   A. 28   B. 30   C. 35   D. 40

37. On an engine lathe, the cutting edge of a boring tool should be set _____ center.

   A. 1/32" above   B. on
   C. 1/16" below   D. 1/16" above

38. The Morse Standard taper is APPROXIMATELY _____ inch per foot.

   A. .250   B. .500   C. .625   D. .750

39. To cut a right hand external American National Standard thread form on a lathe, the compound rest should be swiveled to an angle of _____ degrees.

   A. 70   B. 60   C. 32   D. 29

40. Which of the following tools would be used to enlarge a 1" deep, 3/4" diameter hole to a 7/8" concentric diameter section for the upper 1/2" of its depth?

   A. Expansion reamer   B. Counterbore
   C. Countersink   D. Broach

KEY (CORRECT ANSWERS)

1. C	11. C	21. C	31. D
2. B	12. A	22. A	32. C
3. A	13. B	23. C	33. B
4. A	14. B	24. A	34. C
5. B	15. C	25. D	35. D
6. C	16. A	26. A	36. C
7. C	17. B	27. A	37. B
8. B	18. D	28. A	38. C
9. A	19. D	29. D	39. D
10. C	20. D	30. A	40. B

EXAMINATION SECTION
TEST 1

DIRECTIONS: Each question or incomplete statement is followed by several suggested answers or completions. Select the one that BEST answers the question or completes the statement. *PRINT THE LETTER OF THE CORRECT ANSWER IN TE SPACE AT THE RIGHT.*

1. The hole size for a 1/2"-13" NC tapped hole maintaining a 65% thread height is
   A. 25/64"   B. 7/16"   C. 31/64"   D. 33/64"

2. A good flux for black iron is
   A. zinc chloride   B. rosin
   C. resin   D. sal ammoniac

3. The unified thread system which provides for an interchange of parts manufactured in the United States, Great Britain, and Canada is a combination of the _____ thread and the _____ thread.
   A. American national form; whitworth
   B. sharp V; acme
   C. American national form; acme
   D. American national form; sellers

4. The pan head of self-tapping screw, with a gimlet point, used for fastening light sheet metal, is referred to as type
   A. A   B. B   C. C   D. D

5. Terne plate is black iron coated with a mixture of
   A. lead and tin   B. lead and zinc
   C. lead and nickel   D. tin and zinc

6. The worm gear of a thread chasing dial is designed to mesh with the
   A. feed screw   B. split nut
   C. lead screw   D. gear rack

7. The taper per foot for an American standard taper pin is
   A. 1/16"   B. 1/8"   C. 3/32"   D. 1/4"

8. To give a cutting speed of 35 f.p.m., a 3/4" drill should be run at about _____ r.p.m.
   A. 70   B. 176   C. 280   D. 350

9. The kaws on a pair of combination snips are
   A. curved   B. serrated   C. notched   D. straight

10. The taper that MOST closely resembles the Morse taper is known as the
    A. Pratt and Whitney   B. Sellers
    C. Jarno   D. Brown and Sharpe

11. The gage used to set the threading tool in the lathe is called a(n) _____ gage.

   A. center   B. thread   C. pitch   D. angle

12. Ten-point steel has a carbon content of

   A. .010%   B. .10%   C. 1%   D. 10%

13. The conductor stake used in sheet metal work has

   A. a round, slender horn and a rectangular horn
   B. two tapered horns of different diameters
   C. one slender horn and two shanks
   D. two cylindrical horns of different diameters

14. When draw filing a piece of cold rolled steel 1/2" x 1/2" x 6", the BEST file to use is the

   A. vixon   B. XF
   C. mill   D. double cut smooth

15. Babbitt is an alloy of copper, tin, and

   A. antimony   B. zinc   C. aluminum   D. nickel

16. The hand reamer that lends itself BEST to reaming a pulley hole with a keyway is the _____ reamer.

   A. adjustable hand   B. straight tooth
   C. spiral tooth   D. increment cut

17. An acme thread has an included angle of

   A. 29°   B. 55°   C. 59 1/2°   D. 60°

18. The straight single depth of a 1/2"-13 American national form thread is

   A. .0375   B. .0423   C. .0499   D. .0562

19. A four inch cylinder made of 1 X tin, joined with a #4 grooved seam, should have a stock allowance for the seam equal to

   A. 2 1/2 times the width of the seam plus 4 times the thickness of the metal
   B. 3 times the width of the seam
   C. 3 1/2 times the width of the seam plus twice the thickness of the metal
   D. 3 times the width of the seam plus three times the thickness of the metal

20. The process of heating cold rolled steel, impregnating with a carbonaceous material, and quenching is known as

   A. normalizing   B. nitriding
   C. case-hardening   D. spherodizing

21. A solder made of 60% tin and 40% lead melts at _____ °F.

   A. 370   B. 415   C. 430   D. 461

22. A steel or wrought-iron block, other than the anvil, that is used for forge work is the _____ block.

    A. forming   B. vee   C. shaping   D. swage

23. A gate for a mold should always be shaped so that it

    A. is parallel to the drag surface
    B. slopes toward the mold
    C. slopes away from the mold
    D. connects with the heavy section of the pattern

24. Graphite is sometimes used in foundry practice as a

    A. binder for the sand
    B. binder for small cores
    C. mold facing
    D. material for making gaggers and chaplets

25. A newly developed structural steel that puts weather to work to protect itself and requires no painting is known as

    A. Stan-Steel   B. Ketos
    C. Cor-Ten   D. Armco

26. The process of heating and quenching tool steel from a temperature either within or above the critical temperature range is known as

    A. annealing   B. tempering
    C. hardening   D. normalizing

27. Of the following, the information that is NOT part of the manufacturer's grinding wheel marking symbols is

    A. grain size   B. grade
    C. wheel shape   D. structure

28. The rapid dulling of a twist drill, especially at the outer end of the lips (corners), is evidence that the

    A. drill has excessive lip clearance
    B. drill is revolving too rapidly
    C. point has been ground to an angle of less than 118°
    D. drill is riding on its *heel*

29. The size of a lathe mandrel or arbor is designated

    A. on the small end
    B. in accordance with standards set by individual manufacturers
    C. on the large end
    D. on both ends

30. The numbered lines on the barrel of a micrometer are in increments of   30.____
    A. .001"   B. .005"   C. .025"   D. .100"

KEY (CORRECT ANSWERS)

1. B   16. C
2. A   17. A
3. A   18. C
4. A   19. B
5. A   20. C

6. C   21. A
7. D   22. D
8. B   23. C
9. D   24. C
10. C   25. C

11. A   26. C
12. B   27. C
13. D   28. B
14. C   29. C
15. A   30. D

TEST 2

DIRECTIONS: Each question or incomplete statement is followed by several suggested answers or completions. Select the one that BEST answers the question or completes the statement. *PRINT THE LETTER OF THE CORRECT ANSWER IN THE SPACE AT THE RIGHT.*

1. To tap a hole for 1/8" standard pipe, one should use a tap designated 1/8 -

    A. 13 NSP B. 20 NPT C. 23 NTP D. 27 NPT

2. A promising development in steel technology to produce BETTER steel more efficiently is

    A. modern blooming B. continuous casting
    C. wet rolling D. rapid ingot teaming

3. The spindle bore of an engine lathe is USUALLY equipped with a _____ taper.

    A. Morse B. Brown and Sharpe
    C. Pratt and Whitney D. Sellers

4. The space from the edge of the metal to the center of the rivet line should be AT LEAST _____ times the diameter of the rivet.

    A. 1 1/2 B. 2 C. 3 D. 4

5. A good forging heat for steel is

    A. cherry red (1375° F) B. blood red (1075° F)
    C. light yellow (1975° F) D. white (2200° F)

6. The tools BEST suited to forge a shoulder are the _____ and sledge.

    A. top fuller B. bottom fuller
    C. set hammer D. hardie

7. A base box is the unit of measure for tin plate and contains _____ sheets _____.

    A. 56; 18" x 20" B. 100; 20" x 28"
    C. 112; 14" x 20" D. 128; 18" x 20"

8. Of the following, the stake BEST suited for forming a common funnel is the

    A. creasing B. blow horn
    C. beakhorn D. candlemold

9. The body of sand used to form a recess or opening in a casting is called a

    A. core B. core print
    C. fillet D. cored hole

10. Tin plate with a light coating of tin is called _____ plate.

    A. coke tin B. charcoal tin
    C. dairy D. terne

11. The gage used to measure the thickness of iron and steel sheet metal is

    A. American
    B. United States standard
    C. Brown and Sharpe
    D. stubs

12. If a cross-feed screw on a lathe has eight threads per inch, and the micrometer dial is graduated so that a single division indicates a movement of one one-thousandth of an inch, the micrometer dial will have _____ equal divisions.

    A. 90   B. 100   C. 125   D. 250

13. Screws for use in metal, whose size is designated by a gage number indicating the diameter of the body of the screw, are called

    A. set screws
    B. machine bolts
    C. cap screws
    D. machine screws

14. An accurate method of checking the size of a twist drill would be to use a micrometer to measure the

    A. body of the drill
    B. point of the drill across the land
    C. point of the drill across the margin
    D. flute of the drill

15. If the cutting speed of steel is 75 feet per minute when using a high speed steel cutter to turn a 1 1/2" diameter piece of steel, the spindle speed of the lathe should be _____ RPM.

    A. 75   B. 186   C. 200   D. 340

16. In foundry, the process of making a mold in sand from a pattern with an irregular parting line USUALLY involves

    A. coping down
    B. a lost wax process
    C. a split pattern
    D. a sweep mold

17. The cutting action of a twist drill is aided by a *rake* action which is provided for on the drill by the

    A. web   B. flute   C. land   D. margin

18. The included angle on the head of a standard flat-head machine screw is

    A. 60°   B. 90°   C. 82°   D. 59°

19. The main alloying elements in monel metal are

    A. nickel, zinc, copper
    B. chrome, nickel, copper
    C. copper, zinc, tin
    D. nickel, copper

20. When turning a slender rod in a lathe, springing is minimized by using a

    A. compound rest
    B. follower rest
    C. cross rest
    D. draw-in bar

21. In foundry practice, a strike bar is used for   21._____

    A. loosening the pattern
    B. striking off flashing
    C. separating cope and drag
    D. making sand even with top of flask

22. The forge operation of enlarging the cross-sectional area of a bar is called   22._____

    A. upsetting   B. drawing out
    C. fullering   D. spreading

23. A screw thread that is NOT used much today is the   23._____

    A. acme   B. square
    C. American standard D. S.A.E.

24. One of the first men to produce carbide tools was   24._____

    A. Johannson   B. Metcalf   C. Jarno   D. Moissan

25. The twist drill that is exactly the same diameter as the letter *E* drill is   25._____

    A. 1/4"   B. #40   C. #1   D. 5/16"

26. The cross-sectional shape of a warding file is   26._____

    A. square
    B. tapered wedge
    C. rectangular (wide and thin)
    D. rectangular (wide and thick)

27. The steel that would lend itself BEST for making a center punch is   27._____

    A. high speed   B. 1020 machinery
    C. cold rolled   D. drill rod

28. One thousand 10 oz. rivets weigh about   28._____

    A. 1000 x 10 oz.   B. 10 oz.
    C. 1 lb.   D. 10 lbs.

29. A good flux for tin plate is   29._____

    A. zinc chloride   B. muriatic acid
    C. rosin   D. cut acid

30. The material that gives high-speed steel its hardness and ability to keep an edge is   30._____

    A. tungsten   B. vanadium   C. chromium   D. platinum

KEY (CORRECT ANSWERS)

1.	D	16.	A
2.	B	17.	B
3.	A	18.	C
4.	B	19.	D
5.	C	20.	B
6.	C	21.	D
7.	C	22.	A
8.	B	23.	B
9.	A	24.	D
10.	A	25.	A
11.	B	26.	C
12.	C	27.	D
13.	D	28.	B
14.	C	29.	C
15.	C	30.	B

TEST 3

DIRECTIONS: Each question or incomplete statement is followed by several suggested answers or completions. Select the one that BEST answers the question or completes the statement. *PRINT THE LETTER OF THE CORRECT ANSWER IN THE SPACE AT THE RIGHT.*

1. A metal that has a coating of zinc is known as a(n) _____ metal.　　1._____
   - A. nitrided
   - B. anodized
   - C. galvanized
   - D. normalized

2. A set of hand taps includes _____ taps.　　2._____
   - A. machine, plug, and bottom
   - B. taper, plug, and machine
   - C. taper, machine, and bottom
   - D. taper, plug, and bottom

3. The pitch of the threads in a micrometer sleeve is _____ threads per inch.　　3._____
   - A. 25
   - B. 40
   - C. 100
   - D. 1,000

4. The motion of the shaper ram is.　　4._____
   - A. circular
   - B. rotary
   - C. reciprocating
   - D. semi-circular

5. A split die　　5._____
   - A. is damaged beyond repair
   - B. can be adjusted
   - C. requires two wrenches to operate
   - D. contains two separate cutters

6. The diameter of a twist drill is measured across the　　6._____
   - A. margin
   - B. web
   - C. flutes
   - D. shank

7. A template is a　　7._____
   - A. type of hand shears
   - B. metal cutting saw
   - C. pattern
   - D. type of pin punch

8. The tool post is mounted in the clapper box in a　　8._____
   - A. lathe
   - B. drill press
   - C. milling machine
   - D. shaper

9. To remove a taper shank drill from a drill press, use a　　9._____
   - A. drift punch
   - B. pin punch
   - C. pipe wrench
   - D. chuck key

10. One complete turn of the handle on the index head of a milling machine will turn the work　　10._____
    - A. 180°
    - B. 9°
    - C. 40°
    - D. 90°

57

11. Offsetting the tailstock on the lathe will

    A. facilitate boring
    B. enable threads to be cut accurately
    C. center-drill without oil
    D. produce a taper

12. A rack and pinion on a lathe give movement to the

    A. carriage   B. tailstock
    C. headstock   D. compound rest

13. A knurling tool is used in a

    A. milling machine   B. shaper
    C. lathe   D. drill press

14. The dead center in a lathe is found in the

    A. headstock   B. compound rest
    C. cross slide   D. tailstock

15. Lathe tool bits are made of _____ steel.

    A. low carbon   B. high speed
    C. machine   D. case hardened

16. The products of the blast furnace are

    A. waste gases, steel, and slag
    B. coke, slag, and pig iron
    C. waste gases, pig iron, and slag
    D. waste gases, coke, and slag

17. Solder is composed of _____ and lead.

    A. zinc   B. tin   C. copper   D. spelter

18. On a double thread, the lead is equal to

    A. the pitch   B. one-half the pitch
    C. twice the pitch   D. diameter

19. A vernier scale can be found on a

    A. height gage   B. surface plate
    C. dial indicator   D. telescope gage

20. The lines on the sleeve of a micrometer are _____ of an inch apart.

    A. .075   B. .025   C. .100   D. .001

21. An Allen head screw is tightened with a

    A. regular screwdriver
    B. spanner wrench
    C. cross-shaped screwdriver
    D. hexagon-shaped wrench

22. The handle of a file fits on the 22.____

   A. tang   B. heel   C. tail   D. sole

23. Countersinks for flat head screws have an included angle of 23.____

   A. 60°   B. 75°   C. 82°   D. 90°

24. A hand groover is used to 24.____

   A. remove chips from a groove or keyway
   B. lock a seam
   C. fold over a wired edge
   D. shape soft metal on a lathe

25. An example of a ferrous metal is 25.____

   A. brass   B. aluminum   C. iron   D. copper

26. The cold chisel commonly used to shape a keyway is a 26.____

   A. cape chisel   B. flat chisel
   C. round chisel   D. diamond point

27. A foundry flask is used to 27.____

   A. analyze the sand   B. clean the pattern
   C. support the sand   D. clean the casting

28. A sprue pin is used to 28.____

   A. ram a pattern
   B. provide a hole through which the metal is poured
   C. locate the two halves of a split pattern
   D. clean the slag off molten metal

29. The sand used to separate the cope from the drag is _____ sand. 29.____

   A. parting   B. green   C. core   D. tempered

30. Fillets are used to 30.____

   A. simplify construction of the mold
   B. strengthen the casting
   C. strengthen the pattern
   D. support sand cores

KEY (CORRECT ANSWERS)

1.	C		16.	C
2.	D		17.	B
3.	B		18.	C
4.	C		19.	A
5.	B		20.	B
6.	A		21.	D
7.	C		22.	A
8.	D		23.	C
9.	A		24.	B
10.	B		25.	C
11.	D		26.	A
12.	A		27.	C
13.	C		28.	B
14.	D		29.	A
15.	B		30.	B

TEST 4

DIRECTIONS: Each question or incomplete statement is followed by several suggested answers or completions. Select the one that BEST answers the question or completes the statement. *PRINT THE LETTER OF THE CORRECT ANSWER IN THE SPACE AT THE RIGHT.*

1. The suggested cutting speed for high-speed drills when drilling steel is APPROXIMATELY _____ surface feet per minute. 1._____

   A. 200-250 B. 150-200 C. 100-150 D. 50-100

2. When a strong joint is needed to connect the bottom of a sheet-metal container to the body, the BEST joint to use is a 2._____

   A. burr or flange B. single seam
   C. double seam D. dovetail seam

3. The candle-mould stake 3._____

   A. is used for shaping sheet-metal candlestick holders
   B. has a slender horn for tube forming
   C. is used mainly for corner seam closing
   D. is used for wiring and beading

4. Left-hand aviation snips are designed to 4._____

   A. cut a curve to the left
   B. be used by left-handed people
   C. cut a curve to the right
   D. cut aluminum airplane parts

5. Ammonium chloride is also known as 5._____

   A. sal ammoniac
   B. bauxite
   C. amino acid
   D. a good electro-plating electrolyte

6. As the percentage of lead in soft solder increases, the 6._____

   A. melting point becomes higher
   B. melting point becomes lower
   C. strength of the joint decreases
   D. percentage of zinc decreases

7. To improve the machinability and resistance to corrosion of aluminum, the alloying metal is 7._____

   A. silicon B. copper C. manganese D. magnesium

8. Borax can be used 8._____

   A. as a flux in brazing
   B. for pickling silver

C. as an adhesive in copper enameling
D. as a cutting compound

9. A 42-tooth driving gear rotating at 400 RPM in a clockwise direction is connected to a 14-tooth gear by means of an idler gear.
   The speed and direction of rotation of the (14-tooth) driven gear is

   A. 1200 RPM and rotating clockwise
   B. 1200 RPM and rotating counter-clockwise
   C. 133 1/3 RPM and rotating counter-clockwise
   D. 133 1/3 RPM and rotating clockwise

10. Rouge used in metal polishing is made of

    A. decomposed shale   B. iron oxide
    C. powdered lava   D. silicon carbide

11. The BEST thickness of copper for doing repousse projects is _____ gauge.

    A. 14   B. 18   C. 24   D. 36

12. Copper is often pickled with

    A. a solution of sulphuric acid and water
    B. a solution of ammonium sulphide
    C. powdered tragacenth and alcohol
    D. kasenit

13. Liver of sulphur is also known as

    A. ferric sulphide   B. hyposulphite of soda
    C. potassium sulphide   D. sulphur dioxide

14. *German Silver* is USUALLY made of about

    A. 92% tin, 6% antimony, and 2% copper
    B. 64% copper, 18% nickel, and 18% zinc
    C. 925 parts of silver and 75 parts of copper
    D. 85% copper and 15% zinc

15. Blowholes in castings can be avoided by the use of

    A. a gate   B. vents
    C. a sprue pin   D. a core print

16. Chaplets are used

    A. with match-plate patterns
    B. to support cores
    C. in investment casting
    D. in shell mold casting

17. Muriatic acid is the same as

    A. hydrochloric acid   B. nitric acid
    C. sulphuric acid   D. aqua regia

18. Most of the steel made today is made in a(n). 18.____

    A. open-hearth furnace   B. Bessemer converter
    C. electric furnace   D. blast furnace

19. Nitriding is a process used for hardening 19.____

    A. special steel alloys by using ammonia gas
    B. low carbon steels
    C. steel parts requiring shallow surface hardness
    D. steel by exposing it while heated to a carbonaceous material

20. An aluminum oxide abrasive wheel is intended especially for grinding 20.____

    A. brass   B. iron   C. aluminum   D. steel

21. A scleroscope is used to 21.____

    A. examine crystalline structure
    B. determine hardness
    C. measure with extreme accuracy
    D. identify metal

22. The United States Standard (USS) gauge is used for measuring 22.____

    A. drills from #1 to #80
    B. steel wire, sheets, and plates
    C. copper, brass, and aluminum
    D. machine screw sizes #0 to #12

23. Back gears are USUALLY used on a lathe when 23.____

    A. knurling
    B. boring a hole
    C. reversing the feed
    D. high spindle speed is needed

24. The axes of spur gears are aligned so that they GENERALLY 24.____

    A. intersect at right angles
    B. intersect at acute angles
    C. intersect at obtuse angles
    D. are parallel to each other

25. The BEST file for filing steel on the lathe is a _____ file. 25.____

    A. vixen
    B. double-cut warding
    C. second-cut pillar
    D. long angle single-cut mill

26. In lathe work, the formula to use to determine the correct spindle speed when V = cutting speed in feet per minute, and D = diameter of workpiece in inches, is: 26.____

    A. $RPM = \dfrac{12\pi}{VD}$ B. $RPM = \dfrac{12V}{\pi D}$ C. $RPM = \dfrac{\pi D}{12V}$ D. $RPM = \dfrac{\pi V}{12D}$

27. The CORRECT sequence of drill sizes from smallest to largest is: 27.____

    A. #60, #30, 7/32", M   B. #7, #50, 1/4", F
    C. #14, #2, Q, 1/8"   D. B, R, 3/8", #12

28. The taper per foot on a part 2 5/16" in length and with a 15/16" diameter at one end and   28.____
11/16" at the other end, is

    A. .578"   B. .770"   C. .925"   D. 1.297"

29. The MAJOR diameter of a 5-40 NC machine screw is   29.____

    A. .125"   B. .140"   C. .155"   D. .170"

30. The usual amount left for removal with a reamer is   30.____

    A. 1/8" to 1/16"   B. 1/16" to 1/32"
    C. 1/32" to 1/64"   D. 1/64" to .005"

KEY (CORRECT ANSWERS)

1.	D	16.	B
2.	C	17.	A
3.	B	18.	A
4.	C	19.	A
5.	A	20.	D
6.	A	21.	B
7.	D	22.	B
8.	A	23.	A
9.	A	24.	A
10.	B	25.	D
11.	D	26.	B
12.	A	27.	A
13.	C	28.	D
14.	B	29.	A
15.	B	30.	D

ARITHMETICAL REASONING
EXAMINATION SECTION
TEST 1

DIRECTIONS: Each question or incomplete statement is followed by several suggested answers or completions. Select the one that BEST answers the question or completes the statement. *PRINT THE LETTER OF THE CORRECT ANSWER IN THE SPACE AT THE RIGHT.*

1. A supplier quotes a list price of $172.00 less 15 and 10 percent for twelve tools. The actual cost for these twelve tools is MOST NEARLY 1._____

   A. $146   B. $132   C. $129   D. $112

2. If the diameter of a circular piece of sheet metal is 1 1/2 feet, the area, in square inches, is MOST NEARLY 2._____

   A. 1.77   B. 2.36   C. 254   D. 324

3. The sum of 5'6", 7'3", 9'3 1/2", and 3'7 1/4" is 3._____

   A. 19'8 1/2"   B. 22' 1/2"   C. 25'7 3/4"   D. 28'8 3/4"

4. If the floor area of one shop is 15' by 21'3" and the size of an adjacent shop is 18' by 30'6", then the TOTAL floor area of these two shops is _____ square feet. 4._____

   A. 1127.75   B. 867.75   C. 549.0   D. 318.75

5. The fraction which is equal to 0.875 is 5._____

   A. 7/16   B. 5/8   C. 3/4   D. 7/8

6. The sum of 1/2, 2 1/32, 4 3/16, and 1 7/8 is MOST NEARLY 6._____

   A. 9.593   B. 9.625   C. 9.687   D. 10.593

7. If the base of a right triangle is 9" and the altitude is 12", the length of the third side will be 7._____

   A. 13"   B. 14"   C. 15"   D. 16"

8. If a steel bar 1" in diameter and 12' long weighs 32 lbs., then the weight of a piece of this bar 5'9" long is MOST NEARLY _____ lbs. 8._____

   A. 15.33   B. 15.26   C. 16.33   D. 15.06

9. The diameter of a circle whose circumference is 12" is MOST NEARLY 9._____

   A. 3.82"   B. 3.72"   C. 3.62"   D. 3.52"

10. A dimension of 39/64 inches converted to decimals is MOST NEARLY 10._____

    A. .600"   B. .609"   C. .607"   D. .611"

11. A farm worker was paid a weekly wage of $415.20 for a 44-hour work week. As a result of a new labor contract, he is paid $431.40 a week for a 40-hour work week with time and one-half pay for time worked in excess of 40 hours in any work week.
If he continues to work 44 hours weekly under the new contract, the amount by which his average hourly rate for a 44-hour work week under the new contract exceeds the hourly rate previously paid him lies between _____ and _____, inclusive.

   A. 80¢; $1.00
   B. $1.00; $1.20
   C. $1.25; $1.45
   D. $1.50; $1.70

12. The sum of 4 feet 3 1/4 inches, 7 feet 2 1/2 inches, and 11 feet 1/4 inch is _____ feet _____ inches.

   A. 21; 6 1/4
   B. 22; 6
   C. 23; 5
   D. 24; 5 3/4

13. The number 0.038 is read as

   A. 38 tenths
   B. 38 hundredths
   C. 38 thousandths
   D. 38 ten-thousandths

14. Assume that an employee is paid at the rate of $10.86 per hour with time and a half for overtime past 40 hours in a week.
If he works 43 hours in a week, his gross weekly pay is

   A. $434.40
   B. $438.40
   C. $459.18
   D. $483.27

15. The sum of the following dimensions: 3'2 1/4", 8 7/8", 2'6 3/8", 2'9 3/4", and 1'0" is

   A. 16'7 1/4"
   B. 10'7 1/4"
   C. 10'3 1/4"
   D. 9'3 1/4"

16. Two gears are meshed together and have a gear ratio of 6 to 1.
If the small gear rotates 120 revolutions per minute, the large gear rotates at

   A. 20
   B. 40
   C. 60
   D. 720

17. The vacuum side of a compound gage reads 14 inches of vacuum. The barometer reading is 29.76 inches of mercury. The equivalent absolute pressure of the compound gage reading, in inches of mercury, is MOST likely

   A. 15.06
   B. 15.76
   C. 43.06
   D. 43.76

18. The fraction 5/8 expressed as a decimal is

   A. 0.125
   B. 0.412
   C. 0.625
   D. 0.875

19. If 300 feet of a certain size pipe weighs 450 pounds, the number of pounds that 100 feet will weigh is

   A. 1,350
   B. 150
   C. 300
   D. 250

20. As an oiler, you work for a facility that has automobiles that use, on the average, 600 quarts of one grade of lubricating oil every month.
The number of one-gallon cans of the above oil that should be ordered each month to meet this requirement is

   A. 100
   B. 125
   C. 140
   D. 150

21. The inside dimensions of a rectangular oil gravity tank are: height 15", width 9", length 10".
    The amount of oil in the tank, in gallons, (231 cu.in. = 1 gallon), when the oil level is 9" high, is MOST NEARLY

    A. 2.3   B. 3.5   C. 5.2   D. 5.8

22. If 30 gallons of oil cost $76.80, 45 gallons of oil at the same rate will cost

    A. $91.20   B. $115.20   C. $123.20   D. $131.20

23. If an oiler earns $18,000 in the first six months of a year and receives a 10% raise in salary for the next six months of the same year, his TOTAL earnings for the year will be

    A. $36,000   B. $37,500   C. $37,800   D. $39,600

24. If the cost of lubricating oil increases 15%, then a gallon of oil which used to cost $10.00 will now cost MOST NEARLY

    A. $10.50   B. $11.00   C. $11.50   D. $12.00

25. The sum of 7/8", 3/4", 1/2", and 3/8" is

    A. 2 1/8"   B. 2 1/4"   C. 2 3/8"   D. 2 1/2"

KEY (CORRECT ANSWERS)

1. B
2. C
3. C
4. B
5. D
6. A
7. C
8. A
9. A
10. B

11. A
12. B
13. C
14. D
15. C
16. A
17. B
18. C
19. B
20. D

21. B
22. B
23. C
24. C
25. D

SOLUTIONS TO PROBLEMS

1. Actual cost = ($172)(.85)(.90) = $131.58 ≈ $132

2. Radius = .75', then area = (3.14)(.75)² ≈ 1.77 sq.ft.
   Since 1 sq.ft. = 144 sq.in., the area ≈ 254 sq.in.

3. 5'6" + 7'3" + 9'3 1/2" + 3'7 1/4" = 24'19 3/4" = 25'7 3/4"

4. Total area = (15)(21.25) + (18)(30.5) = 867.75 sq.ft.

5. .875 = 875/1000 = 7/8

6. 1 1/2 + 2 1/32 + 4 3/16 + 1 7/8 = 8 51/32 = 9 19/32 = 9.593

7. Third side = $\sqrt{9^2+12^2} = \sqrt{225} = 15"$

8. Let x = weight. Then, 12/32 = 5.75/x. Solving, x ≈ 15.33 lbs.

9. 12" = (3.14)(diameter), so diameter ≈ 3.82"

10. $\frac{39}{64}$" = .609375" ≈ .609"

11. Under his new contract, the weekly wage for 44 hours can be found by first determining his hourly rate for the first 40 hours = $431.40 ÷ 40 ≈ $10.80. Now, his time and one-half pay will = ($10.80)(1.5) = $16.20. His weekly wage for the new contract = $431.40 + (4)($16.20) = $496.20. His new hourly rate for 44 hours = $496.20 ÷ 44 ≈ $10.34. Under the old contract, his hourly rate for 44 hours was $415.20 ÷ 44 = $9.44. His hourly rate increase = $10.34 - $9.44 = $0.90. (Answer key: between $0.80 and $1.00)

12. 4'3 1/4" + 7'2 1/2" + 11' 1/4" = 22'6"

13. .038 = 38 thousandths

14. ($10.86)(40) + ($16.29)(3) = $483.27

15. 3'2 1/4" + 8 7/8" + 2'6 3/8" + 2'9 3/4" + 1'0" = 8'25 18/8" = 10'3 1/4"

16. The gear ratio is inversely proportional to the gear size. Let x = large gear's rpm. Then, 6/1 = 120/x. Solving, x = 20

17. Subtract 14 from 29.76

18. 5/8 = .625

19. Let x = number of pounds. Then, 300/450 = 100/x. Solving, x = 150

20. 600 quarts = 150 gallons, since 4 quarts = 1 gallon

21. (9")(9")(10") = 810 cu.in. Then, 810 ÷ 231 ≈ 3.5

22. Let x = unknown cost. Then, 30/$76.80 = 45/x. Solving, x = $115.20

23. $18,000 + ($18,000)(1.10) = $37,800

24. ($10.00)(1.15) = $11.50

25. 7/8" + 3/4" + 1/2" + 3/8" = 20/8" = 2 1/2"

TEST 2

DIRECTIONS: Each question or incomplete statement is followed by several suggested answers or completions. Select the one that BEST answers the question or completes the statement. *PRINT THE LETTER OF THE CORRECT ANSWER IN THE SPACE AT THE RIGHT.*

1. A sheet metal plate has been cut in the form of a right triangle with sides of 5, 12, and 13 inches.
   The area of this plate, in square inches, is

   A. 30   B. 32 1/2   C. 60   D. 78

   1._____

2. If steel weighs 480 lbs. per cubic foot, the weight of an 18" x 18" x 2" steel base plate is _____ lbs.

   A. 180   B. 216   C. 427   D. 648

   2._____

3. By trial, it is found that by using 2 cubic feet of sand, a 5 cubic foot batch of concrete is produced.
   Using the same proportions, the amount of sand, in cubic feet, required to produce 2 cubic yards of concrete is MOST NEARLY

   A. 7   B. 22   C. 27   D. 45

   3._____

4. The total number of cubic yards of earth to be removed to make a trench 3'9" wide, 25'0" long, and 4'3" deep is MOST NEARLY

   A. 53.1   B. 35.4   C. 26.6   D. 14.8

   4._____

5. A large number of 2 x 4 studs, some 10'5" long and some 6'5 1/2" long, are required for a job.
   To minimize waste, it would be PREFERABLE to order lengths of _____ feet.

   A. 16   B. 17   C. 18   D. 19

   5._____

6. A 6" pipe is connected to a 4" pipe through a reducer. If 100 cubic feet of water is flowing through the 6" pipe per minute, the flow, in cubic feet, per minute through the 4" pipe is

   A. 225   B. 100   C. 66.6   D. 44.4

   6._____

7. If steel weighs 0.28 pounds per cubic inch, then the weight, in pounds, of a 2" square steel bar 120" long is MOST NEARLY

   A. 115   B. 125   C. 135   D. 155

   7._____

8. A three-inch diameter steel bar two feet long weighs MOST NEARLY (assume steel weighs 480 lbs./cu.ft.) _____ lbs.

   A. 48   B. 58   C. 68   D. 78

   8._____

9. The area of a circular plate will be reduced by 5% if a sector removed from it has an angle of _____ degrees.

   A. 18   B. 24   C. 32   D. 60

   9._____

10. If a 4 1/16 inch shaft wears six thousandths of an inch, the NEW diameter will be _____ inches.

    A. 4.0031 B. 4.0565 C. 4.0578 D. 4.0605

11. A set of mechanical plan drawings is drawn to a scale of 1/8" = 1 foot.
    If a length of pipe measures 15 7/16" on the drawing, the ACTUAL length of the pipe is _____ feet.

    A. 121.5 B. 122.5 C. 123.5 D. 124.5

12. An electrical drawing is drawn to a scale of 1/4" = 1'. If a length of conduit on the drawing measures 7 3/8", the actual length of the conduit, in feet, is

    A. 7.5 B. 15.5 C. 22.5 D. 29.5

13. Assume that you have assigned 6 mechanics to do a job that must be finished in 4 days. At the end of 3 days, your men have completed only two-thirds of the job. In order to complete the job on time and because the job is such that it cannot be speeded up, you should assign a MINIMUM of _____ extra men.

    A. 3 B. 4 C. 5 D. 6

14. Assume that a trench is 42" wide, 5' deep, and 100' long. If the unit price of excavating the trench is $105 per cubic yard, the cost of excavating the trench is MOST NEARLY

    A. $6,805 B. $15,330 C. $21,000 D. $63,000

15. If the scale on a shop drawing is 1/4 inch to the foot, then the length of a part which measures 2 3/8 inches long on the drawing is ACTUALLY _____ feet.

    A. 9 1/2 B. 8 1/2 C. 7 1/4 D. 4 1/4

16. It is necessary to pour a new concrete floor for a shop. If the dimensions of the concrete slab for the floor are to be 27' x 18' x 6", then the number of cubic yards of concrete that must be poured is

    A. 9 B. 16 C. 54 D. 243

17. The jaws of a vise move 1/4" for each complete turn of the handle.
    The number of complete turns necessary to open the jaws 2 3/4" is

    A. 9 B. 10 C. 11 D. 12

18. Assume that a jobbing shop is to submit a price for a contract involving 300 pieces of work. Assume that material costs 50 cents per piece, labor costs $7.50 an hour, and a lathe operator can complete 5 pieces in an hour.
    If overhead is 40% of material and labor costs and the profit is 10% of all costs, the submitted price for the entire job will be

    A. $630.24 B. $872.80 C. $900.00 D. $924.00

19. The following formula is used in connection with the three-wire method of measuring pitch diameters of screw threads: $G = \dfrac{0.57735}{N}$, where G = wire size and N = number of threads per inch.
According to this formula, the proper size of wire for a 1"-8NC thread is MOST NEARLY

   A. .0722"   B. .7217"   C. .0072"   D. .0074"

20. A millimeter is 1/25.4 of an inch and there are 10 millimeters to a centimeter.
If a piece of stock measures 127 centimeters long, the length of the stock, in feet and inches, would be MOST NEARLY

   A. 2'1"   B. 4'2"   C. 8'4"   D. 41'8"

21. For a certain job, you will need 25 steel bars 1 inch in diameter and 4"6" long.
If these bars weigh 3 pounds per foot of length, then the TOTAL weight for all 25 bars is _____ pounds.

   A. 13.5   B. 75.0   C. 112.5   D. 337.5

22. If steel weighs 0.30 pounds per cubic inch, then the weight of a 2 inch square steel bar 90 inches long is _____ pounds.

   A. 27   B. 54   C. 108   D. 360

23. A concrete wall is 36' long, 9' high, and 1 1/2' thick. The number of cubic yards of concrete that were needed to make this wall is

   A. 14   B. 18   C. 27   D. 36

24. If the scale on a shop drawing is 1/2 inch to the foot, then the length of a part which measures 41/4 inches long on the drawing has a length of APPROXIMATELY _____ feet.

   A. 2 1/8   B. 4 1/4   C. 8 1/2   D. 10 3/4

25. If the allowable load on a wooden scaffold is 60 pounds per square foot and the scaffold surface area is 3 feet by 12 feet, then the MAXIMUM total distributed load that is permitted on the scaffold is _____ pounds.

   A. 720   B. 1,800   C. 2,160   D. 2,400

KEY (CORRECT ANSWERS)

1. A
2. A
3. B
4. D
5. B

6. B
7. C
8. A
9. A
10. B

11. C
12. D
13. A
14. A
15. A

16. A
17. C
18. D
19. A
20. B

21. D
22. C
23. B
24. C
25. C

5 (#2)

SOLUTIONS TO PROBLEMS

1. Area = (1/2)(base)(height) = (1/2)(5")(12") = 30 sq.in.

2. Volume = (18") (18") (2") = 648 cu.in. = 648/1720 cu.ft.
   Then, (480)(648/1720) = ≈ 180 lbs.

3. 2 cu.yds. = 54 cu.ft. Let x = required cubic feet of sand. Then, 2/5 = x/54. Solving, x = 21.6 (or about 22)

4. (3.75')(25')(4.25') = 398.4375 cu.ft. ≈ 14.8 cu.yds.

5. 10'5" + 6'5 1/2" = 16'10 1/2", so lengths of 17 feet are needed

6. The amount of water flowing through each pipe must be equal.

7. (2")(2")(120") = 480 cu. in. Then, (480)(.28) ≈ 135 lbs.

8. Volume = $(\pi)(.125')^2(2)$ ≈ .1 cu.ft. Then, (.1)(480) = 48 lbs.

9. (360°)(.05) - 18°

10. 4 1/16 - .006 = 4.0625 - .006 = 4.0565

11. 15 7/16" ÷ 1/8" = 247/16 . 8/1 = 123.5. Then, (123.5)(1 ft.) = 123.5 ft.

12. 7 3/8" ÷ 1/4" = 59/8 . 4/1 = 29.5 Then, (29.5)(1 ft.) = 29.5 ft.

13. (6)(4) = 24 man-days normally required. Since after 3 days only the equivalent of (2/3)(24) = 16 man-days of work has been 1 done, 8 man-days of work is still left. 16 ÷ 3 = 5 1/3, which means the crew is equivalent to only 5 1/3 men. To do the 8 man-days of work, it will require at least 8 - 5 1/3 = 2 2/3 = 3 additional men.

14. (3.5')(5')(100') = 1750 cu.ft. ≈ 64.8 cu.yds. Then, (64.8)($105) ≈ $6805

15. 2 3/8" ÷ 1/4" = 19/8 . 4/1 = 9 1/2 Then, (9 1/2)(1 ft.) = 9 1/2 feet

16. (27')(18')(1/2') = 243 cu.ft. = 9 cu.yds. (1 cu.yd. = 27 cu.ft.)

17. 2 3/4" ÷ 1/4" = 11/4 . 4/1 = 11

18. Material cost = (300)($.50) = $150. Labor cost = ($7.50)(300/5) = $450. Overhead = (.40)($150+$450) = $240. Profit = .10($150+$450+$240) = $84. Submitted price = $150 + $450 + $240 + $84 = $924

19. 6 = .57735" ÷ 8 = .0722"

20. 127 cm = 1270 mm = 1270/25.4" ≈ 50" = 4.2"

21. (25)(4.5') = 112.5' Then, (112.5X3) = 337.5 lbs.

22. (2")(2")(90") = 360 cu.in. Then, (360)(30) = 108 lbs.

23. (36')(9')(1 1/2') = 486 cu.ft. = 18 cu.yds. (1 cu.yd. = 27 cu.ft.)

24. 4 1/4" ÷ 1/2" = 17/4 . 2/1 = 8 1/2. Then, (8 1/2)(1 ft.) = 8 1/2 ft.

25. (12')(3') = 36 sq.ft. Then, (36)(60) = 2160 lbs.

TEST 3

DIRECTIONS: Each question or incomplete statement is followed by several suggested answers or completions. Select the one that BEST answers the question or completes the statement. *PRINT THE LETTER OF THE CORRECT ANSWER IN THE SPACE AT THE RIGHT.*

1. A right triangular metal sheet for a roofing job has sides of 36 inches and 4 feet. The length of the remaining side is

    A. 7 feet
    B. 6 feet
    C. 60 inches
    D. 90 inches

2. A U.S. Standard Gauge thickness is given as 0.15625. This thickness, in fractions of an inch, is MOST NEARLY _____ inches.

    A. 1/8   B. 4/32   C. 5/32   D. 3/64

3. The weight per 100 of sheet metal fasteners is given as 2/3 pound. The APPROXIMATE number of fasteners in a 2-pound package is

    A. 166   B. 200   C. 300   D. 266

4. The decimal equivalent of 27/32 is MOST NEARLY

    A. 0.813   B. 0.828   C. 0.844   D. 0.859

5. If a scaled measurement of 1'3" on the drawing of a sheet metal layout represents an actual length of 10"0", then the drawing has been made to a scale of _____ inch to the foot.

    A. 3/4   B. 1 1/4   C. 1 1/2   D. 1 3/4

6. Two and two-thirds tees can be made from one sheet of steel. If 24 tees must be made, then the number of sheets required is

    A. 6   B. 7   C. 8   D. 9

7. A main duct 20 inches in diameter discharges into two branch ducts. The sum of the areas of the branches is to be equal to the area of the main duct. One branch is 12 inches in diameter. The diameter of the other branch is _____ inches.

    A. 16   B. 12   C. 10   D. 8

8. If steel weighs 480 lbs. per cubic foot, the weight of 10 sheets, each 6 feet by 3 feet by 1/32 inch, is _____ lbs.

    A. 2,700   B. 1,237   C. 270   D. 225

9. The area, in square inches, of a right triangle that has sides of 12 1/2, 10, and 7 1/2 inches is

    A. 18 1/4   B. 37 1/2   C. 75   D. 60

10. In making a container to hold 1 gallon (231 cu.in.) and to be 6 inches in diameter at the top and 8 inches in diameter at the bottom, the height must be, in inches,

    A. 10.0 B. 8.2 C. 4.6 D. 6

11. A sheet metal worker is given a job to make a transition piece from a 8 1/2" diameter duct to an 11 1/4" diameter duct. If the length of the transition piece is 5 1/2" for each inch change in diameter, then the length of the transition piece is

    A. 14 7/8" B. 15" C. 15 1/8" D. 15 1/4"

12. A duct layout is drawn to a scale of 3/8" to a foot. If the length of a run shown on the drawing scales 7 1/2", then the ACTUAL length of the run is

    A. 19'6" B. 19'9" C. 20'0" D. 20'3"

13. An 18" x 24" duct is to be connected to a 24" x 24" duct by means of an eccentric transition piece (3 sides flush). If the taper is to be 1" in 4", then the length of the transition piece is

    A. 6" B. 12" C. 18" D. 24"

14. Twenty-seven pairs of 3/8" diameter rods each 3'3 1/2" long are needed to support a duct.
    If the available rods are ten feet long, then the MINIMUM number of rods that will be needed to make the twenty-seven sets is

    A. 9 B. 12 C. 15 D. 18

15. A rectangular sheet metal air duct with open ends is 12 feet long and 15" x 20" in cross-section. If one square foot of the sheet metal weighs 1/2 pound, then the TOTAL weight of the duct is _____ lbs.

    A. 10 B. 17 1/2 C. 35 D. 150

16. The sum of 1/12 and 1/4 is

    A. 1/3 B. 5/12 C. 7/12 D. 3/8

17. The product of 12 and 2 1/3 is

    A. 27 B. 28 C. 29 D. 30

18. If 4 1/2 is subtracted from 7 1/5, the remainder is

    A. 3 7/10 B. 2 7/10 C. 3 3/10 D. 2 3/10

19. The number of cubic yards in 47 cubic feet is MOST NEARLY

    A. 1.70 B. 1.74 C. 1.78 D. 1.82

20. A wall 8'0" high by 12'6" long has a window opening 4'0" high by 3'6" wide. The net area of the wall (allowing for the window opening) is, in square feet,

    A. 86 B. 87 C. 88 D. 89

21. A worker's hourly rate is $11.36.   21.____
    If he works 11 1/2 hours, he should receive

    A. $129.84   B. $130.64   C. $131.48   D. $132.24

22. The number of cubic feet in 3 cubic yards is   22.____

    A. 81   B. 82   C. 83   D. 84

23. At an annual rate of $.40 per $100, what is the fire insurance premium for one year on a   23.____
    house that is insured for $80,000?

    A. $120   B. $160   C. $240   D. $320

24. A meter equals approximately 1.09 yards.   24.____
    How much longer, in yards, is a 100-meter dash than a 100-yard dash?

    A. 6   B. 8   C. 9   D. 12

25. A train leaves New York City at 8:10 A.M. and arrives in Buffalo at 4:45 P.M. on the same   25.____
    day. How long, in hours and minutes, does it take the train to make the trip?
    _____ hours, _____ minutes.

    A. 6; 22   B. 7; 16   C. 7; 28   D. 8; 35

KEY (CORRECT ANSWERS)

1. C		11. C	
2. C		12. C	
3. C		13. D	
4. C		14. D	
5. C		15. C	
6. D		16. A	
7. A		17. B	
8. D		18. B	
9. B		19. B	
10. D		20. A	

21. B
22. A
23. D
24. C
25. D

SOLUTIONS TO PROBLEMS

1. Let x = remaining side. Converting to inches, $x^2 = 36^2 + 48^2$ So, $x^2 = 3600$. Solving, x = 60 inches.

2. $.15625 = \dfrac{15,625}{100,000} = \dfrac{5}{32}$

3. 2 ÷ 2/3 = 3. Then, (3)(100) = 300 fasteners

4. 27/32 = .84375 ≈ .844

5. 1'3" ÷ 10 = 15" ÷ 10 = 1 1/2"

6. 24 ÷ 2 2/3 = 24/1.3/8 = 9

7. Area of main duct = $(\pi)(10^2) = 100\pi$. One of the branches has an area of $(\pi)(6^2) = 36\pi$. Thus, the area of the 2nd branch = $100\pi - 36\pi = 64\pi$. The 2nd branch's radius must be 8" and its diameter must be 16".

8. Volume = (1/384')(6')(3') = .046875 cu.ft. Then, 10 sheets have a volume of .46875 cu.ft. Now, (.46875)(480) = 225 lbs.

9. Note that $(7\ 1/2)^2 + (10)^2 = (12\ 1/2)^2$, so that this is a right triangle. Area = (1/2)(10")(7 1/2") = 37 1/2 sq.in.

10. $231 = \dfrac{h}{3}[(\pi)(3)^2 + (\pi)(4)^2 + \sqrt{(9\pi)(16\pi)}]$, where h = required height. Then,

    $231 = \dfrac{h}{3}(9\pi + 16\pi + 12\pi)$. Simplifying, $231 = 37\pi h/3$.
    Solving, h ~ 5.96" or 6"

11. 11 1/4 - 8 1/2 = 2 3/4. Then, (2 3/4)(5 1/2) = 11/4 .11/2 = 15 1/8

12. 7 1/2" ÷ 3/8" = 15/2 .8/3 = 20 Then, (20)(1 ft.) = 20 feet

13. 24" - 18" = 6" Then, (6")(4) = 24"

14. 3'3 1/2" = 39.5". Now, (27)(2)(39.5") = 2133". 10 ft. = 120".
    Finally, 2133 ÷ 120 = 17.775, so 18 rods are needed.

15. Surface area = (2)(12')(1 1/4') + (2)(12')(1 2/3') = 70 sq.ft.
    Then, (70)(1/2 lb.) - 35 lbs.

16. 1/12 + 1/4 = 4/12 = 1/3

17. $(12)(2\ 1/3) = 12/1 \cdot 7/3 = 28$

18. $7\ 1/5 - 4\ 1/2 = 7\ 2/10 - 4\ 5/10 = 6\ 12/10 - 4\ 5/10 = 2\ 7/10$

19. 47 cu.ft. = 47/27 cu.yds. = 1.74 cu.yds.

20. $(8')(12.5') - (4')(3.5') = 86$ sq.ft.

21. $(\$11.36)(11.5) = \$130.64$

22. 1 cu.yd. = 27 cu.ft., so 3 cu.yds. = 81 cu.ft.

23. $\$80,000 \div \$100 = 800$. Then, $(800)(\$.40) = \$320$

24. 100 meters = 109 yds. Then, 109 - 100 = 9 yds.

25. 4:45 P.M. - 8:10 AM. = 8 hrs. 35 min.

BASIC FUNDAMENTALS OF LATHES AND LATHE MACHINING OPERATIONS

CONTENTS

	Page
I. THE ENGINE LATHE	1
II. FACTORS RELATED TO MACHINING OPERATIONS	11
III. PRELIMINARY PROCEDURES	14
IV. MACHINING OPERATIONS	20

LATHE AND LATHE MACHINING OPERATIONS

Although machine shop work is generally done by men in other ratings, there may be times when you will find the lathe essential to complete a repair job. There are a number of different types of lathes installed in the machine shops of various shops, including the engine lathe, horizontal turret lathe, vertical turret lathe, and several variations of the basic engine lathe, such as bench, toolroom, and gap lathes. All lathes, except the vertical turret type, have one thing in common in that for all usual machining operations the workpiece is held and rotated about a horizontal axis, while being formed to size and shape by a cutting tool. In the vertical turret lathe, the workpiece is rotated about a vertical axis. Of the various types of lathes, the type you are most likely to use is the engine lathe, therefore this chapter deals only with lathes of that type and the machining operations you may be required to perform.

THE ENGINE LATHE

An engine lathe such as is shown in figure 12-1, or one similar to it, is found in every machine shop, however small. It is used principally for turning, boring, facing, and screw cutting, but it may also be used for drilling, reaming, knurling, grinding, spinning, and spring winding. The work held in the engine lathe can be revolved at any one of a number of different speeds, and the cutting tool can be accurately controlled by hand or power for longitudinal and cross feed. (Longitudinal feed is the movement of the cutting tool parallel to the axis of the lathe; cross feed is the movement of the cutting tool perpendicular to the axis of the lathe.)

Lathe size is determined by two measurements: (1) the diameter of work it will swing over the bed and (2) the length of the bed. For example, a 14-inch x 6-foot lathe will swing work up to 14 inches in diameter, and has a bed that is 6 feet long.

Engine lathes are built in various sizes ranging from small bench lathes having a swing of 9 inches to very large lathes for turning work of large diameter such as low pressure turbine rotors. The 16-inch lathe is the average size for general purposes, and is the size usually installed on ships having only one lathe.

PRINCIPAL PARTS

To learn the operation of a lathe, you must first become familiar with the names and functions of the principal parts. Lathes of different manufacture differ somewhat in details of construction, but all are built to perform the same general functions. As you read the description of each part, find its location on the lathe by referring to figure 12-1 and the figures which follow. (For specific details on the features of construction and operating techniques, refer to the manufacturer's technical manual for the machine you are using.)

Bed and Ways

The bed is the base or foundation of the working parts of the lathe. The main features of its construction are the ways which are formed on its upper surface and run the full length of the bed. They provide the means for maintaining the tailstock and carriage, which slide on them, in alignment with the headstock, which is permanently secured by bolts at one end (at operator's left).

Headstock

The headstock carries the headstock spindle and the mechanism for driving it. In the belt-driven type, shown in figure 12-2, the driving

LATHE AND LATHE MACHINING OPERATIONS

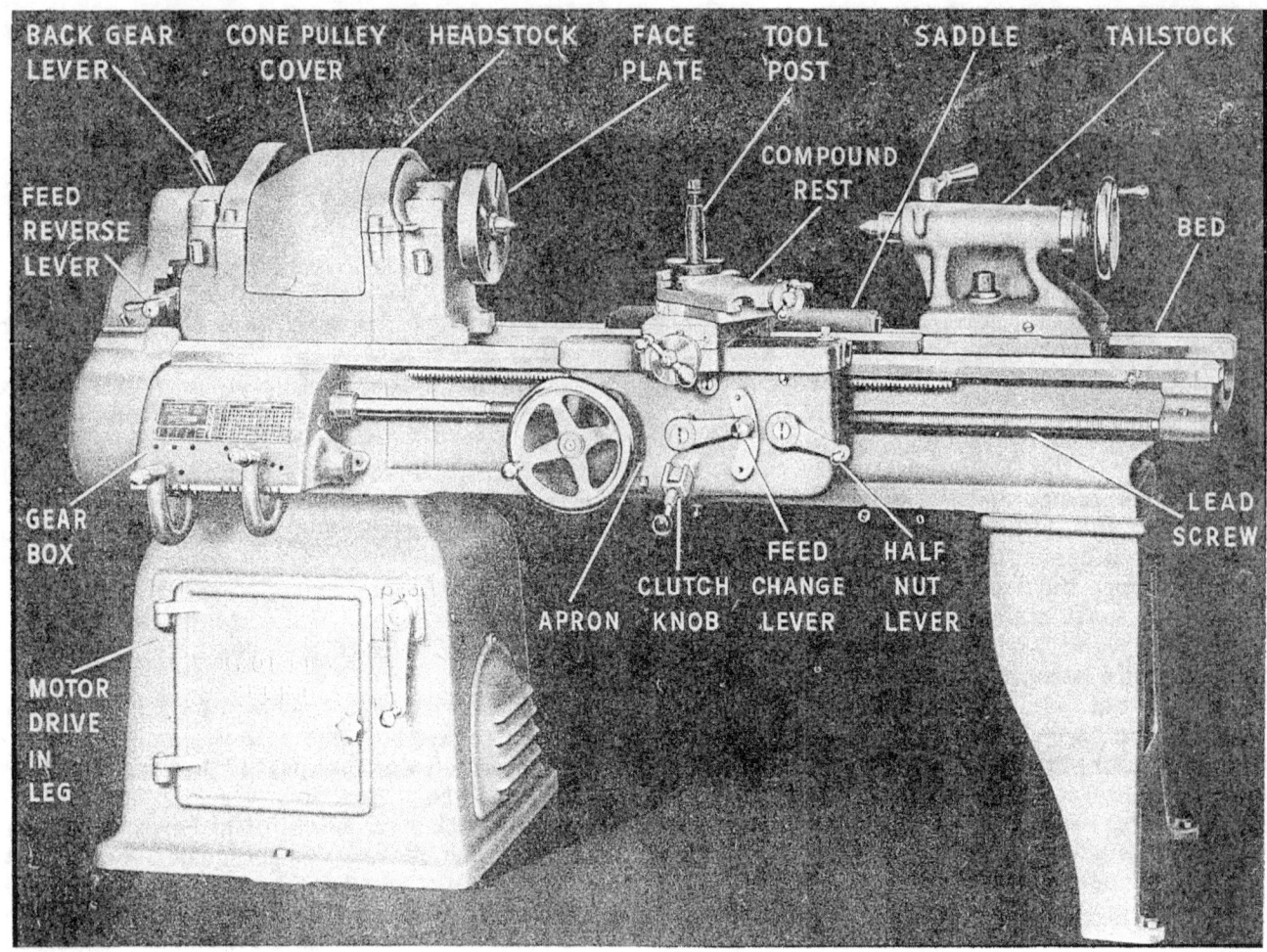

Figure 12-1.—An engine lathe.

mechanism consists merely of a cone pulley that drives the spindle direct or through back gears. When driving direct, the spindle revolves with the cone pulley; when driving through the back gears, the spindle revolves more slowly than the cone pulley, which, in this case, turns freely on the spindle. Thus two speeds are obtainable with each position of the belt on the cone; if the cone pulley has four steps as illustrated, eight spindle speeds can be obtained.

The geared headstock shown in figure 12-3 is more complicated but more convenient to operate, because speed changes are accomplished by the mere shifting of gears. It is similar to an automobile transmission except that it has more gear-shift combinations and therefore a greater number of speed changes.

A speed index plate attached to the headstock indicates the lever positions for obtaining the different spindle speeds.

Tailstock

The primary purpose of the tailstock is to hold the DEAD center to support one end of work being machined on centers. However, it can also be used to hold tapered shank drills, reamers, and drill chucks. It is movable on the ways along the length of the bed to accommodate work of varying lengths and can be clamped in the desired position by means of the tailstock clamping nut.

Before inserting a dead center, drill, or reamer, carefully clean the tapered shank and wipe out the tapered hole of the spindle. When holding drills or reamers in the tapered hole

28.71X
Figure 12-2.—Belt-driven type headstock.

of a spindle, be sure they are tight enough so they will not revolve. If allowed to revolve, they will score the tapered hole and destroy its accuracy.

Carriage

The function of the carriage is to carry the compound rest, which in turn carries the cutting tool in the tool post. Figure 12-4 shows how the carriage travels along the bed over which it slides on the outboard ways.

The carriage is provided with T-slots or tapped holes for clamping work for boring or milling. When used in this manner the carriage movement feeds the work to the cutting tool, which is revolved by the headstock spindle.

You can lock the carriage in any position on the bed by tightening up on the carriage clamp screw. This is done only when doing such work as facing or cutting-off, for which longitudinal feed is not required. Normally the carriage clamp should be kept in the released position.

Always move the carriage by hand to be sure it is free before applying the automatic feed.

Apron

The apron is attached to the front of the carriage and contains the mechanism for controlling the movement of the carriage for longitudinal feed and thread cutting, and the lateral movement of the cross-slide.

Feed Rod

The feed rod transmits power to the apron to drive the longitudinal and cross-feed mechanisms. The feed rod is driven by the spindle through a train of gears, and the ratio of its speed to that of the spindle can be varied by means of change gears to produce various rates of feed. The rotating feed rod drives gears in the apron, and these gears in turn drive the longitudinal and cross-feed mechanisms through friction clutches.

Lead Screw

The lead screw is used for thread cutting. Along its length, it has accurately cut Acme threads, which engage the threads of the half-nuts in the apron when the half-nuts are clamped over it. When the lead screw turns in the closed half-nuts, the carriage moves along the ways a distance equal to the lead of the thread in each revolution of the lead screw. Since the lead screw is driven by the spindle through a gear train which connects them (fig. 12-5), the rotation of the lead screw bears a direct relation to the rotation of the spindle. Therefore, it may be seen that when the half-nuts are engaged, the longitudinal movement of the carriage is directly controlled by the spindle rotation, and consequently the cutting tool is moved a definite distance along the work for each revolution that it makes.

Compound Rest

The compound rest provides a rigid adjustable mounting for the cutting tool. The compound rest assembly has the following principal parts

1. The compound rest SWIVEL, which can be swung around to any desired angle and clamped in position. It is graduated over an arc of 90° on each side of its center position to

LATHE AND LATHE MACHINING OPERATIONS

Figure 12-3.—Sliding gear type headstock.

facilitate setting to the angle selected. This feature is used when machining short, steep tapers such as the angle on bevel gears, valve disks, and lathe centers.

2. The compound rest TOP or TOP SLIDE is mounted on the swivel section of a dovetailed slide. It is moved by means of the compound rest feed screw. This arrangement permits feeding at any angle (determined by the angular setting of the swivel section), while the cross-slide feed provides only for feeding at right angles to the axis of the lathe. The graduated collars on the cross feed and compound rest feed screws read in thousandths of an inch for fine adjustment in regulating the depth of cut.

ATTACHMENTS AND ACCESSORIES

Accessories are the tools and equipment used in routine lathe machining operations. Attachments are special fixtures which may be secured to the lathe to extend the versatility of the lathe to include taper cutting, milling, and grinding. Some of the common accessories and attachments used on lathes are described in the following paragraphs.

Tool Post

The sole purpose of the tool post is to provide a rigid support for the tool. It is mounted in the T-slot of the compound rest top. A forged tool or a toolholder is inserted in the slot in the tool post. By tightening a setscrew, the whole unit is firmly clamped in place with the tool in the desired position.

Toolholders

Commonly used lathe toolholders are illustrated in figure 12-6. Notice the angles that the tool bit sets in the holder. These angles must be considered with respect to the angles

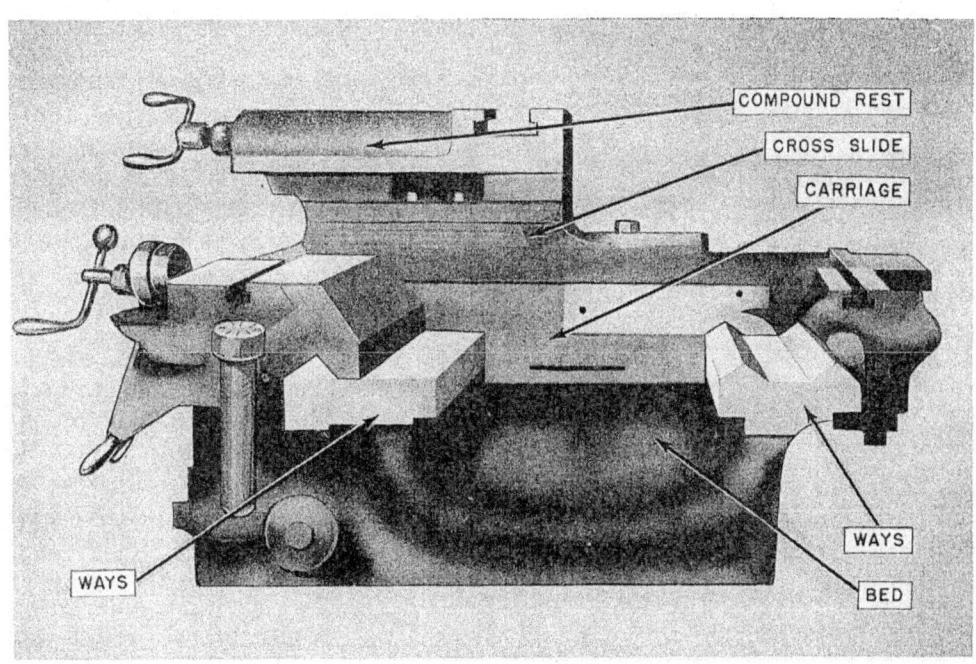

Figure 12-4.—Side view of a carriage mounted on bed.

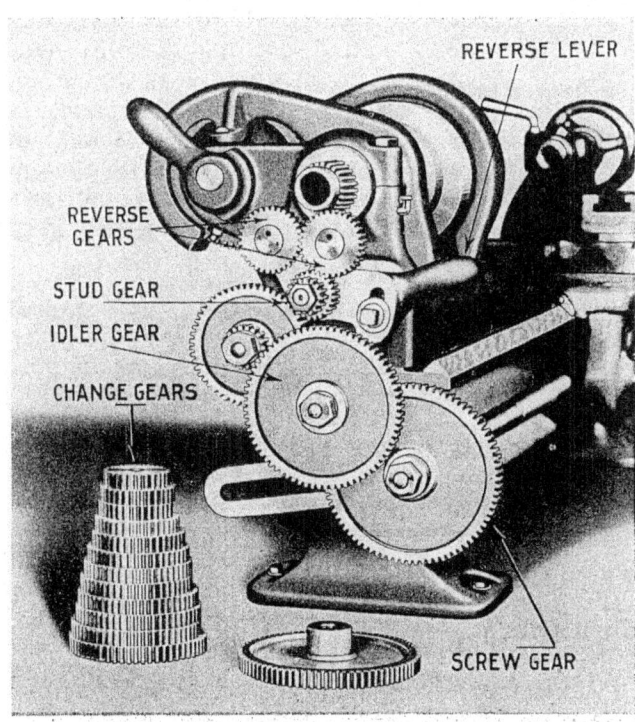

Figure 12-5.—Lead screw gear train.

ground in the tools and the angle that the toolholder is set with respect to the axis of the work.

Engine Lathe Tools

Figure 12-7 shows the most popular shapes of ground lathe tool cutter bits and their application. In the following paragraphs each of the types shown is described.

LEFT-HAND TURNING TOOL.—This tool is ground for machining work when fed from left to right, as indicated in A, figure 12-7. The cutting edge is on the right side of the tool and the top of the tool slopes down away from the cutting edge.

ROUND-NOSED TURNING TOOL.—This tool is for general all-round machine work and is used for taking light roughing cuts and finishing cuts. Usually, the top of the cutter bit is ground with side rake so that the tool may be fed from right to left. Sometimes this cutter bit is ground flat on top so that the tool may be fed in either direction (B, fig. 12-7).

RIGHT-HAND TURNING TOOL.—This is just the opposite of the left-hand turning tool and is

LATHE AND LATHE MACHINING OPERATIONS

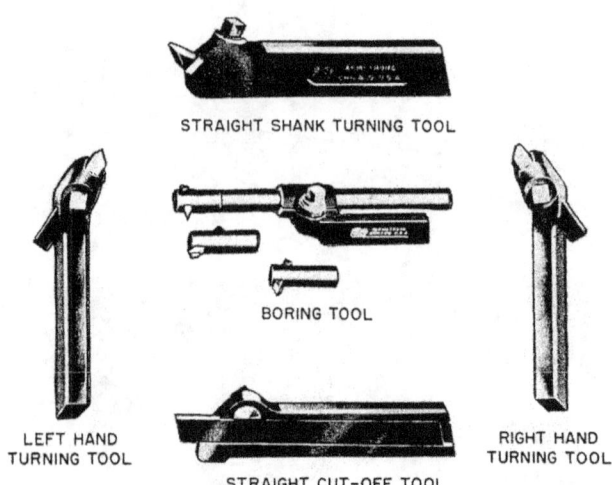

Figure 12-6.—Common types of tool holders.

designed to cut when fed from right to left (C, fig. 12-7). The cutting edge is on the left side. This is an ideal tool for taking roughing cuts and for general all-round machine work.

LEFT-HAND FACING TOOL.—This tool is intended for facing on the left-hand side of the work, as shown in D, figure 12-7. The direction of feed is away from the lathe center. The cutting edge is on the right-hand side of the tool and the point of the tool is sharp to permit machining a square corner.

THREADING TOOL.—The point of the threading tool is ground to a 60° included angle for machining V-form screw threads (E, fig. 12-7). Usually, the top of the tool is ground flat and there is clearance on both sides of the tool so that it will cut on both sides.

RIGHT-HAND FACING TOOL.—This tool is just the opposite of the left-hand facing tool and is intended for facing the right end of the work and for machining the right side of a shoulder. (See F, fig. 12-7.)

SQUARE-NOSED PARTING TOOL.—The principal cutting edge of this tool is on the front. (See G, fig. 12-7.) Both sides of the tool must have sufficient clearance to prevent binding and should be ground slightly narrower at the back than at the cutting edge. This tool is convenient for machining necks, grooves, squaring corners, and for cutting off.

BORING TOOL.—The boring tool is usually ground the same shape as the left-hand turning tool so that the cutting edge is on the front side of the cutter bit and may be fed in toward the headstock.

INTERNAL-THREADING TOOL.—The internal-threading tool is the same as the threading tool in E, figure 12-7, except that it is usually much smaller. Boring and internal-threading tools may require larger relief angles when used in small diameter holes.

Lathe Chucks

The lathe chuck is a device for holding lathe work. It is mounted on the nose of the spindle. The work is held by jaws which can be moved in radial slots toward the center to clamp down on the sides of the work. These jaws are moved in and out by screws turned by a chuck wrench applied to the sockets located at the outer ends of the slots.

The 4-jaw independent lathe chuck, part A in figure 12-8, is the most practical for general work. The four jaws are adjusted one at a time, making it possible to hold work of various shapes and to adjust the center of the work to coincide with the center of the lathe. The jaws are reversible.

The 3-jaw universal or scroll chuck, part B in figure 12-8, can be used only for holding round or hexagonal work. All three jaws are moved in and out together in one operation. They move universally to bring the work on center automatically. This chuck is easier to operate than the four-jaw type, but when its parts become worn its accuracy in centering cannot be relied upon. Proper lubrication and constant care in use are necessary to ensure reliability.

The draw-in collet chuck is used to hold small work for machining in the lathe. It is the most accurate type of chuck made and is intended for precision work. Figure 12-9 shows the parts assembled in place in the lathe spindle.

The collet chuck which holds the work is a split-cylinder with an outside taper that fits into the tapered closing sleeve and screws into the threaded end of the hollow drawbar. Screwing up on the drawbar by turning the handwheel pulls the collet back into the tapered sleeve, thereby closing it firmly over the work, and centering it accurately and quickly. The size of the hole in the collet determines the diameter of the work it can accommodate.

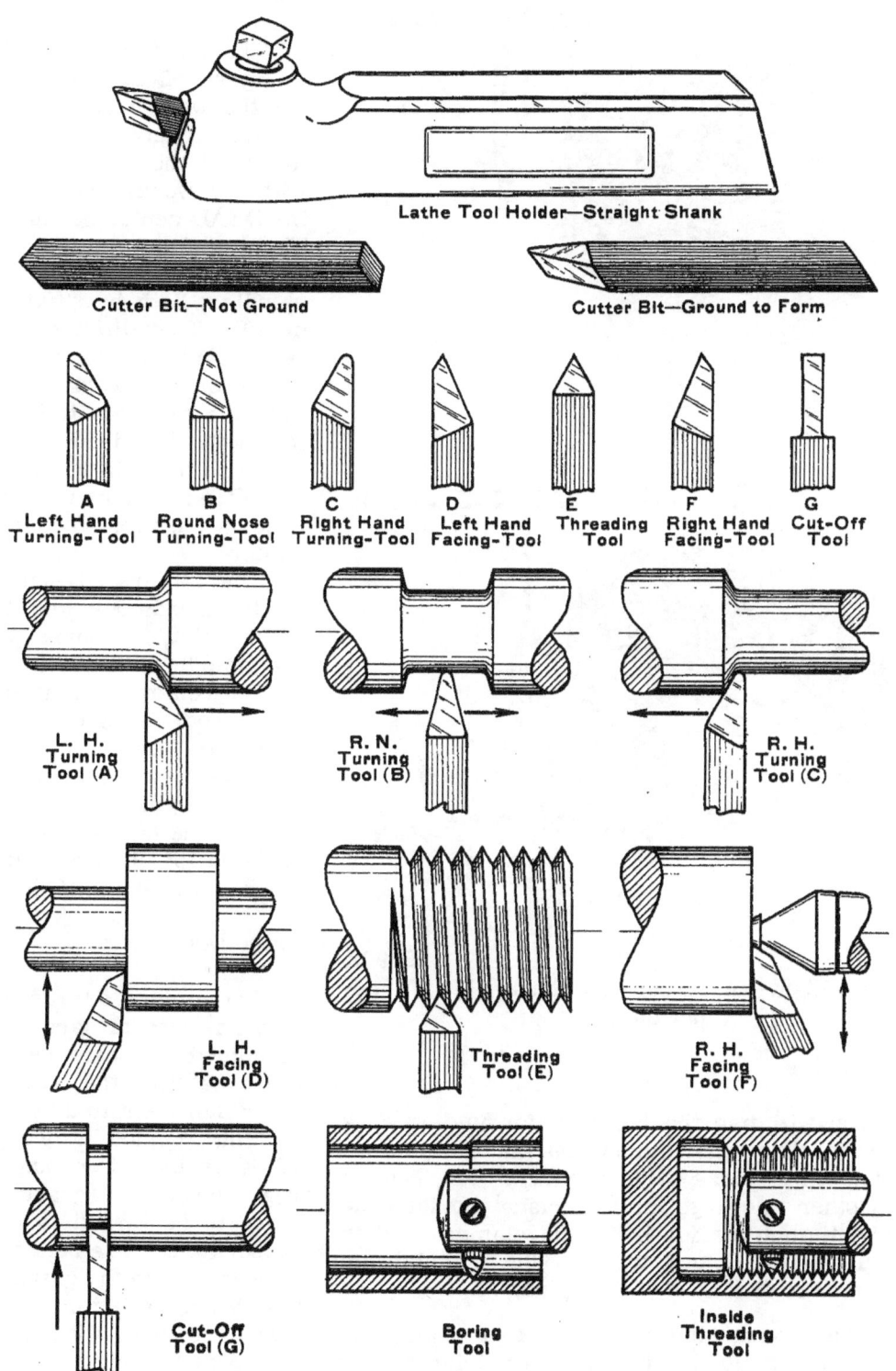

Figure 12-7.—Lathe tools and their application.

LATHE AND LATHE MACHINING OPERATIONS

the work and thereby transmits rotary motion to the work.

Lathe Centers

The function of the 60° lathe centers shown in figure 12-10 is to provide a means for holding the work between points so it can be turned accurately on its axis. The head spindle center is called the LIVE center because it revolves with the work. The tailstock center is called the DEAD center because it does not turn. Both live and dead centers have shanks turned to a Morse taper to fit the tapered holes in the spindles; both have points finished to an angle of 60°. They differ only in that the dead center is hardened and tempered to resist the wearing effect of the work revolving on it. The live center revolves with the work, and it is usually left soft. The dead center and live center must never be interchanged.

NOTE: There is a groove around the hardened tail center to distinguish it from the live center.

The centers fit snugly in the tapered holes of the headstock and tailstock spindles. If chips, dirt, or burrs prevent a perfect fit in the spindles, the centers will not run true.

To remove the headstock center, insert a brass rod through the spindle hole and tap the center to jar it loose; it can then be picked out with the hand. To remove the tailstock center, run the spindle back as far as it will go by turning the handwheel to the left. When the end of the tailstock screw bumps the back of center, it will force it out of the tapered hole.

Lathe Dogs

Lathe dogs are used in conjunction with a driving plate or faceplate to drive work being machined on centers, the frictional contact alone between the live center and the work not being sufficient to drive it.

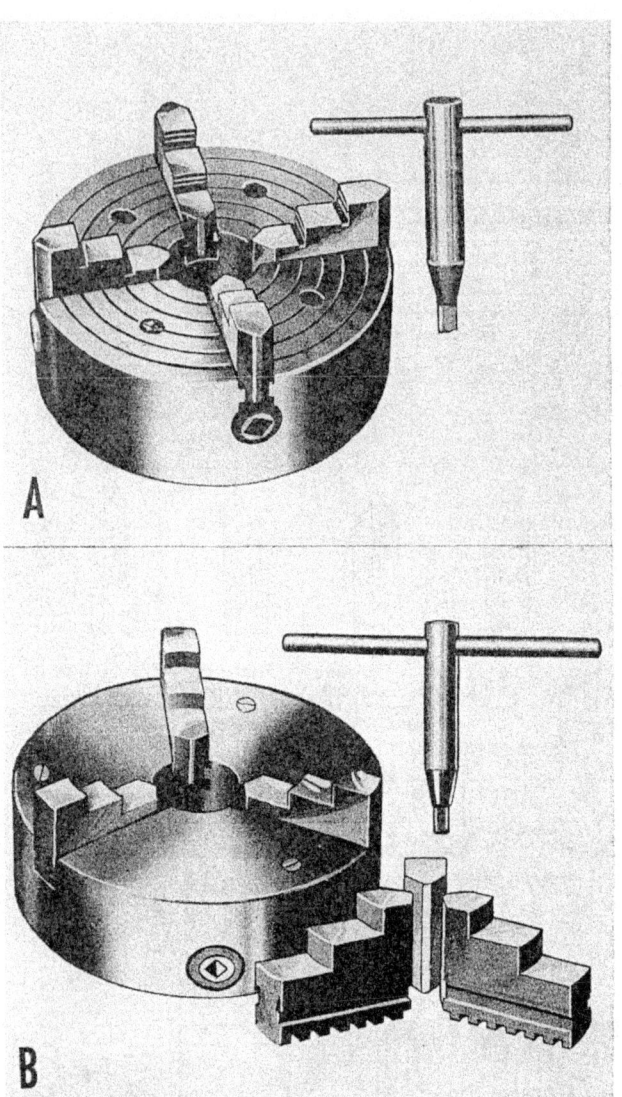

28.90X
Figure 12-8.—A. Four-jaw chuck. B. Three-jaw chuck.

Faceplates

You will use the faceplate for holding work of such shape and dimensions that it cannot be swung on centers or in a chuck. The T-slots and other openings on its surface provide convenient anchors for bolts and clamps used in securing the work to it. The faceplate is mounted on the nose of the spindle.

The driving plate is similar to a small faceplate and is used principally for driving work that is held between centers. The radial slot receives the bent tail of a lathe dog clamped to

The common lathe dog shown at left in figure 12-11 is used for round work or work having a regular section (square, hexagon, octagon). The piece to be turned is held firmly in hole A by setscrew B. The bent tail C projects through a slot or hole in the driving plate or faceplate, so that when the latter revolves with the spindle it turns the work with it. The clamp dog illustrated at the right in figure 12-11 may be used for rectangular or irregular shaped work. Such work is clamped between the jaws.

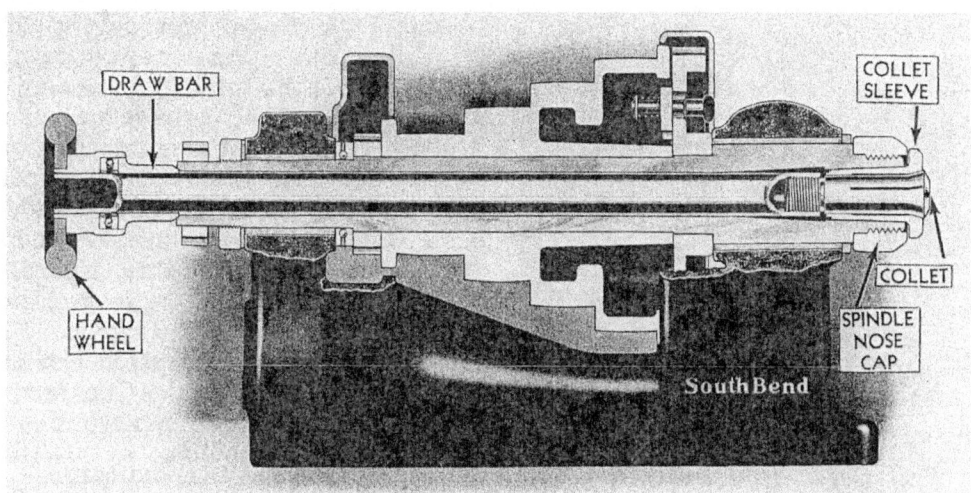

Figure 12-9.—Draw-in collet chuck.

Center Rest

The center rest, also called the steady rest, is used for the following purposes:

1. To provide an intermediate support or rest for long slender bars or shafts being machined between centers. It prevents them from springing under cut, or sagging as a result of their otherwise unsupported weight.

2. To support and provide a center bearing for one end of work, such as a spindle, being bored or drilled from the end when it is too long to be supported by a chuck alone. The center rest is clamped in the desired position on the bed on which it is properly aligned by the ways, as illustrated in figure 12-12. It is important that the jaws (A) be carefully adjusted to allow the work (B) to turn freely and at the same time keep it accurately centered on the axis of the lathe. The top half of the frame is hinged at C to facilitate placing it in position without removing the work from the centers or changing the position of the jaws.

Follower Rest

The follower rest is used to back up work of small diameter to keep it from springing under the stress of cutting. It gets its name from the fact that it follows the cutting tool along the work. As shown in figure 12-13, it is attached directly to the saddle by bolts B. The adjustable jaws bear directly on the finished diameter of the work opposite the cutting tool.

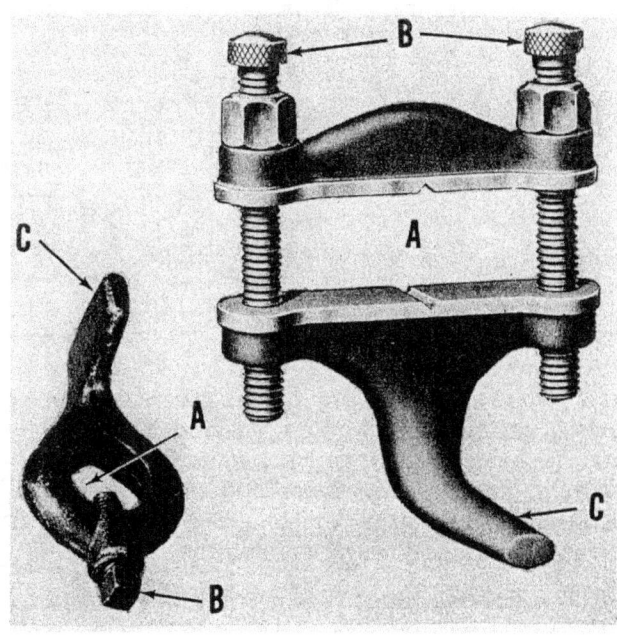

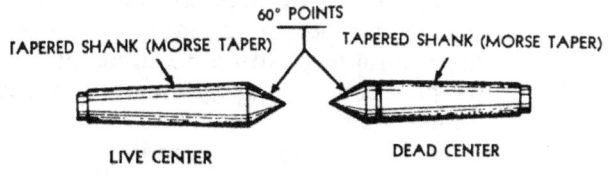

Figure 12-10.—Sixty-degree lathe centers.

Figure 12-11.—Lathe dogs.

LATHE AND LATHE MACHINING OPERATIONS

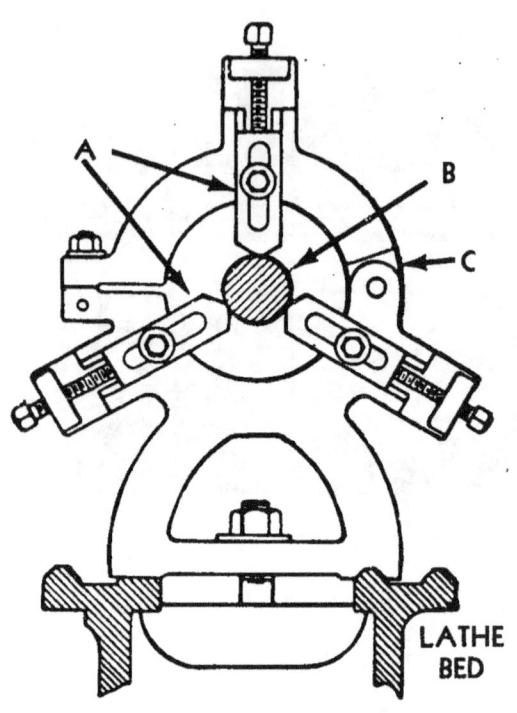

Figure 12-12.—Center rest.

Taper Attachment

The taper attachment, illustrated in figure 12-14, is used for turning and boring tapers. It is bolted to the back of the carriage saddle. In operation, it is so connected to the cross-slide that it moves the cross-slide laterally as the carriage moves longitudinally, thereby causing the cutting tool to move at an angle to the axis of the work to produce a taper.

The angle of the taper it is desired to cut is set on the guide bar of the attachment. The guide bar support is clamped to the lathe bed.

Since the cross-slide is connected to a shoe that slides on this guide bar, the tool follows along a line that is parallel to the guide bar and hence at an angle to the work axis corresponding to the desired taper.

The operation and application of the taper attachment will be further explained under the subject of taper work.

Thread Dial Indicator

This attachment, shown in figure 12-15, eliminates the necessity of reversing the lathe to return the carriage to the starting point to catch the thread at the beginning of each successive cut that is taken. The dial, which is geared to the lead screw, indicates when to clamp the half-nuts on the lead screw for the next cut.

The threading dial consists of a worm wheel which is attached to the lower end of a shaft and meshed with the lead screw. On the upper end of the shaft is the dial. As the lead screw revolves, the dial is turned and the graduations on the dial indicate points at which the half-nuts may be engaged.

Carriage Stop

You can attach this device to the bed at any point where it is desired to stop the carriage. It is used principally when turning, facing, or boring duplicate parts, as it eliminates the necessity of repeated measurements of the same dimension. In operation, the stop is set at the point where it is desired to stop the feed. Just before reaching this point, the operator shuts off the automatic feed and carefully runs the carriage up against the stop. Carriage stops are provided with or without micrometer adjustment. Figure 12-16 shows a micrometer carriage stop. It is clamped on the ways in the approximate position required and then adjusted to the exact setting by means of the micrometer adjustment.

NOTE: Do not confuse this stop with the automatic carriage stop that automatically stops the carriage by disengaging the feed or stopping the lathe.

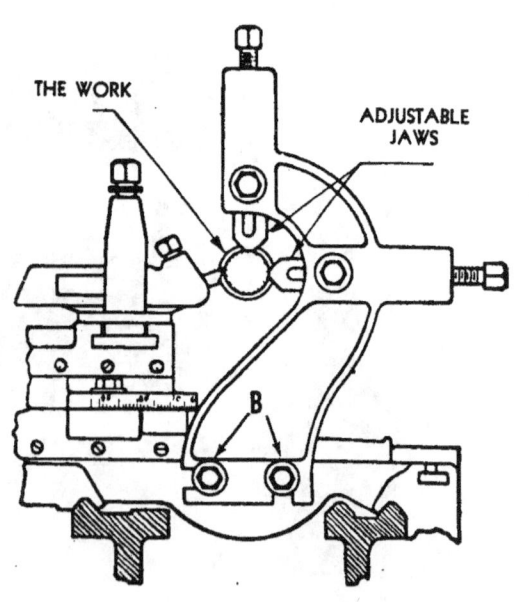

Figure 12-13.—Follower rest.

Figure 12-14.—A taper attachment.

FACTORS RELATED TO MACHINING OPERATIONS

A knowledge of many factors is required if you are to be proficient in performing machine work with a lathe. Some of these factors are considered in the following paragraphs.

PHASES OF THE OPERATION

Before attempting the operation of any lathe, make sure you know how to run it. Read all operating instructions supplied with the machine. Ascertain the location of the various controls and how to operate them. When you are satisfied that you know how they work, start the motor, but first check to see that the spindle clutch and the power feeds are disengaged. Then become familiar with all phases of operation, as follows:

1. Shift the speed change levers into the various combinations; start and stop the spindle after each change. Get the feel of this operation.

2. With the spindle running at its slowest speed, try out the operation of the power feeds and observe their action. Take care not to run the carriage too near the limits of its travel. Learn how to reverse the direction of feeds and how to disengage them quickly. Before engaging either of the power feeds, operate the hand controls to be sure parts involved are free for running.

3. Try out the operation of engaging the lead screw for thread cutting. Remember that the feed mechanism must be disengaged before the half-nuts can be closed on the lead screw.

4. Practice making changes with the QUICK-CHANGE GEAR MECHANISM by referring to the thread and feed index plate on the lathe you intend to operate. Remember that changes made in the gear box are done with the lathe running slowly, but the lathe must be stopped for large changes made by shifting gears in the main gear train.

MAINTENANCE

Maintenance is an important part of operational procedure for lathes. The first requisite is PROPER LUBRICATION. Make it a point to oil your lathe daily where oil holes are provided. Oil the ways daily—not only for lubrication but to protect their scraped surfaces. Oil

LATHE AND LATHE MACHINING OPERATIONS

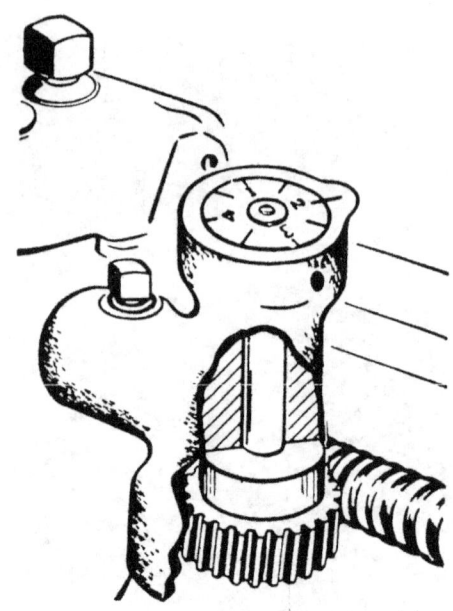

Figure 12-15.—Thread dial indicator.

the lead screw often while in use; this is necessary to preserve its accuracy, for a worn lead screw lacks precision in thread cutting. Make sure the headstock is filled up to the oil level; drain it out and replace it when the oil becomes dirty or gummy. If your lathe is equipped with an automatic oiling system for some parts, make sure all those parts are getting oil. Make it a habit to CHECK frequently for lubrication of all moving parts.

Figure 12-16.—Micrometer carriage stop.

Don't treat your machine roughly. When you shift gears for changing speed or feed, remember that you are putting solid gear teeth into mesh with each other; ease the gears into engagement. Disengage the clutch and stop the lathe before shifting.

Before engaging the longitudinal feed, be certain that the carriage CLAMP SCREW is loose and that the CARRIAGE can be moved by hand. Avoid running the carriage against the headstock or tailstock while under power feed; it puts an unnecessary strain on the lathe and may jam the gears.

Do not neglect the motor just because it may be out of sight; check its LUBRICATION. If it does not run properly, notify the Electrician's Mate whose duty it is to care for it. He will cooperate with you to keep it in good condition. In the case of belt drive from the motor to lathe, avoid getting oil or grease on the belt when oiling the lathe or motor.

Keep your lathe CLEAN. A clean and orderly machine is an indication of a good mechanic. Dirt and chips on the ways, on the lead screw, and on the cross-feed screws will cause serious wear and impair the accuracy of the machine.

Never put wrenches, files, or other tools on the ways. If you must keep tools on the bed, a board should be provided to protect the finished surfaces of the ways.

Never use the bed or carriage as an anvil; remember that the lathe is a precision machine and nothing must be allowed to destroy its accuracy.

CUTTING SPEEDS AND FEEDS

CUTTING SPEED is the rate at which the surface of the work passes the point of the cutting tool. It is expressed in feet per minute.

To find the cutting speed, multiply the circumference of the work (in inches) by the number of revolutions it makes per minute (rpm) and divide by 12 (Circumference = diameter x 3.1416). The result is the peripheral or cutting speed in feet per minute (fpm). For example, a 2-inch diameter piece turning at 100 rpm will produce a cutting speed of

$$\frac{(2 \times 3.1416) \times 100}{12} = 52.36 \text{ fpm}$$

Conversely, the rpm required to obtain a given cutting speed is found by dividing the product of the given cutting speed and 12 by the circumference of the work (in inches).

FEED is the amount the tool advances in each revolution of the work. It is usually expressed in thousandths of an inch per revolution of the spindle. The index plate on the quick-change gear box indicates the setup for obtaining the feed desired. The amount of feed to use is best determined from experience.

Cutting speeds and tool feeds are determined by various considerations: the hardness and toughness of the metal being cut; the quality, shape, and sharpness of the cutting tool; the depth of the cut; the tendency of the work to spring away from the tool; and the strength and power of the lathe. Since conditions vary, it is good practice to find out what the tool and work will stand, and then select the most practicable and efficient speed and feed consistent with the finish desired.

If the cutting speed is too slow, the job takes longer than necessary and often the work produced is unsatisfactory. On the other hand, if the speed is too great the tool edge will dull quickly, and frequent grinding will be necessary. The cutting speeds possible are greatly affected by the use of a suitable cutting lubricant. For example, steel which can be rough turned dry at 60 rpm can be turned at about 80 rpm when flooded with a good cutting lubricant.

The accompanying chart gives the approximate recommended cutting speeds for different metals, using high-speed steel tool bits. Figures indicate feet per minute (fpm).

When ROUGHING parts down to size, use the greatest depth of cut and feed per revolution that the work, the machine, and the tool will stand at the highest practicable speed. In this connection it may be mentioned that on many pieces where tool failure is the limiting factor in the size of roughing cut, it is usually possible to reduce the speed slightly and increase the feed to a point where the metal removed is much greater. This will prolong tool life. Consider an example where the depth of cut is 1/4 inch, the feed 20 thousandths of an inch per revolution, and the speed 80 fpm. If the tool will not permit additional feed at this speed, it is usually possible to drop the speed to 60 fpm and increase the feed to about 40 thousandths of an inch per revolution without having tool trouble. The speed is, therefore, reduced 25 percent but the feed increased 100 percent, so that the actual time required to complete the work is less with the second setup.

Type of metal	Roughing cut	Finishing cut	Thread-cutting
Cast iron	60	80	25
Machine steel	90	125	35
Tool steel	50	75	20
Brass	150	200	50
Bronze	90	100	25
Aluminum	200	300	50

On the FINISH TURNING OPERATION a very light cut is taken, since most of the stock has been removed on the roughing cut. A fine feed can usually be used, making it possible to run at a high surface speed. A 50-percent increase in speed over the roughing speed is commonly used. In particular cases the finishing speed may be twice the roughing speed. In any event, the work should be run as fast as the tool will withstand to obtain the maximum speed in this operation. A sharp tool should be used when finish turning.

COOLANTS

A cutting lubricant serves two main purposes—it cools the tool by absorbing a portion of the heat and reduces the friction between the tool and the metal being cut. A secondary purpose is to keep the cutting edge of the tool flushed clean.

The best lubricants to use for cutting metal must often be determined by experiment. Ordinary oil is often used, but soapy water or soda water is better for iron and steel shafting and if used in conjunction with a sharp tool and light finish cut, the work will be smooth enough to polish without filing. Other cutting lubricants are mineral lard oil, kerosene, and turpentine. Special cutting compounds containing such ingredients as tallow, graphite, and white lead, marketed under various names, are also used, but these are expensive and used mainly in manufacturing where high cutting speeds are the rule.

The usual lubricants for turning the listed metals are:

Metal	Lubricant
Cast iron	Usually worked dry.
Mild steel	Oil or soapy water.
Hard steel	Mineral lard oil.

LATHE AND LATHE MACHINING OPERATIONS

Monel metal	Dry (or mineral lard oil).
Bronze	Dry (or mineral lard oil).
Brass	Dry (kerosene or turpentine sometimes used on the hard compositions).
Copper	Dry (or mixture of lard oil and turpentine).
Babbitt	Dry (or mixture of lard oil and kerosene).
Aluminum	Dry (or kerosene or mixture of lard oil and kerosene).

For threading, a lubricant is more important than for straight turning. Mineral lard oil is recommended for threading in all steels and cast iron, kerosene mixed with oil for aluminum, white lead mixed with oil (to the consistency of glue) for monel metal, and kerosene or turpentine for brass compositions.

CHATTER

If you are unaware of the meaning of the word "chatter," you will learn all too soon while working with a machine tool of any description.

Briefly, chatter is vibration in either the tool or the work. The finished work surface appears to have a grooved or lined finish instead of the smooth surface that is to be expected. The vibration is set up by a weakness in the work, work support, tool, or tool support, and is about the most elusive thing to find in the entire field of machine work. As a general rule, strengthening the various parts of the tool support train will help. It is also advisable to support the work by a center rest or follower rest.

Possibly the fault may be in the machine adjustments. Gibs may be too loose; bearings may, after a long period of heavy service, be worn; the tool may be sharpened improperly, etc. If the machine is in perfect condition, the fault may be in the tool or tool setup. Grind the tool with a point or as near a point as the finish specified will permit; avoid a wide round leading edge on the tool. Reduce the overhang of the tool as much as possible and be sure that all the gib and bearing adjustments are properly made. See that the work receives proper support for the cut, and, above all, do not try to turn at a surface speed that is too high. Excessive speed is probably the greatest cause of chatter, and the first thing you should do when chatter occurs is to reduce the speed.

DIRECTION OF FEED

Regardless of how the work is held in the lathe, the tool should feed toward the headstock. This results in most of the pressure of the cut being exerted on the workholding device and spindle thrust bearings. When it is necessary to feed the cutting tool toward the tailstock, take lighter cuts at reduced feeds. In facing, the general practice is to feed the tool from the center of the workpiece out toward the periphery.

PRELIMINARY PROCEDURES

Before starting a lathe machining operation, always ensure that the machine is set up for the job you are doing. If the work is mounted between centers, check the alignment of the dead center with the line center and make any changes required. Ensure that the tool holder and cutting tool are set at the proper height and angle. Check the workholding accessory to ensure that the workpiece is held securely. Use the center rest or follower rest for support of long workpieces.

PREPARING THE CENTERS

The first step in preparing the centers is to see that they are accurately mounted in the headstock and tailstock spindles. The centers and the tapered holes in which they are fitted must be perfectly clean. Chips and dirt left on the contact surfaces will impair accuracy by preventing a perfect fit of the bearing surfaces. Make sure that there are no burrs in the spindle hole. If burrs are found they should be removed by careful scraping or reaming with a Morse taper reamer. Burrs will produce the same inaccuracies as chips or dirt.

Center points must be accurately finished to an angle of 60°. Figure 12-17 shows the method of checking this angle with a center gage. The large notch of the center gage is intended for this particular purpose. If this test shows that the point is not perfect it must be trued in the lathe by taking a cut over the point with the compound rest set at 30°. The hardened tail center must be annealed before it can be machined in this manner, or it can be ground if a grinding attachment is available.

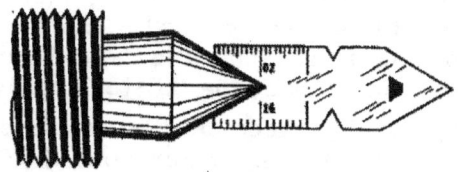

Figure 12-17.—Checking center point with center gage.

CHECKING ALIGNMENT

To turn a shaft straight and true between centers, it is necessary that the centers be in a plane parallel to the ways of the lathe. The tailstock may be moved laterally to accomplish this alignment by means of two adjusting screws after it has been released from the ways. At the rear of the tailstock are two zero lines, and the centers are approximately aligned when these lines coincide. This approximate alignment may be checked by moving the tailstock up until the centers almost touch, and observing their relative positions as shown in figure 12-18. For very accurate work, especially if it is long, the following test is necessary to correct small errors in alignment not otherwise detected.

The work to be turned, or a piece of stock of similar length, is mounted on the centers. With a turning tool in the tool post, take a small cut to a depth of a few thousandths of an inch at the headstock end of the work. Then remove the work from the centers to allow the carriage to be run back to the tailstock without withdrawing the tool. Do not touch the tool setting. Replace the work in the centers, and with the tool set at the previous depth take another cut coming in from the tailstock end. Compare the diameters over these cuts with a micrometer. If the diameters are exactly the same, the centers are in perfect alignment. If they are different, the tailstock must be adjusted in the direction required by means of the set-over adjusting screws. Repeat the above test and adjustment until a cut at each end produces equal diameter.

Positive alignment of centers may also be checked by placing a test bar between centers and bringing both ends of the bar to a zero reading as indicated by a dial indicator clamped in the tool post. The tailstock must be clamped to the ways and the test bar properly adjusted between centers when taking the indicator readings.

Another method that may be used for positive alignment of lathe centers is to take a light cut over the work held between centers. Then measure the work at each end with a micrometer, and if the readings are found to differ, adjust the tailstock accordingly. Repeat the procedure until alignment is obtained.

SETTING THE TOOLHOLDER AND CUTTING TOOL

The first requirement for setting the tool is to have it rigid. Make sure the tool sets squarely in the tool post and that the setscrew is tight. Reduce overhang as much as possible to prevent springing when cutting. If the tool has too much spring, the point of the tool will catch in the work causing chatter and damaging both the tool and the work. The distances represented by A and B in figure 12-19 show the correct overhang for the tool bit and the holder.

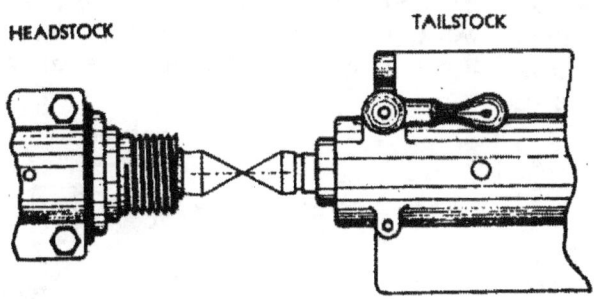

Figure 12-18.—Aligning lathe centers.

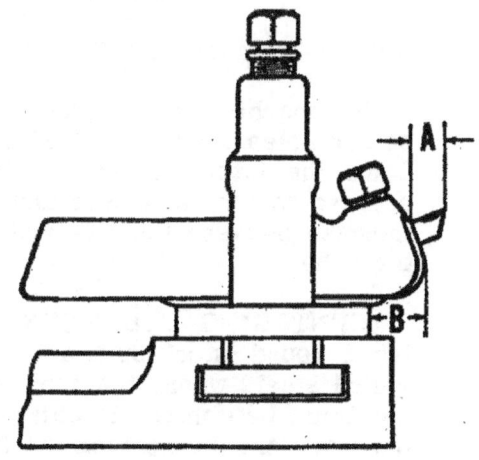

Figure 12-19.—Tool overhang.

The point of the tool must be correctly positioned on the work. The cutting edge is placed slightly above the center for straight turning of steel and cast iron, and exactly on the center for all other work. To set the tool at the height desired, raise or lower the point of the tool by moving the wedge in or out of the tool post ring. By placing the point opposite the tail center point, the setting can be accurately adjusted.

HOLDING THE WORK

Accurate work cannot be performed if work is improperly mounted. Requirements for proper mounting are:
1. The work center line must be accurately centered with the axis of the lathe spindle.
2. The work must be rigidly held while being turned.
3. The work must not be sprung out of shape by the holding device.
4. The work must be adequately supported against any sagging caused by its own weight and against springing caused by the action of the cutting tool.

There are four general methods of holding work in the lathe: (1) between centers, (2) on a mandrel, (3) in a chuck, and (4) on a faceplate. Work may also be clamped to the carriage for boring and milling, in which case the boring bar or milling cutter is held and driven by the headstock spindle.

Other methods of holding work to suit special conditions are: (1) one end on the live center or in a chuck and the other end supported in a center rest, and (2) one end in a chuck and the other end on the dead center.

Holding Work Between Centers

To machine a workpiece between centers, center holes must be drilled in each end to receive the lathe centers. A lathe dog is then secured to the workpiece and then the work is mounted between the live and dead centers of the lathe.

CENTERING THE WORK.—To center finished round stock such as drill rod or cold-rolled steel, where the ends are to be turned and must be concentric with the unturned body, the work can be held on the head spindle in a universal chuck or a draw-in collet chuck. If the work is long and too large to be passed through the spindle, a center rest must be used to support one end. The centering tool is held in a drill chuck in the tail spindle and is fed to the work by the tailstock handwheel (fig. 12-20).

If a piece must be centered very accurately, the tapered center hole should be bored after center drilling to correct any run-out of the drill. This is done by grinding a tool bit to a center gage at a 60° angle. Then with the tool holder held in the tool post, set the compound rest at 30° with the line of center as shown in figure 12-21. Set the tool exactly on the center for height and adjust to the proper angle with the center gage as shown at A. By feeding the tool as shown at B, any run-out of the center is corrected. The tool bit should be relieved under the cutting edge as shown at C to prevent the tool from dragging or rubbing in the hole.

For centerdrilling a workpiece, the combined drill and countersink is the most practical tool. These combined drills and countersinks vary in size and the drill points also vary. Sometimes a drill point on one end will be 1/8 inch in diameter, and the drill point on the opposite end 3/16 inch in diameter. The angle of the centerdrill is always 60° so that the countersunk hole will fit the angle of the lathe center point.

If a centerdrill is not available, the work may be centered with a small twist drill. Let the drill enter the work a sufficient length on each end; then follow with a special countersink, the point of which is 60°.

In centerdrilling, a drop or two of oil should be used on the drill. The drill should be fed slowly and carefully so as not to break the tip. Extreme care is needed when the work is heavy, because it is then more difficult to "feel" the proper feed of the work on the centerdrill.

If the centerdrill breaks while countersinking and part of the broken drill remains in the work, this part must be removed. Sometimes it can be driven out by a chisel or jarred loose,

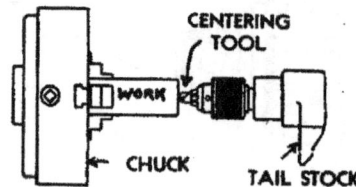

28.111
Figure 12-20.—Drilling center hole.

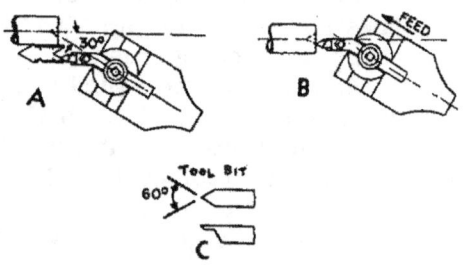

Figure 12-21.—Boring center hole.

but it may stick so hard that it cannot be removed. In that case the broken part of the drill should be annealed and drilled out.

The importance of proper center holes in the work and a correct angle on the point of the lathe centers cannot be overemphasized. To do an accurate job between centers on the lathe, countersunk holes must be of the proper size and depth, and the points of the lathe centers must be true and accurate.

MOUNTING THE WORK.—Figure 12-22 shows correct and incorrect methods of mounting work between centers. In the correct example, the driving dog is attached to the work and rigidly held by the setscrew. The tail of the dog rests in the slot of the faceplate and extends beyond the base of the slot so that the work rests firmly on both the headstock center and tailstock center.

In the incorrect example, you will note that the tail of the dog rests on the bottom of the slot on the faceplate at A, thereby pulling the work away from the center points, as shown at

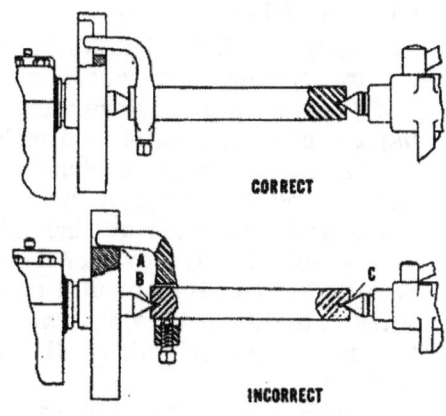

Figure 12-22.—Examples of work mounted between centers.

B and C, and causing the work to revolve eccentrically.

When mounting work between centers for machining, there should be no end play between the work and the dead center. However, if held too tightly by the tail center when revolving, the work will heat the center point and destroy both the center and the work. For the same reason, the tail center must be lubricated with a heavy mixture of white lead and oil.

Holding Work on a Mandrel

Many parts, such as bushings, gears, collars, and pulleys, require all the finished external surfaces to run true with the hole which extends through them. That is, the outside diameter must be true with the inside diameter or bore.

General practice is to finish the hole to a standard size, within the limit of the accuracy desired. Thus a 3/4-inch standard hole would ordinarily be held from 0.7505 inch or a tolerance of one-half thousandth of an inch above or below the true standard size of exactly 0.750 inch. First drill or bore the hole to within a few thousandths of an inch of the finished size; then remove the remainder of the material with a machine reamer, following with a hand reamer if the limits are extremely close.

The piece is then pressed on a mandrel tight enough so the work will not slip while being machined and a dog is clamped on the mandrel which is mounted between centers. Since the mandrel surface runs true with respect to the lathe axis, the turned surfaces of the work on the mandrel will be true with respect to the hole in the piece.

A mandrel is simply a round piece of steel of convenient length which has been centered and turned true with the centers. Commercial mandrels are made of tool steel, hardened and ground with a slight taper (usually 0.0005 inch per inch). On sizes up to 1 inch the small end is usually one-half thousandth of an inch under the standard size of the mandrel, while on larger sizes this dimension is usually one thousandth of an inch under standard. This taper allows the standard hole in the work to vary according to the usual shop practice, and still provides a drive to the work when the mandrel is pressed into the hole. The taper is not great enough to distort the hole in the work. The countersunk centers of the mandrel are lapped for accuracy. The ends are turned smaller than the body of the mandrel and provided with flats which give a driving surface for the lathe dog.

Holding Work in Chucks

The independent chuck and universal chuck are more often used than other workholding devices in performing lathe operations. The universal chuck is used for holding relatively true cylindrical work when accurate concentricity of the machined surface and holding power on the chuck is secondary to time required to do the job. When the work is irregular in shape, must be accurately centered, and must be held securely for heavy feeds and depth of cuts, the independent chuck should be used.

FOUR-JAW INDEPENDENT CHUCK.—Figure 12-23 shows a rough casting mounted in a four-jaw independent lathe chuck on the spindle of the lathe. Before truing the work, determine which part you wish to have turn true. To mount this casting in the chuck, proceed as follows:

1. Adjust the chuck jaws to receive the casting. Each jaw should be concentric with the ring marks indicated on the face of the chuck. If there are no ring marks, be guided by the circumference of the body of the chuck.

2. Fasten the work in the chuck by turning the adjusting screw on jaw No. 1 and jaw No. 3, a pair of jaws which are opposite each other. Next tighten jaws No. 2 and No. 4.

3. At this stage the work should be held in the jaws just tight enough so it will not fall out of the chuck while being trued.

4. Revolve the spindle slowly and, with a piece of chalk, mark the high spot (A in fig. 12-23) on the work while it is revolving. Steady your hand on the tool post while holding the chalk.

5. Stop the spindle. Locate the high spot on the work and adjust the jaws in the proper direction to true the work by releasing the jaw opposite the chalk mark and tightening the one nearest the mark.

6. Sometimes the high spot on the work will be located between adjacent jaws. In that case, loosen the two opposite jaws and tighten the jaws adjacent to the high spot.

THREE-JAW UNIVERSAL CHUCK.—The three-jaw universal or scroll chuck is made so that all jaws move together or apart in unison. A universal chuck will center almost exactly at the first clamping, but after a period of use it is not uncommon to find inaccuracies of from 2 to 10 thousandths of an inch in centering the work, and consequently the run-out of the work must be corrected. Sometimes this may be done by inserting a piece of paper or thin shim stock between the jaw and the work on the high side.

After the positioning has been done in a chuck, be sure to tighten all the screws so that each jaw is tight against the piece to prevent it from slipping under cut.

When checking thin sections, be careful not to clamp the work too tightly, as then the diameter of the piece will be machined when it is in a distorted position. When the pressure of the jaws is released after the cut, there will be as many high spots as there are jaws, and the turned surface will not be true.

CARE OF CHUCKS.—To preserve a chuck's accuracy, handle it carefully and keep it clean and free from grit. Never force a chuck jaw by using a pipe as an extension on the chuck wrench.

Before mounting a chuck, remove the live center and fill the hole with a rag to prevent chips and dirt from getting into the taper hole of the spindle. Removal of the center is necessary to prevent the possibility of its being ruined when drilling work held in the chuck (the operator may inadvertently drill right through the center).

Clean and oil the threads of the chuck and the spindle nose.—Dirt or chips on the threads will not allow the chuck to run true when it is screwed up to the shoulder. Screw the chuck

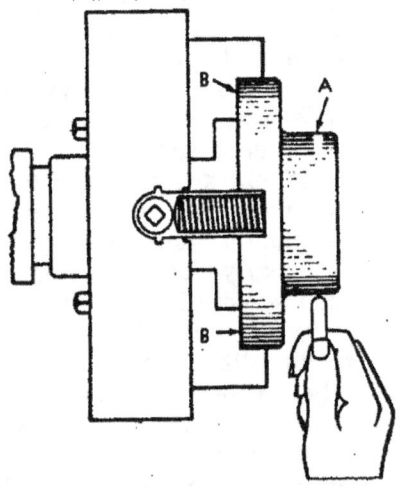

28.119
Figure 12-23.—Work mounted in a 4-jaw chuck.

on carefully. Avoid bringing it up against the shoulder so fast that the chuck comes up with a shock. This will strain the spindle and the threads and make removal difficult. Never use mechanical power in screwing on the chuck. Rotate the spindle with the left hand while holding the chuck in the hollow of the right arm.

To remove a small chuck, place an adjustable jaw wrench on one of the jaws and start it by a smart blow with the hand on the handle of the wrench. To remove a heavy chuck, rotate it against a block of wood held between a jaw and the lathe bed. When mounting or removing a heavy chuck, lay a board across the bed ways to protect them; the board will serve as a support for the chuck as it is put on or taken off.

The above comments on mounting and removing chucks also apply to faceplates.

Holding Work on a Faceplate

A faceplate is used for mounting work which cannot be chucked or turned between centers. This may occur because of the peculiar shape of the work. A faceplate may be used when holes are to be accurately machined in flat work, or when large and irregularly shaped work is to be faced on the lathe.

Work is secured to the faceplate by bolts, clamps, or any suitable clamping means. The holes and slots in the faceplate are used for anchoring the holding bolts. Angle plates may be used to present the work at the desired angle, as shown in figure 12-24.

Note the counterweight added for balance.

For work to be mounted accurately on a faceplate, the surface of the work in contact with the faceplate must be accurately faced. For very accurate work, the faceplate itself should be refaced by taking a light cut over its surface. It is good practice to place a piece of paper between the work and the faceplate to prevent slipping.

Before securely clamping the work, it must be moved about on the surface of the faceplate until the point to be machined is centered accurately over the axis of the lathe. Suppose you wish to bore a hole, the center of which has been laid out and marked with a prick punch. First clamp the work to the approximate position on the faceplate. Then prepare a rod with a countersunk center hole to fit the tailstock center at one end, and with an accurate center point on the other end. Slide the tailstock up and place the rod with the point in the prick punch mark

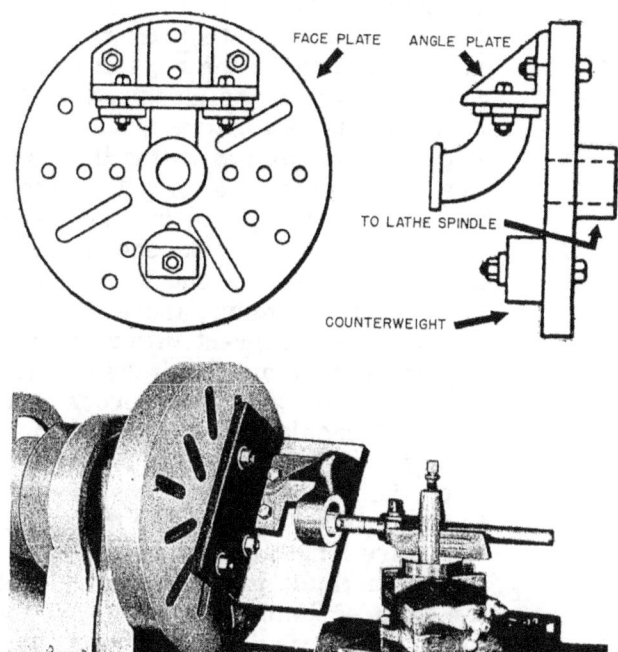

Figure 12-24.—Work clamped to an angle plate.

28.124X

on the work and the other end on the tail center. Then revolve the work slowly. If the punch mark is off center, the point of the rod will describe a small circle (appear to wobble); if it is right on center the rod will remain stationary. For very accurate centering, a dial indicator held in the tool post and applied to the rod will indicate a very small movement of the rod (to a thousandth of an inch).

Using the Center Rest and Follower Rest

In addition to being supported at the ends by the lathe centers, long slender work often requires support between ends while being turned; otherwise the work would spring away from the tool and chatter. The center rest is used to support such work so it can be accurately turned with a faster feed and cutting speed than would be possible without it.

The center rest should be placed where it will give the greatest support to the piece to be turned. This is usually at about the middle of its length.

Ensure that the center point between the jaws of the center rest coincides exactly with the axis of the lathe spindle. To do this, place a short piece of stock in a chuck and machine it to the

LATHE AND LATHE MACHINING OPERATIONS

diameter of the workpiece to be supported. Without removing the stock from the chuck, clamp the center rest on the ways of the lathe and adjust the jaws to the machined surface. Without changing the jaw settings, slide the center rest into position for supporting the workpiece. Remove the stock used for setting the center rest and set the workpiece in place. Use a dial indicator to true the workpiece at the chuck. Figure 12-25 shows how a chuck and center rest are used when machining the end of a workpiece.

The follower rest differs from the center rest in that it moves with the carriage and provides support against the forces of the cut only. The tool should be set to the diameter selected and a "spot" turned about 5/8 to 3/4 inch wide. Then the follower rest jaws should be adjusted to the finished diameter to follow the tool along the entire length to be turned.

Use a thick mixture of white lead and oil on the jaws of the center rest and follower rest to prevent "seizing" and scoring the workpiece. Check the jaws frequently to see that they do not become hot. The jaws may expand slightly if they get hot thus pushing the work out of alignment (when using the follower rest) or binding (when using the center rest).

Holding Work in a Draw-In Collet Chuck

The draw-in collet chuck is used for very fine accurate work of small diameter. Long work can be passed through the hollow drawbar, and short work can be placed directly into the collet from the front. The collet is tightened on the work by rotating the drawbar to the right. This draws the collet into the tapered closing sleeve; the opposite operation releases the collet.

Accurate results are obtained when the diameter of the work is exactly the same size as the dimension stamped on the collet. In some cases, the diameter may vary as much as 0.002 inch; that is, the work may be 0.001 inch smaller or larger than the collet size. If the work diameter varies more than this, it will impair the accuracy and efficiency of the collet. That is why a separate collet should be used for each small variation of work diameter, especially if precision is desired.

MACHINING OPERATIONS

Up to this point you have studied the preliminary steps leading up to the performance of machine work in the lathe. You have learned how to mount the work and the tool, and which tools are used for various purposes. Now, to be considered is the method of using the proper tools in combination with the lathe to perform various machining operations.

FACING

Facing is the machining of the end surfaces and shoulders of a workpiece. In addition to squaring the ends of the work, facing provides a means of accurately cutting the work to length. Generally in facing the workpiece, only light cuts are required as the work will have been cut to approximate length or rough machined to the shoulder.

Figure 12-26 shows the method of facing a cylindrical piece. The work is placed on centers and driven by a dog. A right-hand side tool is used as shown, and a light cut is taken on the end of the work, feeding the tool (by hand crossfeed) from the center toward the outside. One or two chips are taken to remove sufficient stock to true the work. Then place the dog on the other end of the work and face it to the proper length. A steel rule is used to measure off the length. Another rule or straightedge held on the end that has just been faced provides an accurate base from which to measure. Be sure there is no fin or burr on the edge to keep the straightedge from bearing accurately on the finished end. Use a sharp scriber to mark off the dimension desired.

Figure 12-27 shows the application of a turning tool in finishing a shouldered job having a

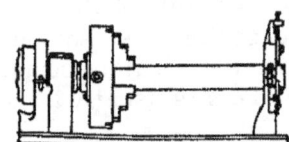

28.126X
Figure 12-25.—Work mounted in a chuck and center rest.

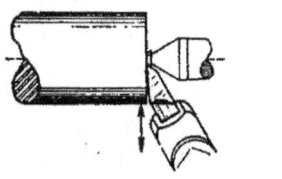

28.129X
Figure 12-26.—Facing a cylindrical piece.

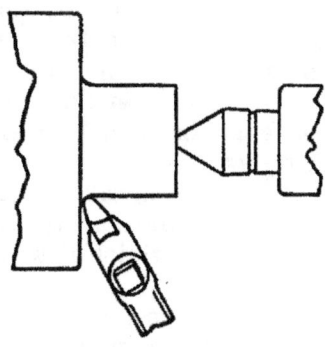

Figure 12-27.—Facing a shoulder.

28.130X

fillet corner. A finish cut is taken on the small diameter. The fillet is machined with a light cut; then the tool is used to face from the fillet to the outside diameter of the work.

In facing large surfaces the carriage should be locked in position, since only cross-feed is required to traverse the tool across the work. With the compound rest set at 90° (parallel to the axis of the lathe), the micrometer collar can be used to feed the tool to the proper depth of cut in the face. For greater accuracy in obtaining a given size in finishing a face, the compound rest may be set at 30°. In this position, one-thousandth of an inch movement of the compound rest will move the tool exactly a half of a thousandth of an inch in a direction parallel to the axis of the lathe. (In a 30°-60° right triangle, the length of the side opposite the 30° angle is equal to one-half the length of the hypotenuse.)

TURNING

Turning is the machining of excess stock from the periphery of the workpiece to reduce the diameter. In most lathe machining requiring removal of large amounts of stock, a series of roughing cuts is taken to remove most of the excess stock; then a finishing cut is taken to accurately "size" the workpiece.

Rough Turning

When a great deal of stock is to be removed, heavy cuts should be taken in order to complete the job in the least possible time. This is called rough turning.

The proper tool should be selected for taking a heavy chip. The speed of the work, and the amount of feed of the tool should be as great as the tool will stand.

When taking a roughing cut on steel, cast iron, or any other metal that has a scale upon its surface, be sure to set the tool deep enough to get under the scale in the first cut. Unless you do, the scale on the metal will dull the point of the tool.

The work should be rough machined to almost the finished size; then care in measuring is required.

Bear in mind the fact that the diameter of the work being turned is reduced by an amount equal to twice the depth of the cut; thus, if you desire to reduce the diameter of a piece by one-fourth of an inch, one-eighth of an inch of metal must be removed from the surface.

Figure 12-28 shows the position of the tool for taking a heavy chip on large work. The tool should be set so that if anything occurs while machining to change the position of the tool, it will not dig into the work, but rather it will move in the direction of the arrow—away from the work. Setting the tool in the above position sometimes prevents chatter.

Finish Turning

When the work has been rough turned to within about 1/32 inch of the finished size, take a finishing cut. A fine feed, the proper lubricant, and above all a keen-edged tool are necessary to produce a smooth finish. Caliper carefully to be sure that you are machining the work to the proper dimension. Stop the lathe when measuring with calipers.

Where very close limits are to be held, it is advisable to see that the work is not hot when the finish cut is taken. Cooling of the piece will leave it undersized if it has been turned to the exact size.

On work that is to be finished by a cylindrical grinder, a limited amount of stock is usually left for grinding to the finished dimensions.

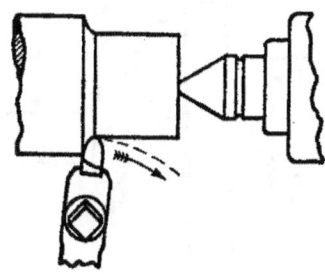

28.132X

Figure 12-28.—Position of tool for heavy cut.

LATHE AND LATHE MACHINING OPERATIONS

Perhaps the most difficult operation for a beginner in machine work is to make accurate measurements. So much depends on the accuracy of the work that you should make every effort to become proficient in the use of measuring instruments. A certain "feel" in the application of calipers is developed through experience alone; do not be discouraged if your first efforts do not produce perfect results. Practice taking caliper measurements on pieces of known dimensions. You will acquire skill if you are persistent.

Turning to a Shoulder

Machining to a shoulder is often done by locating the shoulder with a parting tool. The parting tool is inserted about 1/32 inch back of the shoulder line, and enters the work within 1/32 inch of the smaller diameter of the work. Then the stock may be machined by taking heavy chips up to the shoulder thus made. Shouldering eliminates detailed measuring and speeds up production.

Figure 12-29 illustrates the method of shouldering. A parting tool has been used at P and the turning tool is taking a chip. It will be unnecessary to waste any time in taking measurements. You can devote your time to rough machining until the necessary stock is removed. Then you can take a finishing cut to accurate measurement.

BORING

Boring is the machining of holes or any interior cylindrical surface. The piece to be bored must have a drilled or cored hole, and the hole must be large enough to insert the tool. The boring process merely enlarges the hole to the desired size or shape. The advantage of boring is that a perfectly true round hole is obtained, and two or more holes of the same or different diameters may be bored at one setting, thus ensuring absolute alinement of the axis of the holes.

It is the usual practice to bore a hole to within a few thousandths of an inch of the desired size and then finish it with a reamer to the exact size.

Work to be bored may be held in a chuck, bolted to the faceplate, or bolted to the carriage. Long pieces must be supported at the free end in a center rest.

When the boring tool is fed into the hole in work being rotated on a chuck or faceplate, the process is called single point boring. It is the same as turning except that the cutting chip is taken from the inside. The cutting edge of the boring tool resembles that of a turning tool. Boring tools may be of the solid forged type or the inserted cutter bit type.

When the work to be bored is clamped to the top of the carriage, a boring bar is held between centers and driven by a dog. The work is fed to the tool by the automatic longitudinal feed of the carriage. Three types of boring bars are shown in figure 12-30.

Note the countersunk center holes at the ends to fit the lathe centers.

Figure 12-30A shows a boring bar fitted with a fly cutter held by a headless setscrew. The other setscrew, bearing on the end of the cutter, is for adjusting the cutter to the work.

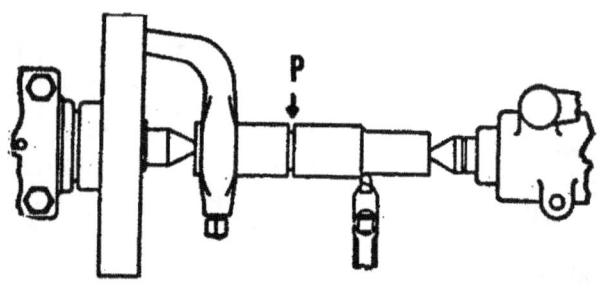

28.133X
Figure 12-29.—Machining to a shoulder

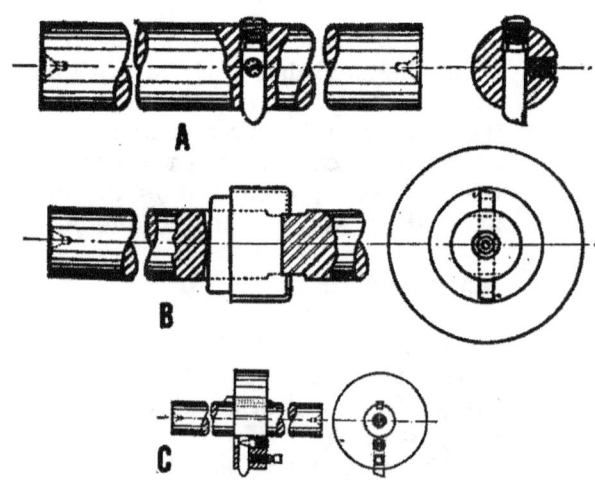

28.134
Figure 12-30.—Boring bars.

Figure 12-30B shows a boring bar fitted with a two-edge cutter held by a taper key. This is more of a finishing or sizing cutter, as it cuts on both sides and is used for producton work.

The boring bar shown in figure 12-30C is fitted with a cast-iron head to adapt it for boring work of large diameter. The head is fitted with a fly cutter similar to the one shown in figure 12-30A. The setscrew with the tapered point adjusts the cutter to the work.

TAPERS

The term taper may be defined as the gradual lessening of the diameter or thickness of a piece of work toward one end. The amount of taper in any given length of work is found by subtracting the size of the small end from the size of the large end. Taper is usually expressed as the amount of taper per foot of length, or as an angle.

We will take two examples as an illustration.

EXAMPLE 1.—Find the taper per foot of a piece of work 2 inches long: Diameter of small end is 1 inch; diameter of the large end is 2 inches.

The amount of the taper is 2 inches minus 1 inch, which equals 1 inch. The length of the taper is given as 2 inches. Therefore, the taper is 1 inch in 2 inches of length. In 12 inches of length it would be 6 inches. (See fig. 12-31)

EXAMPLE 2.—Find the taper per foot of a piece 6 inches long. Diameter of small end is 1 inch; diameter of large end is 2 inches.

The amount of taper is the same as in problem 1, that is, 1 inch. However, the length of this taper is 6 inches; hence the taper per foot is

1 inch x 12/6 = 2 inches per foot (fig. 12-31).

From the foregoing, it may be seen that the length of a tapered piece is very important in computing the taper. If you bear this in mind when machining tapers you will not go wrong. Using the formula:

$$\text{Taper per foot} = T \times \frac{12}{L},$$

where T represents the amount of taper in length L, both expressed in inches.

Now let us consider the angle of the taper. In a round piece of work, the included angle of the taper is twice the angle that the surface makes with the axis or center line. In straight

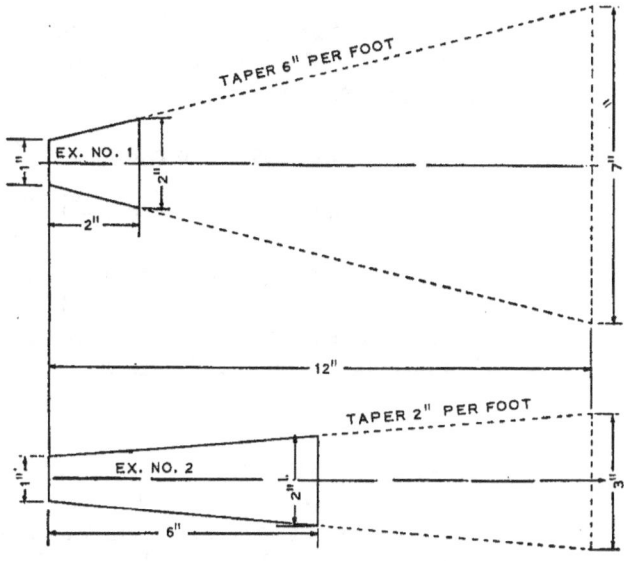

Figure 12-31.—Tapers.

turning, it will be recalled that the diameter of a piece is reduced by twice the depth of the cut taken from its surface. For the same reason, the included angle of the taper is twice the angle that the path of the cutting tool makes with the axis or center line of the piece being turned. There are tables or charts in all machinist's handbooks that give the angles for different amounts of taper per foot.

There are several well-known tapers that are recognized as standards for machines on which they are used. These standards make it possible to make or obtain parts to fit the machine in question without the necessity of detailed measuring and fitting. By designating the name and number of the standard taper being used, the length, the diameter of the small and large ends, the taper per foot, and all other pertinent measurements are immediately obtainable by reference to appropriate tables found in all machinist's handbooks.

There are three standard tapers with which you should be familiar: (1) the MORSE TAPER (approximately 5/8 inch per foot) used for the taper holes in lathe and drill press spindles and the attachments that fit them, such as lathe centers, drill shanks, etc.; (2) the BROWN & SHARPE TAPER (1/2 inch per foot except No. 10 which is 0.5161 inch per foot) used for milling machine spindle shanks; and (3) the JARNO TAPER (0.6 inch per foot) used by some manufacturers because of its simplicity, it being the only taper that is constant and does not require a table to find the various dimensions pertaining to its parts; e.g.

$$\text{Diameter of large end} = \frac{\text{taper number}}{8}$$

$$\text{Diameter of small end} = \frac{\text{taper number}}{10}$$

$$\text{Length of taper} = \frac{\text{taper number}}{2}$$

The taper for pipe ends, 3/4 inch per foot, is also considered a standard.

TURNING TAPERS

In ordinary straight turning, the cutting tool moves along a line parallel to the axis of the work, causing the finished job to be the same diameter throughout. If, however, in cutting, the tool moves at an angle to the axis of the work, a taper will be produced. Therefore, to turn a taper, it is necessary either to mount the work in the lathe so the axis upon which it turns is at an angle to the axis of the lathe, or to cause the cutting tool to move at an angle to the axis of the lathe.

There are three methods in common use for turning tapers:

1. SETTING OVER THE TAILSTOCK, which moves the dead center away from the axis of the lathe and hence causes work supported between centers to be at an angle with the axis of the lathe.

2. USING THE COMPOUND REST set at an angle and causing the cutting tool to be fed at the desired angle to the axis of the lathe.

3. USING THE TAPER ATTACHMENT, which also causes the cutting tool to move at an angle to the axis of the lathe.

In the first method, the cutting tool is fed by the longitudinal feed parallel to the lathe axis, but a taper is produced because the work axis is at an angle. In the second and third methods, the work axis coincides with the lathe axis, but a taper is produced because the cutting tool moves at an angle.

SETTING OVER THE TAILSTOCK.— The tailstock top may be moved laterally on its base by means of adjusting screws. In straight turning, you will recall that these adjusting screws were used to align the dead center with the tail center by moving the tailstock to bring it on the center-line. For taper turning, we deliberately move the tailstock off center, and the amount we move it determines the taper produced. The amount of setover can be approximately set by means of the zero lines inscribed on the base and top of the tailstock as shown in figure 12-32. Then for final adjustment, the setover is measured with a scale between center points as illustrated in figure 12-33.

In turning a taper by this method, the distance between centers is of utmost importance. To illustrate, figure 12-34 shows two very different tapers produced by the same amount of setover of the tailstock, because in one case the length of the work between centers is greater than in the other. THE CLOSER THE DEAD CENTER IS TO THE LIVE CENTER, THE STEEPER THE TAPER PRODUCED.

Suppose it is desired to turn a taper on the full length of a piece 12 inches long with one end having a diameter of 3 inches, and the other end a diameter of 2 inches. The small end is to be 1 inch smaller than the large end; so we set the tailstock over one-half this amount or 1/2 inch in this case. Thus, at one end the cutting tool will be 1/2 inch closer to the center of the work than at the other end; so the diameter of the finished job will be 2 x 1/2 or 1 inch less at the small end. Since the piece is 12 inches long, we have produced a taper of 1 inch per foot. Now, if you wish to produce a taper of 1 inch per foot on a piece only 6 inches long, the small end would be only 1/2 inch less in diameter than the large end, so the tailstock would be set over 1/4 inch or one-half of the distance used for the 12-inch length.

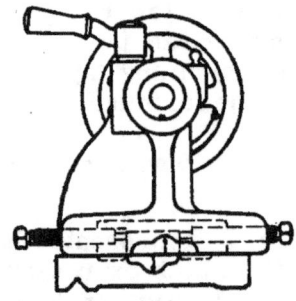

28.139X
Figure 12-32.—Tailstock set-over for taper turning.

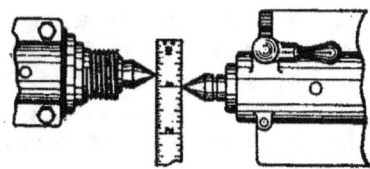

Figure 12-33.—Measuring set-over of dead center.

From the foregoing, it is seen that the set-over is proportional to the length between centers and may be computed by the following formula:

$$S = \frac{T}{2} \times \frac{L}{12}$$

where S = setover in inches, T = taper per foot in inches, and

$\frac{L}{12}$ = length in feet.

Remember that L is length of work from live center to dead center. If the work is on a mandrel, L is the length of the mandrel between centers.

The setover tailstock method cannot be used for steep tapers because the setover necessary would be too great and the work would not be properly supported by the lathe centers. It is obvious that with setover there is not a true bearing between the work centers and the lathe center points, and that the bearing surface becomes less and less satisfactory as the setover is increased.

After turning a taper by the tailstock setover method, don't forget to realign the centers for straight turning of your next job.

USING THE COMPOUND REST.—The compound rest is generally used for short, steep tapers. It is set at the angle which the taper is to make with the centerline (that is half the included angle of the taper). The tool is then fed to the work at this angle by means of the compound rest feed screw. The length of taper that can be machined is necessarily short because of limited travel of the compound rest top.

Truing a lathe center is one example of the use of the compound rest for taper work. Other examples are the refacing of an angle type valve disk, the machining of the face of a bevel gear, and similar work. Such jobs are often referred to as working to an angle rather than as taper work.

The graduations marked on the compound rest provide a quick means for setting to the angle desired. When set at zero, the compound rest is perpendicular to the lathe axis. When set at 90° on either side, the compound rest is parallel to the lathe axis.

On the other hand, when the angle to be cut is measured from the centerline, the setting of the compound rest corresponds to the complement of that angle—(the complement of an angle is that angle which added to it makes a right angle; that is, angle plus complement = 90°). For example, to machine a 50° included angle (25° angle with centerline), the compound rest is set at 90°—25°, or 65°.

When a very accurate setting of the compound rest is to be made to a fraction of a degree, for example, run the carriage up to the faceplate and set the compound rest with a vernier bevel protractor set to the required angle. The blade of the protractor is held on the flat surface of the faceplate, and the stock is held against the finished side of the compound rest.

USING THE TAPER ATTACHMENT.— For turning and boring long tapers with accuracy, the taper attachment is indispensable. It is especially useful in duplicating work; identical tapers can be turned and bored with one setting of the taper guide bar.

The guide bar is set at an angle to the lathe axis corresponding to the taper desired. By means of a shoe which slides on the guide bar as the carriage moves longitudinally, the tool cross slide is moved laterally. The resultant movement of the cutting tool is along a line that is parallel to the guide bar, and therefore a taper is produced whose angular measurement is the same as that set on the guide bar. The guide bar is graduated in degrees at one end, and in inches per foot of taper at the other end to facilitate rapid setting.

When preparing to use the taper attachment, run the carriage up to the approximate position of the work to be turned. Set the tool on line

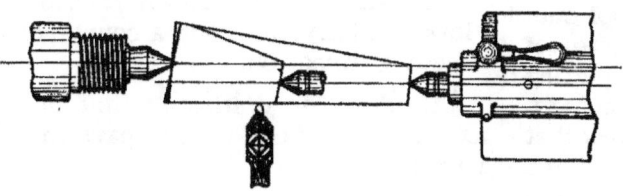

Figure 12-34.—Set-over of tailstock showing importance of considering length of work.

with the centers of the lathe. Then bolt or clamp the holding bracket to the ways of the bed (the attachment itself is bolted to the back of the carriage saddle) and tighten clamp C, figure 12-35. The taper guide bar now controls the lateral movement of the cross slide. Set the guide bar for the taper desired and the attachment is ready for operation. The final adjustment of the tool for size must be made by means of the compound rest feed screw, since the crossfeed screw is inoperative.

TAPER BORING

Taper boring may be accomplished only by the use of the compound rest or the taper attachment.

The rules that are applicable to outside taper turning also apply to the boring of tapered holes. The cutting point of the tool is placed on center and, if the taper attachment is used, care must be exercised to eliminate the backlash of the slide fittings so that the hole will not be bored straight at the start. Measurement of the size and taper of the hole is generally made with a taper plug gage by the cut and try method. After a cut or two has been taken, the bore is cleaned, the gage rubbed lightly with chalk, inserted in the hole, and twisted slightly to cause the chalk to show where the gage is bearing. Any necessary corrections may then be made and the boring continued until the taper is brought to size. A very light application of prussian blue to the gage will give better results than chalk for accurate work.

When making a blind tapered hole, such as may be required in drill sockets, it is best to drill the hole carefully to the correct depth with a drill of the same size as specified for the small end of the hole. This gives the advantage of boring to the right size without the removal of metal at the extreme bottom of the bore, which is rather difficult, particularly in small, deep holes.

For turning and boring tapers, the tool cutting edge should be set exactly at the center of the work. That is, set the point of the cutting edge even with the height of the lathe centers.

In testing the taper on a piece of work that is to fit a spindle and is nearly finished, make a chalk mark along the element or side of the taper piece. Place the work in the taper hole it is to fit and turn carefully by hand. Then remove the work and the chalk mark will show where the taper is bearing. If it is a perfect fit, it will indicate along the entire line of the chalk mark. If it is not, it will show where the adjustment is needed. Make the adjustment, take another light chip and test again. Be sure the taper is correct before turning to the finished diameter.

Figure 12-36 shows a Morse standard taper plug and a taper socket gage. They not only give the proper taper, but also show the proper distance that the taper should enter the spindle.

SCREW THREADS

The thread forms you will be working with most are V-form threads, Acme threads, and square threads. Each of these thread forms is used for specific applications. V-form threads are commonly used on fastening devices such as bolts and nuts as well as on machine parts. Acme screw threads are generally used for transmitting motion such as that between the lead screw and lathe carriage. Square threads are used to increase mechanical advantage and to provide good clamping ability as in the screw jack or vise screw.

Terminology

There are several terms used in describing screw threads and screw thread systems which you must know before you can calculate and machine screw threads. Figure 12-37 illustrates the application of some of the following terms:

External Thread.— A thread on the external surface of a cylinder.

Internal Thread.— A thread on the internal surface of a hollow cylinder.

Right-Hand Thread.— A thread which, when viewed axially, winds in a clockwise and receding direction.

Left-Hand Thread.— A thread which, when viewed axially, winds in a counterclockwise and receding direction.

Lead.— The distance a threaded part moves axially in a fixed mating part in one complete revolution.

Pitch.— The distance between corresponding points on adjacent threads.

Single Thread.— A single (single start) thread having the lead equal to the pitch.

Figure 12-35.—Turning a taper using taper attachment.

Multiple Thread.—A multiple (multiple start) thread has a lead which is equal to the pitch multiplied by the number of starts.

Class of Threads.— Classes of threads are distinguished from each other by the amount of tolerance or tolerance and allowance specified.

Thread Form.— The axial plane profile of a thread for a length of one pitch.

Flank.—The side of the thread.

Crest.—The top of the thread (bounded by the major diameter on external threads; by the minor diameter on internal threads).

Root.— The bottom of the thread (bounded by the minor diameter on external threads; by the major diameter on internal threads).

Thread Angle.— The angle formed by adjacent flanks of a thread.

Major Diameter.—The diameter of a cylinder that bounds the crest of an external thread or the root of an internal thread.

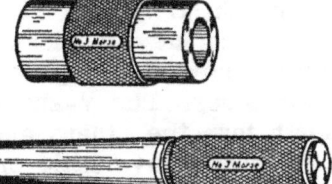

Figure 12-36.—Morse taper socket gage and plug gage.

LATHE AND LATHE MACHINING OPERATIONS

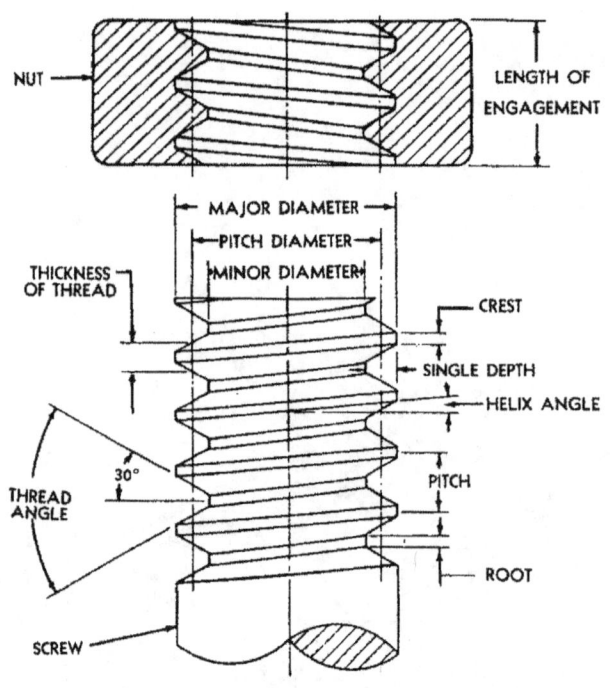

28.145
Figure 12-37.—Screw thread nomenclature.

Minor Diameter.— The diameter of a cylinder that bounds the root of an external thread or the crest of an internal thread.

Height of Thread.— The distance from the crest to the root of a thread measured perpendicular to the axis of the threaded piece (also called depth of thread).

Slant Depth.— The distance from the crest to the root of a thread measured along the angle forming the side of the thread.

Thread Series.— Groups of diameter pitch combinations which are distinguished from each other by the number of threads per inch to a specific diameter. The common thread series are the coarse series and the fine series.

Forms of Threads

V-FORM THREADS.— The three forms of V-threads are the V-sharp, the American National and the American Standard. All of these threads have a 60 degree included angle between their sides. The V-sharp thread has a greater depth than the others and the crest and root of this thread have little or no flat. The external American Standard thread has slightly less depth than the external American National thread but is otherwise similar. The American Standard thread is actually a modification of the American National thread. This modification was made so that a unified series of threads, which permits interchangeability of standard threaded fastening devices manufactured in the United States, Canada, and the United Kingdom, could be included in the threading system used in the United States. The Bureau of Ships and naval procurement activities use American Standard threading system specifications whenever possible; this system is recommended for use by all naval activities.

To cut a V-form screw thread, you need to know (1) the pitch of the thread, (2) the straight depth of the thread, (3) the slant depth of the thread, and (4) the width of the flat at the root of the thread. The pitch of a thread is the basis for calculating all other dimensions and is equal to 1 divided by the number of threads per inch. Twice the straight depth of an internal thread subtracted from the outside diameter of the externally threaded part is the basis for determining the bore diameter of a mating part to the threaded internally. When the thread cutting tool is fed into the workpiece at one-half of the included angle of the thread, the slant depth is the dimension necessary to determine how far to feed the tool into the work. The point of the threading tool must have a flat equal to the width of the flat at the root of the thread (external or internal thread, as applicable). If the flat at the point of the tool is too wide, the resulting thread will be too thin if the cutting tool is fed in the correct amount. If the flat is too narrow, the thread will be too thick.

The following formulas will provide you with the information you need to know for cutting V-form threads:

V-SHARP THREAD

Pitch $= \frac{1}{n} = 1 \div$ number of threads per inch

Depth of thread = 0.866 x pitch = 0.866p.
Slant depth of thread = pitch

AMERICAN NATIONAL THREAD

Pitch $= 1 \div$ number of threads per inch $= \frac{1}{n}$

Depth of external thread - 0.64952 x pitch
= 0.64952p

Depth of internal thread = 0.541266 x pitch
= 0.541266p

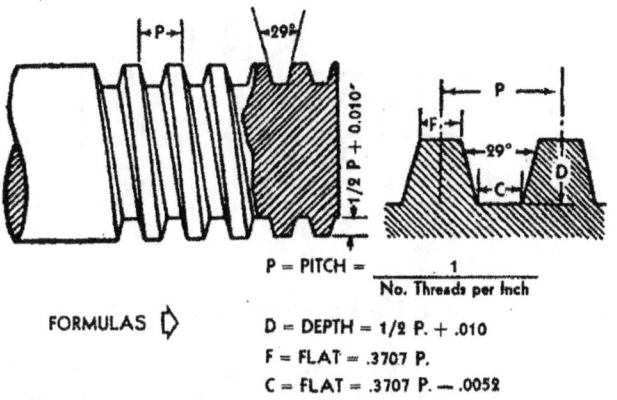

FORMULAS

P = PITCH = $\dfrac{1}{\text{No. Threads per inch}}$

D = DEPTH = 1/2 P. + .010
F = FLAT = .3707 P.
C = FLAT = .3707 P. − .0052

28.147X

Figure 12-39.—Acme thread and formulas.

Width of flat at point of tool for external and internal threads = 0.125 x pitch = 0.125p
Slant depth of external thread = 0.750 x pitch = 0.750p
Slant depth of internal thread = 0.625 x pitch = 0.625p

AMERICAN STANDARD THREAD

Pitch = 1 ÷ number of threads per inch = $\dfrac{1}{n}$

Depth of external thread = 0.61343 x pitch = 0.61343p
Depth of internal thread = 0.541266 x pitch = 0.541266p
Width of flat at point of tool for external threads = 0.166 x pitch = 0.166p
Width of flat at point of tool for internal threads = 0.125 x pitch = 0.125p
Slant depth of external thread = 0.708 x pitch = 0.708p
Slant depth of internal thread = 0.625 x pitch = 0.625p

To produce the correct thread profile, the cutting tool must be accurately ground to the correct angle and contour. Also the cutting tool must be set in the correct position. Figure 12-38 shows how a tool must be ground and set.

The point of the tool must be ground to an angle of 60°, as shown in A of figure 12-38. A center gage or a thread-tool gage is used for grinding the tool to the exact angle required. The top of the tool is usually ground flat, with no side rake or back rake. However, for cutting threads in steel, side rake is sometimes used.

The threading tool must be set square with the work, as shown in B and C of figure 12-38. The

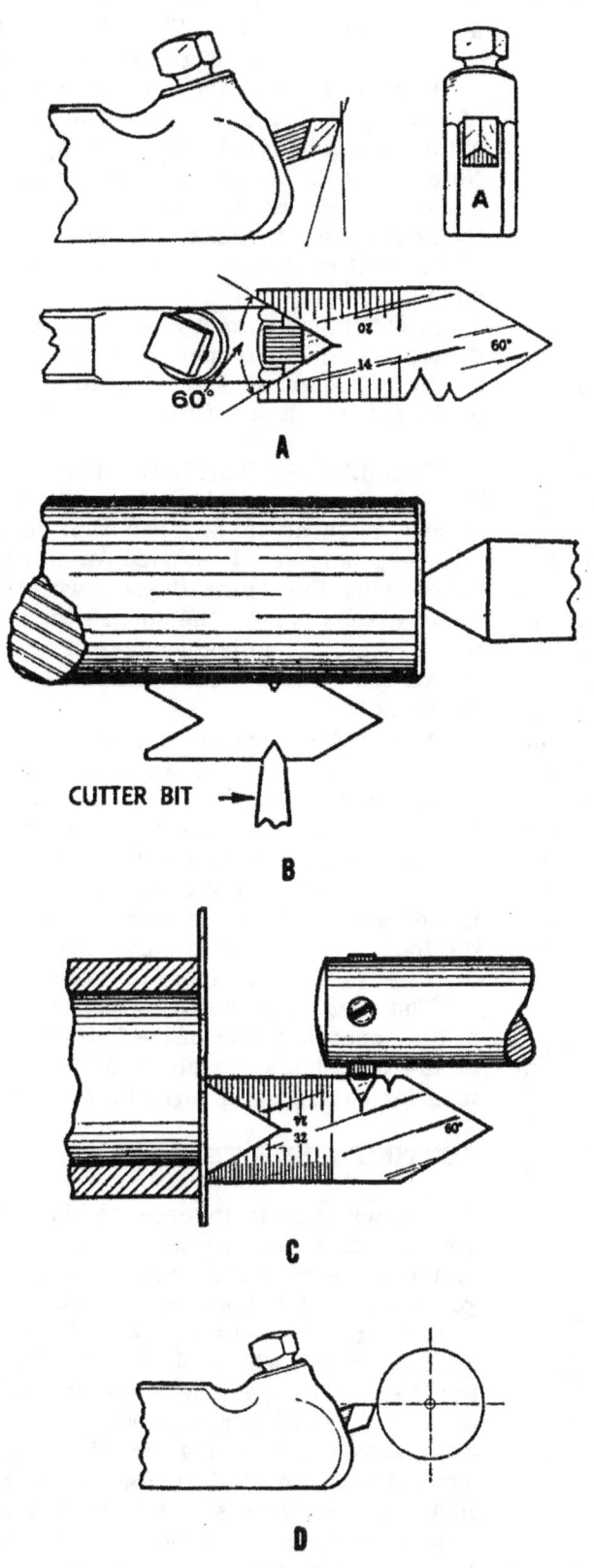

28.146X

Figure 12-38.—Threading tool setup for V-form threads.

LATHE AND LATHE MACHINING OPERATIONS

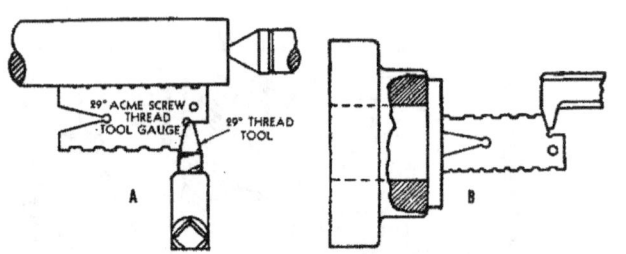

Figure 12-40.—Use of Acme thread tool gage.

center gage is used to adjust the point of the threading tool and if the tool is carefully set, a perfect thread will result. Of course, if the threading tool is not set perfectly square with the work, the angle of the thread will be incorrect.

For cutting external threads, the top of the threading tool should be placed exactly on center as shown in D of figure 12-38. Note that the top of the tool is ground flat and is in exact alignment with the lathe center. This is necessary to obtain the correct angle of the thread.

Size of the threading tool for cutting an internal thread is important. The tool head must be small enough to be backed out of the thread and still leave enough clearance to be drawn from the threaded hole without injuring the thread. However, the boring bar which holds the threading tool for internal threading should be as large in diameter and as short as possible to prevent springing.

THE ACME SCREW THREAD.—The Acme screw thread is used on valve stems, the lead screw of a lathe, and other places where a strong thread is required. The top and bottom of the threads are similar to a square thread

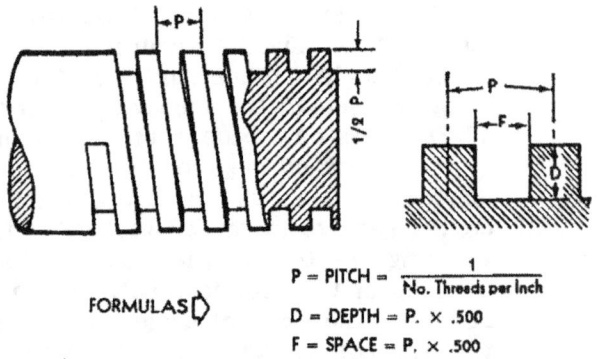

Figure 12-41.—Square thread and formulas.

in that they are flat. The sides of the thread have an included angle of 29° (fig. 12-38).

Figures 12-40A and 12-40B show the method of setting an Acme threading tool for cutting an external and internal Acme thread, respectively. Note that a 29° Acme thread gage is used in the same manner as the center gage was used for V-form screw threads. Adjust the cutting edge of the tool to line it up exactly with the beveled edge of the gage.

In cutting an Acme thread, there should be a clearance of 0.010 inch between the top of the thread of the screw and the bottom of the thread of the nut in which it fits.

THE SQUARE THREAD.—The square thread (fig. 12-41) is used where heavy threads are required, such as in jack screws, press screws and feed screws. It is used for much the same purpose as the Acme thread, which is used in many places where the square thread was formerly used. The disadvantage of square threads is that the straight sides eliminate sideplay adjustment.

The cutting edge width of the tool for cutting square screw threads is exactly one-half the pitch, but the width of the edge of the tool for threading nuts is from 0.001 inch to 0.003 inch larger. This permits a sliding fit on the screw.

The threading tool for cutting square threads is set square with the work. Since the edge of the tool is square, it is only necessary to adjust the edge to the surface of the work.

The clearance between the top of the thread of the screw and that of the bottom of the thread of the nut should be about 0.005 inch to 0.006 inch for each inch of thread diameter.

CUTTING SCREW THREADS

Cutting screw threads on the lathe is accomplished by connecting the headstock spindle of the lathe with the lead screw by a series of gears so that a positive carriage feed is obtained, and the lead screw is driven at the required speed with relation to the headstock spindle. The gearing between the headstock spindle and lead screw may be arranged so that any desired pitch of the thread may be cut. For example, if the lead screw has 8 threads per inch and the gears are arranged so that the headstock spindle revolves four times while the lead screw revolves once, the thread cut will be four times as fine as the thread on the lead screw, or 32 threads per inch. By means of the quick-change gear box, the proper gearing arrangement can be made quickly and easily by placing the levers as indicated on the index plate for the thread desired.

When the lathe is set up to control the carriage movement for cutting the desired thread pitch, the next consideration is shaping the thread. The cutting tool is ground to the shape required for the form of the thread to be cut, that is V, Acme, square, etc. The depth of the thread is obtained by adjusting the cross slide.

MOUNTING WORK IN THE LATHE.—When mounting work between lathe centers for cutting screw threads, be sure the lathe dog is securely attached before starting to cut the thread. If the dog should slip, the thread will be ruined. Never remove the lathe dog from the work until the thread has been completed. If it is necessary to remove work from the lathe before the thread is completed, be sure that the lathe dog is replaced in the same slot of the driving plate.

When threading work in the lathe chuck, be sure the chuck jaws are tight and the work is well supported. The chuck must be tight enough on the spindle to prevent unscrewing when the lathe is reversed. Never remove the work from the chuck until the thread is finished.

When threading long slender shafts, use a follower rest. The center rest must be used for supporting one end of long work that is to be threaded on the inside.

POSITION OF COMPOUND REST FOR CUTTING SCREW THREADS.—Ordinarily on threads of fine lead, the tool is fed straight into the work in successive cuts. For coarse threads, it is better to set the compound rest at one-half of the included angle of the thread and feed in along the side of the thread. For the last few finishing cuts, the tool should be fed straight in with the crossfeed of the lathe to make a smooth, even finish on both sides of the thread.

When cutting V-form threads and when maximum production is desired, it is customary to place the compound rest of the lathe at an angle of 29°, as shown in figure 12-42A. When the compound rest is set in this position, and the compound-rest screw is used for adjusting the depth of cut, most of the metal is removed by the left side of the threading tool (fig. 12-42B). This permits the chip to curl out of the way better than if the tool is fed straight in, and prevents tearing the thread. Since the angle on the side of the threading tool is 30°, the right side of the tool will shave the thread smooth and produce a better finish; although it does not

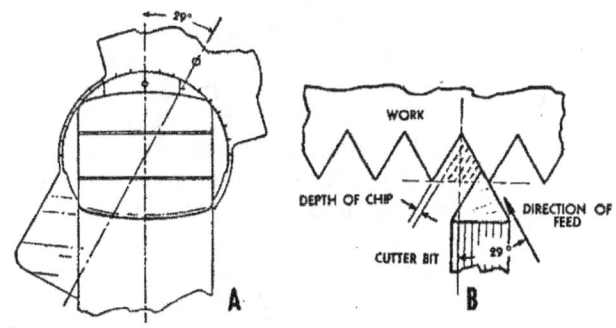

Figure 12-42.—Compound rest set at 29°.

remove enough metal to interfere with the main chip, which is taken by the left side of the tool.

USING THE THREAD-CUTTING STOP.—On account of the lost motion caused by the play necessary for smooth operation of the change gears, lead screw, half-nuts, etc., the thread-cutting tool must be withdrawn quickly at the end of each cut. If this is not done, the point of the tool will dig into the thread and may be broken off.

To reset the tool accurately for each successive cut, and to regulate the depth of the chip, the thread-cutting stop is useful.

First, set the point of the tool so that it just touches the work, then lock the thread-cutting stop and turn the thread-cutting stop screw A (fig. 12-43) until the shoulder is tight against stop B (fig. 12-43). When ready to take the first chip, run the tool rest back by turning the crossfeed screw to the left several times and move the tool to the point where the thread is to start. Then turn the crossfeed screw to the right until

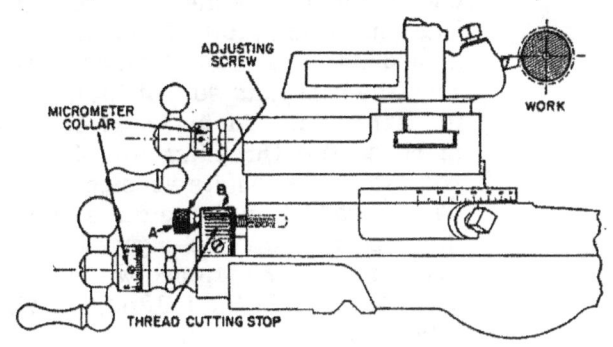

Figure 12-43.—Adjustable thread-cutting stop mounted on carriage saddle (clamped to dovetail).

LATHE AND LATHE MACHINING OPERATIONS

the thread-cutting stop screw strikes the thread-cutting stop. The tool is now in the original position, and by turning the compound-rest feed screw in 0.002 inch or 0.003 inch the tool will be in a position to take the first cut (fig. 12-43).

For each successive cut after the carriage is returned to its starting point, the tool can be reset accurately to its previous position. Turn the crossfeed screw to the right until the shoulder of screw A strikes stop B. Then the depth of the next cut can be regulated by adjustment of the compound rest feed screw as for the first chip.

For cutting an internal thread, the adjustable thread-cutting stop should be set with the head of the adjusting screw on the inside of the stop. In this case, the tool is withdrawn by moving it toward the center or axis of the lathe.

The micrometer collar on the crossfeed screw may be used in place of the thread-cutting stop, if desired.

To do this, first bring the point of the threading tool up so that it just touches the work; then adjust the micrometer collar on the crossfeed screw to zero. All adjustments for obtaining the desired depth of cut should be made with the compound-rest screw. Withdraw the tool at the end of each cut by turning the crossfeed screw to the left one complete turn; return the tool to the starting point and turn the crossfeed screw to the right one turn, stopping at zero. The compound rest feed screw may then be adjusted for any desired depth.

ENGAGING THE THREAD FEED MECHANISM.—When threads are being cut on a lathe, the half nuts are clamped over the lead screw to engage the threading feed and released at the end of the cut by means of the threading lever. The threading dial (illustrated in fig. 12-15) provides a means for determining the time to engage the half nuts so that the cutting tool follows the same path during each cut. When an index mark on the threading dial is aligned with the witness mark on its housing, the half nuts may be engaged. For some thread pitches however, the half nuts may be engaged only when certain index marks are aligned with the witness mark. On most lathes the half nuts can be engaged as follows:

For all even-numbered threads per inch, close the half-nuts at any line on the dial.

For all odd-numbered threads per inch, close the half-nuts at any numbered line on the dial.

For all threads involving one-half of a thread in each inch, such as 11 1/2, close the half-nuts at any odd-numbered line.

CUTTING THE THREAD.—After setting up the lathe, as explained previously, take a very light trial cut just deep enough to scribe a line on the surface of the work, as shown in figure 12-44A. The purpose of this trial cut is to be sure that the lathe is arranged for cutting the desired pitch of thread.

To check the number of threads per inch, place a rule against the work, as shown in figure 12-44B so that the end of the rule rests on the point of a thread or on one of the scribed lines. Count the scribed lines between the end of the rule and the first inch mark, and this will give you the number of threads per inch.

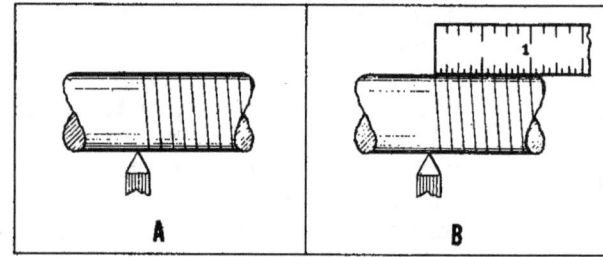

28.152X

Figure 12-44.—The first cut.

It is quite difficult to count accurately fine pitches of screw threads, as described above. A screw pitch gage used as illustrated in figure 12-45 is very convenient for checking the finer screw threads. This gage consists of a number of sheet metal plates in which are cut the exact form of threads of the various pitches and each plate is stamped with a number indicating the number of threads per inch for which it is to be used.

Final check for both diameter and pitch of the thread may be made with the nut that is to be used or with a ring thread gage, if one is available. The nut should fit snugly without play or

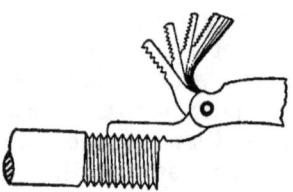

28.153X

Figure 12-45.—Screw pitch gage.

shake but should not bind on the thread at any point.

RESETTING THE TOOL.—If the thread-cutting tool needs resharpening or gets out of alignment, or if you are chasing the threads on a previously threaded piece, you must reset the tool so that it will follow the original thread groove. This may be done by using the compound rest feed screw and crossfeed screw to jockey the tool to the proper position, by disengaging the change gears and turning the spindle until the tool is positioned properly, or by loosening the lathe dog (if used) and turning the work until the tool is in proper position with the thread groove. In either case the micrometer collars on the crossfeed screw and compound rest screw will usually have to be reset.

Before adjusting the tool in the groove, use the appropriate thread gage to set the tool square with the workpiece. Then with the tool a few thousandths of an inch away from the workpiece, start the machine and engage the threading mechanism. When the tool has moved to a position such as is shown in figure 12-46, stop the lathe without disengaging the thread mechanism.

The most practical and commonly used method for resetting a threading tool for machining angular form threads is the compound rest and crossfeed positioning method. By adjusting the compound rest slide forward or back the tool is moved parallel to the axis of the work as well as toward or away from the work. When the point of the tool coincides with the original thread groove (see alternate view of tool in figure 12-46), the crossfeed screw is used to bring the tool point directly into the groove. When a good fit between the cutting tool and thread groove is obtained the micrometer collar on the crossfeed screw is set on zero and the micrometer collar on the compound rest feed screw is set to the depth of cut previously taken or to zero as required. (Note: Be sure that the thread mechanism is engaged and the tool is set square with the work before adjusting the position of the tool along the axis of the workpiece.)

If it is inconvenient to use the compound rest for readjusting the threading tool, the lathe dog (if used) may be loosened; turn the work so that the threading tool will match the groove, and tighten the lathe dog. If possible, however, avoid the necessity of doing this.

Another method that is sometimes used, is to disengage the reverse gears or the change gears; turn the headstock spindle until the point of the threading tool enters the groove in the work, and then engage the gears.

FINISHING THE END OF A THREADED PIECE.—The end of a thread may be finished by any one of several methods. The 45° chamfer on the end of a thread, as shown in figure 12-47A, is commonly used for bolts, and cap screws. For machined parts and special screws, the end is often finished by rounding with a forming tool, as shown in figure 12-47B.

It is difficult to stop the threading tool abruptly, so some provision is usually made for clearance at the end of the cut. In figure 12-47A, a hole has been drilled at the end of the thread, and in figure 12-47B, a neck or groove has been cut around the shaft. The groove is preferable, as the lathe must be run very slowly in order to obtain satisfactory results with the drilled hole.

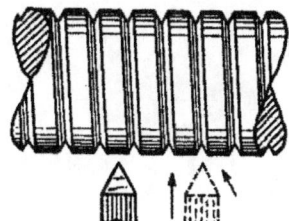

28.154X

Figure 12-46.—Tool must be reset to original Groove.

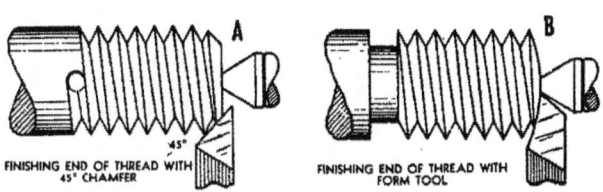

28.155X

Figure 12-47.—Finishing the end of a threaded piece.

BASIC FUNDAMENTALS OF MEASURING TOOLS AND TECHNIQUES

CONTENTS

		Page
I.	RULES AND TAPES	1
II.	SIMPLE CALIPERS	5
III.	VERNIER CALIPER	10
IV.	MICROMETER	14
V.	SQUARES	20
VI.	MISCELLANEOUS GAGES	24

BASIC FUNDAMENTALS OF MEASURING TOOLS AND TECHNIQUES

In performing many jobs during your career, you will be required to take accurate measurements of materials and objects. It is common practice in the shop to fabricate material for installation in a shop or in the field. For example, suppose you need a box of certain size to fit a space in a compartment. You would have to take measurements of the space and send them to a shop where the box would be built. This example suggests that the measurements you took and those taken in the process of building the box must be accurate. However, the accuracy of the measurements will depend on the measuring tools used and one's ability to use them correctly.

Measuring tools are also used for inspecting a finished product or partly finished product. Inspection operations include testing or checking a piece of work by comparing dimensions of the workpiece to the required dimensions given on a drawing or sketch. Again, the measurements taken must be accurate and accuracy depends on one's ability to use measuring tools correctly.

After studying this chapter, you should be able to select the appropriate measuring tool to use in doing a job and be able to operate properly a variety of measuring instruments.

I. RULES AND TAPES

There are many different types of measuring tools in use in the shop. Where exact measurements are required, a micrometer caliper (mike) is used. Such a caliper, when properly used, gives measurements to within .001 of an inch accuracy. On the other hand, where accuracy is not extremely critical, the common rule or tape will suffice for most measurements.

Figure 1 shows some of the types of rules and tapes commonly used. Of all measuring tools, the simplest and most common is the steel rule. This rule is usually 6 or 12 inches in length, although other lengths are available. Steel rules may be flexible or nonflexible, but the thinner the rule, the easier it is to measure accurately because the division marks are closer to the work.

Generally a rule has four sets of graduations, one on each edge of each side. The longest lines represent the inch marks. On one edge, each inch is divided into 8 equal spaces; so each space represents 1/8 in. The other edge of this side is divided into sixteenths. The 1/4-in. and 1/2-in. marks are commonly made longer than the smaller division marks to facilitate counting, but the graduations are not, as a rule, numbered individually, as they are sufficiently far apart to be counted without difficulty. The opposite side is similarly divided into 32 and 64 spaces per inch, and it is common practice to number every fourth division for easier reading.

There are many variations of the common rule. Sometimes the graduations are on one side only, sometimes a set of graduations is added across one end for measuring in narrow spaces, and sometimes only the first inch is divided into 64ths, with the remaining inches divided into 32nds and 16ths.

A metal or wood folding rule may be used for measuring purposes. These folding rules are usually 2 to 6 feet long. The folding rules cannot be relied on for extremely accurate measurements because a certain amount of play develops at the joints after they have been used for a while.

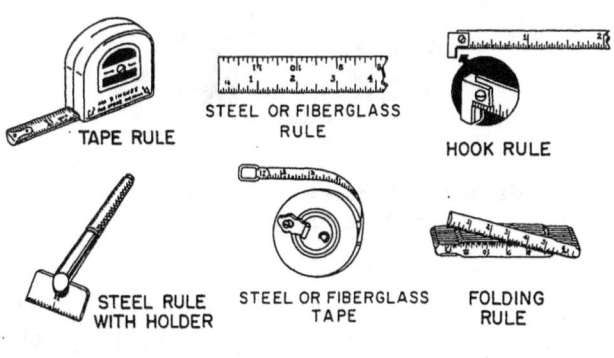

Figure 1.—Some common types of rules.

MEASURING TOOLS AND TECHNIQUES

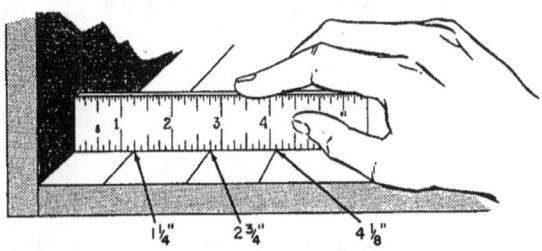

Figure 2.—Measuring with and reading a common rule.

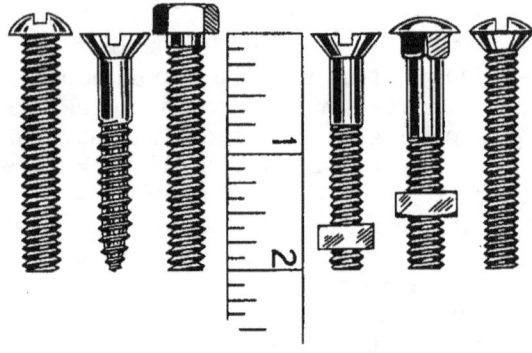

Figure 3.—Measuring the length of a bolt or screw.

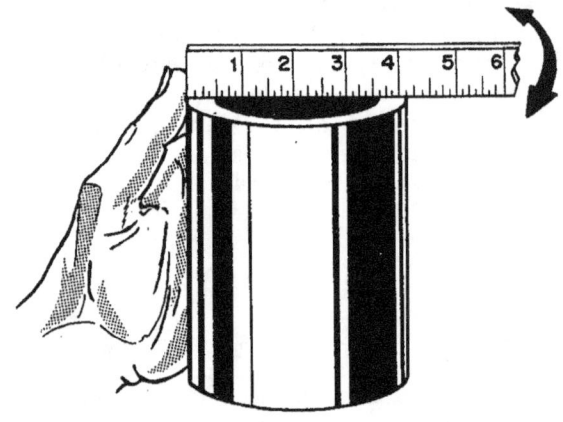

Figure 4.—Measuring the outside diameter of a pipe.

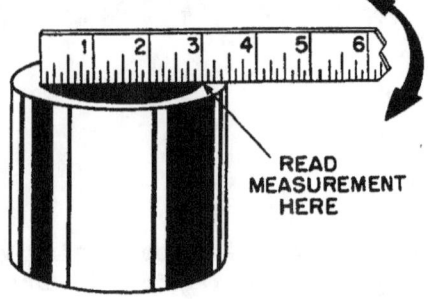

Figure 5.—Measuring the inside diameter of a pipe.

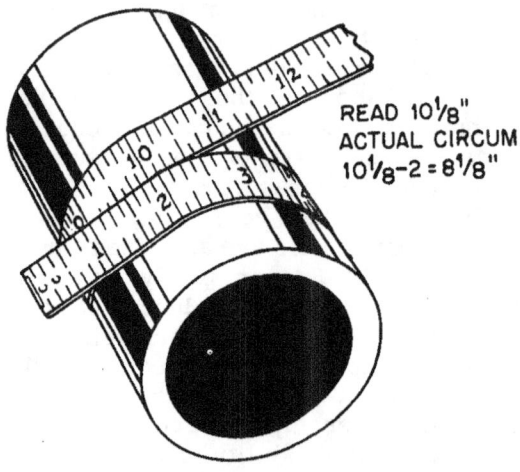

Figure 6.—Measuring the circumference of a pipe with a tape.

Steel tapes are made from 6 to about 300 ft. in length. The shorter lengths are frequently made with a curved cross section so that they are flexible enough to roll up, but remain rigid when extended. Long, flat tapes require support over their full length when measuring, or the natural sag will cause an error in reading.

The flexible-rigid tapes are usually contained in metal cases into which they wind themselves when a button is pressed, or into which they can be easily pushed. A hook is provided at one end to hook over the object being measured so one man can handle it without assistance. On some models, the outside of the case can be used as one end of the tape when measuring inside dimensions.

MEASURING PROCEDURES

To take a measurement with a common rule, hold the rule with its edge on the surface of the object being measured. This will eliminate parallax and other errors which might result

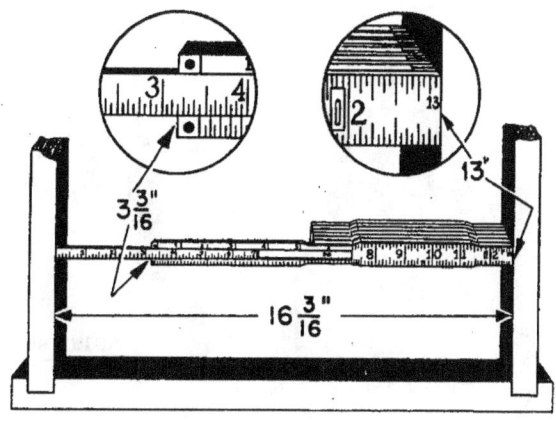

Figure 7.—Using a folding rule to measure an inside dimension.

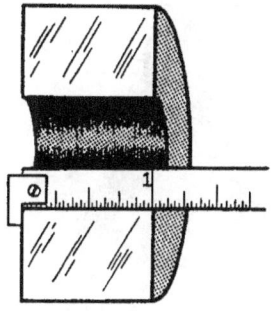

Figure 9.—Measuring the thickness of stock through a hole.

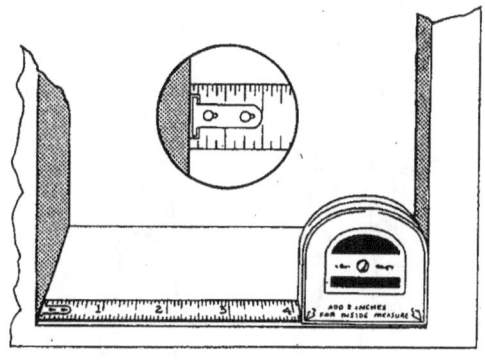

Figure 8.—Measuring an inside dimension with a tape rule.

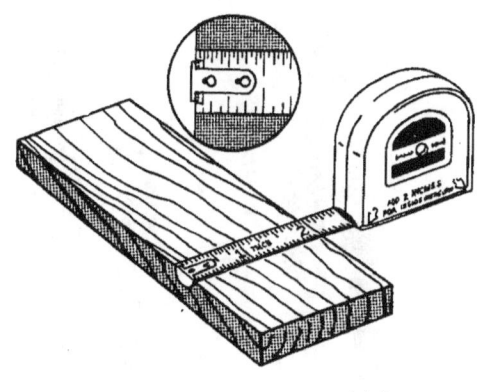

Figure 10.—Measuring an outside dimension using a tape rule.

due to the thickness of the rule. Read the measurement at the graduation which coincides with the distance to be measured, and state it as being so many inches and fractions of an inch. (Fig. 2.) Always reduce fractions to their lowest terms, for example, 6/8 inch would be called 3/4 inch. A hook or eye at the end of a tape or rule is normally part of the first measured inch.

Bolts or Screws

The length of bolts or screws is best measured by holding them up against a rigid rule or tape. Hold both the bolt or screw to be measured and the rule up to your eye level so that your line of sight will not be in error in reading the measurement. As shown in figure 3, the bolts or screws with countersink type heads are measured from the top of the head to the opposite end, while those with other type heads are measured from the bottom of the head.

Outside Pipe Diameters

To measure the outside diameter of a pipe, it is best to use some kind of rigid rule. A folding wooden rule or a steel rule is satisfactory for this purpose. As shown in figure 4, line up the end of the rule with one side of the pipe, using your thumb as a stop. Then with the one end held in place with your thumb, swing the rule through an arc and take the maximum reading at the other side of the pipe. For most practical purposes, the measurement obtained

MEASURING TOOLS AND TECHNIQUES

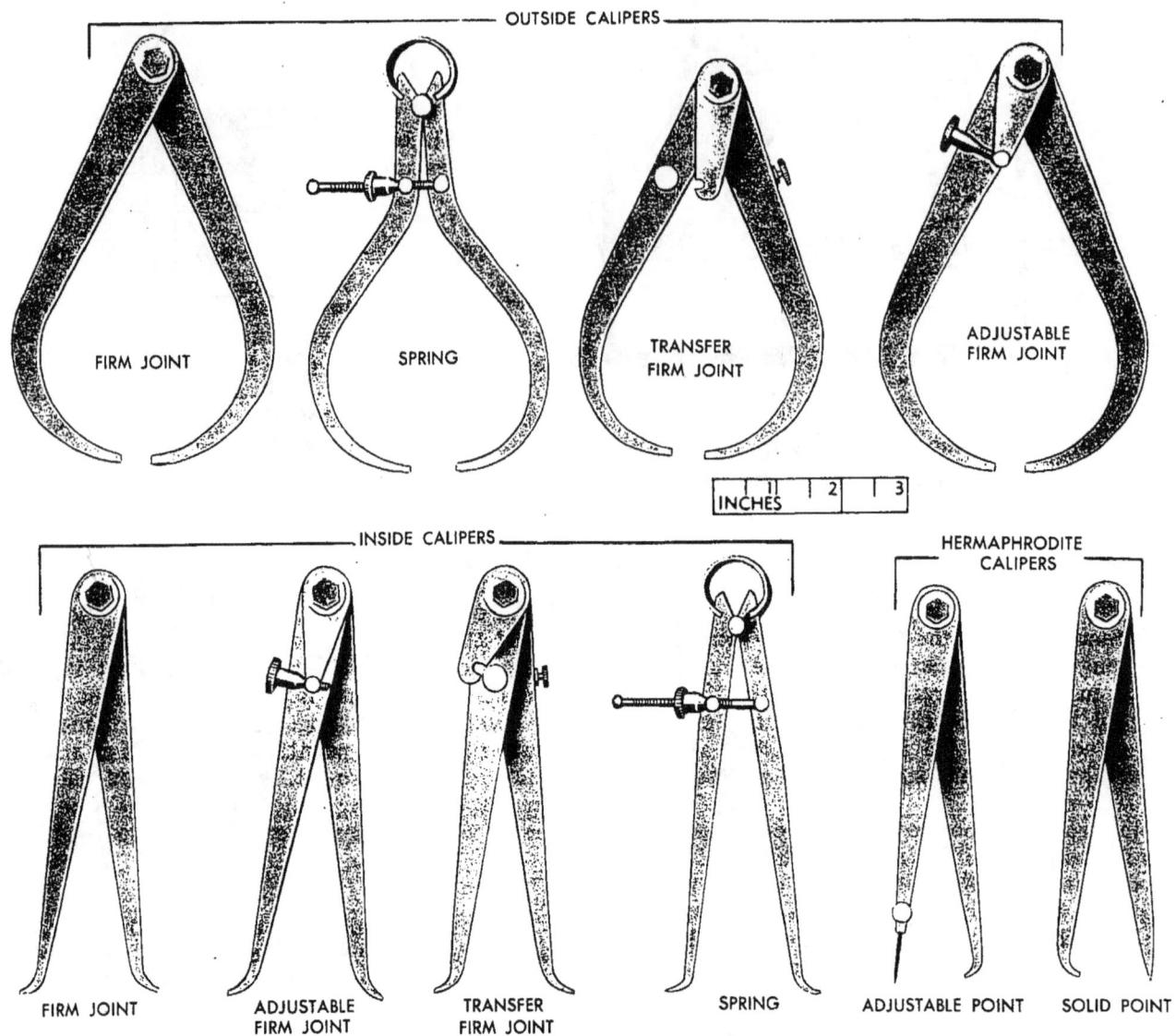

Figure 11.—Simple calipers—noncalibrated.

by using this method is satisfactory. It is necessary that you know how to take this measurement as the outside diameter of pipe is sometimes the only dimension given on pipe specifications.

Inside Pipe Diameters

To measure the inside diameter of a pipe with a rule, as shown in figure 5, hold the rule so that one corner of the rule just rests on the inside of one side of the pipe. Then, with one end thus held in place, swing the rule through an arc and read the diameter across the maximum inside distance. This method is satisfactory for an approximate inside measurement.

Pipe Circumferences

To measure the circumference of a pipe, a flexible type rule that will conform to the cylindrical shape of the pipe must be used. A tape rule or a steel tape is adaptable for this job. When measuring pipe, make sure the tape has been wrapped squarely around the axis of the pipe (i.e., measurement should be taken in a plane perpendicular to the axis) to ensure that the reading will not be more than the actual circumference of the pipe. This is extremely important when measuring large diameter pipe.

Hold the rule or tape as shown in figure 6. Take the reading, using the 2-inch graduation, for example, as the reference point. In this case the correct reading is found by subtracting 2 inches from the actual reading. In this way the first 2 inches of the tape, serving as a handle, will enable you to hold the tape securely.

Inside Dimensions

To take an inside measurement, such as the inside of a box, a folding rule that incorporates a 6- or 7-inch sliding extension is one of the best measuring tools for this job. To take the inside measurement, first unfold the folding rule to the approximate dimension. Then extend the end of the rule and read the length that it extends, adding the length of the extension to the length on the main body of the rule. (Fig. 7.) In this illustration the length of the main body of the rule is 13 inches and the extension is pulled out 3 3/16 inches. In this case the total inside dimension being measured is 16 3/16 inches.

In figure 8 notice in the circled insert that the hook at the end of the particular rule shown is attached to the rule so that it is free to move slightly. When an outside dimension is taken by hooking the end of the rule over an edge, the hook will locate the end of the rule even with the surface from which the measurement is being taken. By being free to move, the hook will retract away from the end of the rule when an inside dimension is taken. To measure an inside dimension using a tape rule, extend the rule between the surfaces as shown, take a reading at the point on the scale where the rule enters the case, and add 2 inches. The 2 inches are the width of the case. The total is the inside dimension being taken.

To measure the thickness of stock through a hole with a hook rule, insert the rule through the hole, hold the hook against one face of the stock, and read the thickness at the other face. (Fig. 9.)

Outside Dimensions

To measure an outside dimension using a tape rule, hook the rule over the edge of the stock. Pull the tape out until it projects far enough from the case to permit measuring the required distance. The hook at the end of the rule is designed so that it will locate the end of the rule at the surface from which the measurement is being taken. (Fig. 10.) When taking a measurement of length, the tape is held parallel to the lengthwise edge. For measuring widths, the tape should be at right angles to the lengthwise edge. Read the dimension of the rule exactly at the edge of the piece being measured.

It may not always be possible to hook the end of the tape over the edge of stock being measured. In this case it may be necessary to butt the end of the tape against another surface or to hold the rule at a starting point from which a measurement is to be taken.

Distance Measurements

Steel or fiberglass tapes are generally used for making long measurements. Secure the hook end of the tape. Hold the tape reel in the hand and allow it to unwind while walking in the direction in which the measurement is to be taken. Stretch the tape with sufficient tension to overcome sagging. At the same time make sure the tape is parallel to an edge or the surface being measured. Read the graduation on the tape by noting which line on the tape coincides with the measurement being taken.

CARE

Rules and tapes should be handled carefully and kept lightly oiled to prevent rust. Never allow the edges of measuring devices to become nicked by striking them with hard objects. They should preferably be kept in a wooden box when not in use.

To avoid kinking tapes, pull them straight out from their cases—do not bend them backward. With the windup type, always turn the crank clockwise—turning it backward will kink or break the tape. With the spring-wind type, guide the tape by hand. If it is allowed to snap back, it may be kinked, twisted, or otherwise damaged. Do not use the hook as a stop. Slow down as you reach the end.

II. SIMPLE CALIPERS

Simple calipers are used in conjunction with a scale to measure diameters. The calipers most commonly used are shown in figure 11.

MEASURING TOOLS AND TECHNIQUES

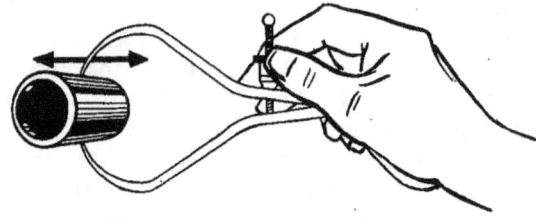

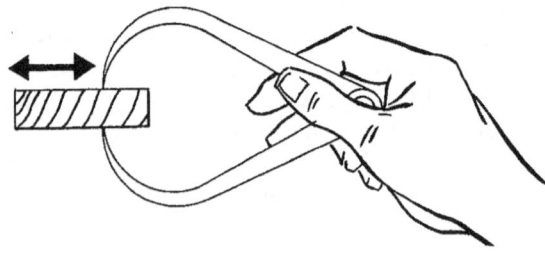

Figure 12.—Using an outside caliper.

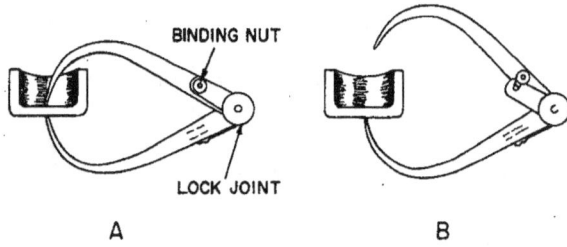

Figure 13.—Measuring the thickness of the bottom of a cup.

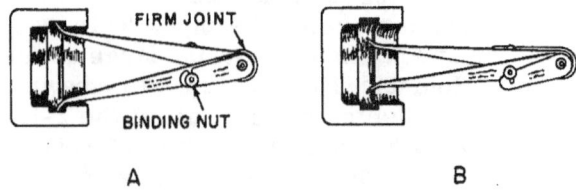

Figure 14.—Measuring a hard to reach inside dimension with an inside caliper.

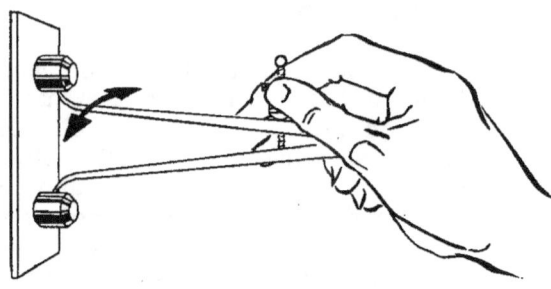

Figure 15.—Measuring the distance between two surfaces with an inside caliper.

Outside calipers for measuring outside diameters are bow-legged; those used for inside diameters have straight legs with the feet turned outward. Calipers are adjusted by pulling or pushing the legs to open or close them. Fine adjustment is made by tapping one leg lightly on a hard surface to close them, or by turning them upside down and tapping on the joint end to open them.

Spring-joint calipers have the legs joined by a strong spring hinge and linked together by a screw and adjusting nut. For measuring chamfered cavities (grooves), or for use over flanges, transfer calipers are available. They are equipped with a small auxiliary leaf attached to one of the legs by a screw. (Fig. 11.) The measurement is made as with ordinary calipers; then the leaf is locked to the leg.

The legs may then be opened or closed as needed to clear the obstruction, then brought back and locked to the leaf again, thus restoring them to the original setting.

A different type of caliper is the hermaphrodite, sometimes called odd-leg caliper. This caliper has one straight leg ending in a sharp point, sometimes removable, and one bow leg. The hermaphrodite caliper is used chiefly for locating the center of a shaft, or for locating a shoulder.

USING CALIPERS

A caliper is usually used in one of two ways. Either the caliper is set to the dimension of the work and the dimension transferred to a scale, or the caliper is set on a scale and the work machined until it checks with the dimension set up on the caliper. To adjust a caliper to a scale dimension, one leg of the caliper should be held firmly against one end of the scale and the other leg adjusted to the desired dimension. To adjust a caliper to the work, open the legs wider than the work and then bring them down to the work.

CAUTION: Never place a caliper on work that is revolving in a machine.

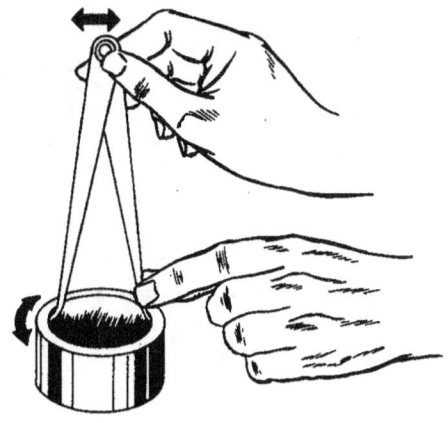

Figure 16.—Measuring an inside diameter with an inside caliper.

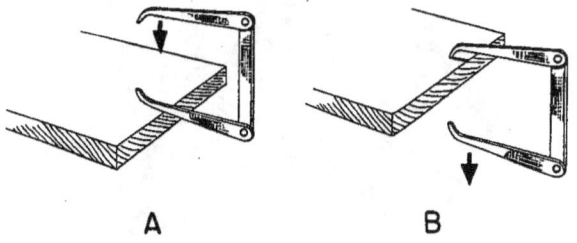

Figure 18.—Decreasing and increasing the setting of a firm joint caliper.

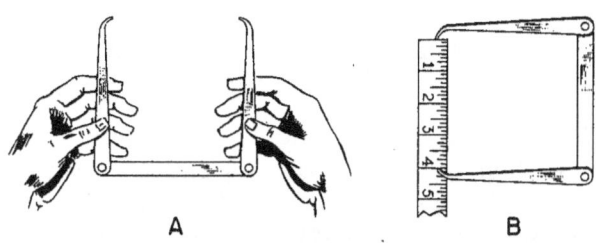

Figure 17.—Setting a combination firm joint caliper.

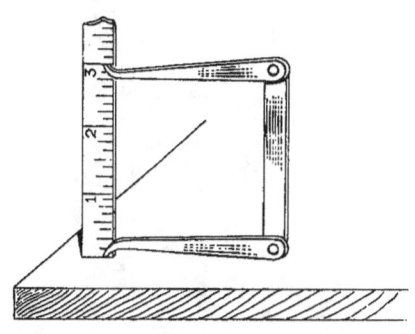

Figure 19.—Setting a combination firm joint caliper for inside measurements.

Measuring The Diameter of Round or
The Thickness of Flat Stock

To measure the diameter of round stock, or the thickness of flat stock, adjust the outside caliper so that you feel a slight drag as you pass it over the stock. (See fig. 12.) After the proper "feel" has been attained, measure the setting of the caliper with a rule. In reading the measurement, sight over the leg of the caliper after making sure the caliper is set squarely with the face of the rule.

Measuring Hard to Reach
Dimensions

To measure an almost inaccessible outside dimension, such as the thickness of the bottom of a cup, use an outside transfer firm-joint caliper as shown in figure 13. When the proper "feel" is obtained, tighten the lock joint. Then loosen the binding nut and open the caliper enough to remove it from the cup. Close the caliper again and tighten the binding nut to seat in the slot at the end of the auxiliary arm. The caliper is now at the original setting, representing the thickness of the bottom of the cup. The caliper setting can now be measured with a rule.

To measure a hard to reach inside dimension, such as the internal groove shown in figure 14, a lock-joint inside caliper should be used. The procedure followed for measuring a hard to reach outside dimension is used.

Measuring The Distance
Between Two Surfaces

To measure the distance between two surfaces with an inside caliper, first set the caliper to the approximate distance being measured. Hold the caliper with one leg in contact with one of the surfaces being measured. (See fig. 15.) Then as you increase the setting of the caliper, move the other leg from left to right. Feel for

MEASURING TOOLS AND TECHNIQUES

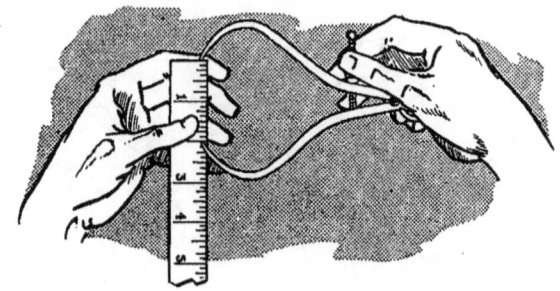

Figure 20.—Setting an outside spring caliper.

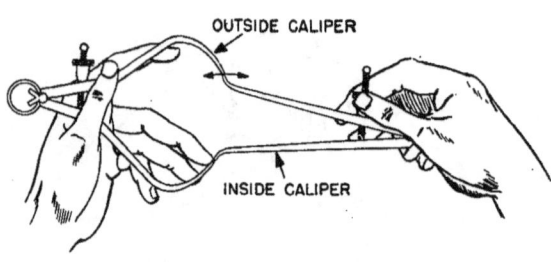

Figure 22.—Transferring a measurement from an outside to an inside caliper.

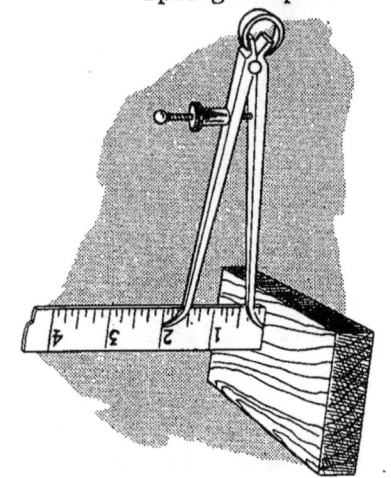

Figure 21.—Setting an inside spring caliper.

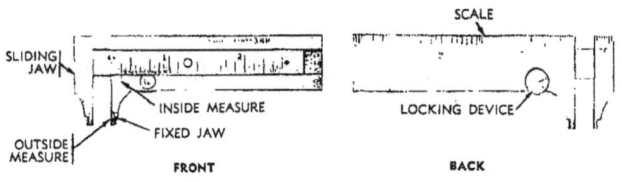

Figure 23.—Caliper square (slide caliper).

the slight drag indicating the proper setting of the caliper. Then remove the caliper and measure the setting with a rule.

Measuring Hole Diameters

To measure the diameter of a hole with an inside caliper, hold the caliper with one leg in contact with one side of the hole (fig. 16) and, as you increase the setting, move the other leg from left to right, and in and out of the hole. When you have found the point of largest diameter, remove the caliper and measure the caliper setting with a rule.

Setting A Combination
Firm Joint Caliper

To set a combination firm joint caliper with a rule, when the legs are in position for outside measurements, grasp the caliper with both hands, as shown in figure 17A, and adjust both legs to the approximate setting. By adjusting both legs, the shape of the tool will be approximately symmetrical. Thus it will maintain its balance and be easier to handle.

Check this approximate setting as shown in figure 17B. Sight squarely across the leg at the graduations on the rule to get the exact setting required.

If it is necessary to decrease or increase the setting, tap one leg of the caliper, as shown in figure 18. The arrow indicates the change in setting that will take place.

When the caliper is set for inside measurements, the same directions for adjusting the setting apply. Figure 19 shows how the end of the rule and one leg of the caliper are rested on the bench top so that they are exactly even with each other when the reading is taken.

Setting Outside And Inside
Spring Calipers

To set a particular reading on an outside spring caliper, first open the caliper to the approximate setting. Then, as shown in figure 20, place one leg over the end of the rule, steadying it with index finger. Make the final setting by sighting over the other leg of the

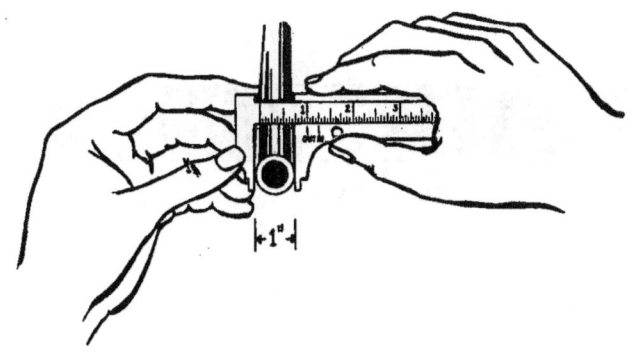

Figure 24.—Measuring an outside dimension with a pocket slide caliper.

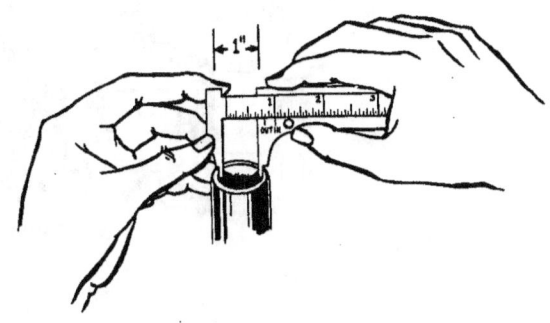

Figure 25.—Measuring an inside dimension with a slide caliper.

caliper, squarely with the face of the rule at the reading, and turning the knurled adjusting nut until the desired setting is obtained.

To set an inside spring caliper to a particular reading, place both caliper and rule on a flat surface as shown in figure 21. The rule must be held squarely or normal (90° in both directions) to the surface to ensure accuracy. Adjust the knurled adjusting nut, reading the setting on the rule with line of sight normal to the face of the rule at the reading.

Transferring Measurements From One Caliper To Another

To transfer a measurement from one spring caliper to another, hold the calipers as shown in figure 22. Note that one of the man's fingers is extended to steady the point of contact of the two lower caliper legs. In this figure the inside caliper is being adjusted to the size of the outside caliper. As careful measurements with calipers depend on one's sense of touch, which is spoken of as "feel," calipers are best held lightly. When you notice a slight drag, the caliper is at the proper setting.

CARE

Keep calipers clean and lightly oiled, but do not overoil the joint of firm joint calipers or you may have difficulty in keeping them tight. Do not throw them around or use them for screwdrivers or pry bars. Even a slight force may spring the legs of a caliper so that other measurements made with it are never accurate. Remember they are measuring instruments and must be used only for the purpose for which they are intended.

SLIDE CALIPER

The main disadvantage of using ordinary calipers is that they do not give a direct reading of a caliper setting. As explained earlier, you must measure a caliper setting with a rule. To overcome this disadvantage, use slide calipers (fig. 23). This instrument is occasionally called a caliper rule.

Slide calipers can be used for measuring outside, inside, and other dimensions. One side of the caliper is used as a measuring rule, while the scale on the opposite side is used in measuring outside and inside dimensions. Graduations on both scales are in inches and fractions thereof. A locking screw is incorporated to hold the slide caliper jaws in position during use. Stamped on the frame are two words, "IN" and "OUT." These are used in reading the scale while making inside and outside measurements, respectively.

To measure the outside diameter of round stock, or the thickness of flat stock, move the jaws of the caliper into firm contact with the surface of the stock. Read the measurement at the reference line stamped OUT. (See fig. 24.)

When measuring the inside diameter of a hole, or the distance between two surfaces, insert only the rounded tips of the caliper jaws into the hole or between the two surfaces. (See fig. 25.) Read the measurement on the reference line stamped IN.

Note that two reference lines are needed if the caliper is to measure both outside and inside dimensions, and that they are separated

MEASURING TOOLS AND TECHNIQUES

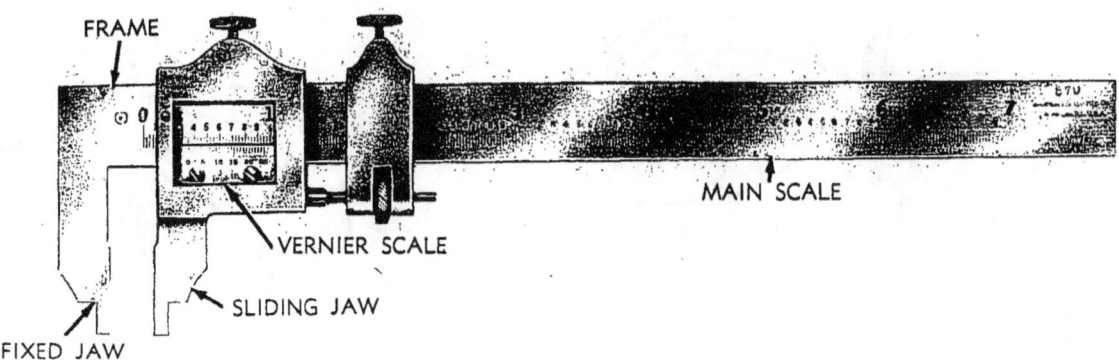

Figure 26.—Vernier caliper.

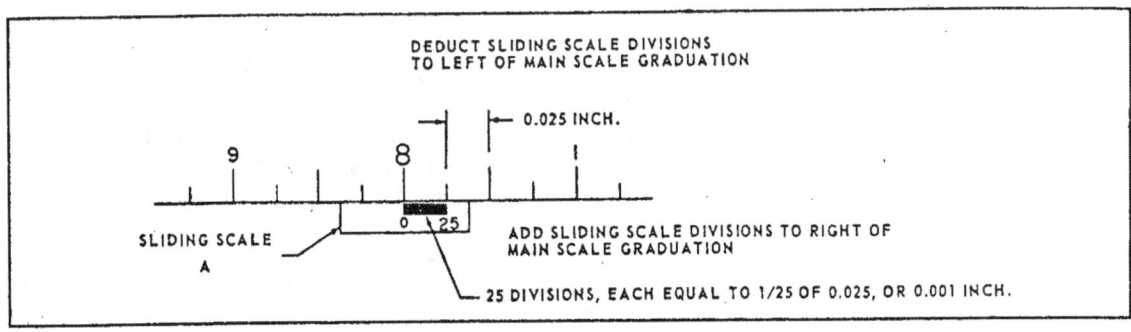

Figure 27.—Vernier scale principle.

by an amount equal to the outside dimension of the rounded tips when the caliper is closed.

Pocket models of slide calipers are commonly made in 3-in. and 5-in. sizes and are graduated to read in 32nds and 64ths. Pocket slide calipers are valuable when extreme precision is not required. They are frequently used for duplicating work when the expense of fixed gages is not warranted.

III. VERNIER CALIPER

A vernier caliper (fig. 26) consists of an L-shaped member with a scale engraved on the long shank. A sliding member is free to move on the bar and carries a jaw which matches the arm of the L. The vernier scale is engraved on a small plate that is attached to the sliding member.

Perhaps the most distinct advantage of the vernier caliper, over other types of caliper, is the ability to provide very accurate measurements over a large range. It can be used for both internal and external surfaces. Pocket models usually measure from zero to 3 in., but sizes are available all the way to 4 ft. In using the vernier caliper, you must be able to measure with a slide caliper and be able to read a vernier scale.

PRINCIPLES OF THE VERNIER SCALE

It would be possible to etch graduations 1/1000 inch (0.001) in. apart on a steel rule or sliding caliper as shown in figure 27. This enlarged illustration shows two graduated scales. The top scale has divisions which are 0.025 inches apart. The small sliding lower scale has 25 0.001 inch graduations which can divide any of the main scale divisions of 0.025 inch into 25 parts. When the first graduation marked "O" on this small scale aligns with a graduation on the main scale, the last, or 25th will also align with a graduation on the main scale as shown. Consequently, the small 0.00

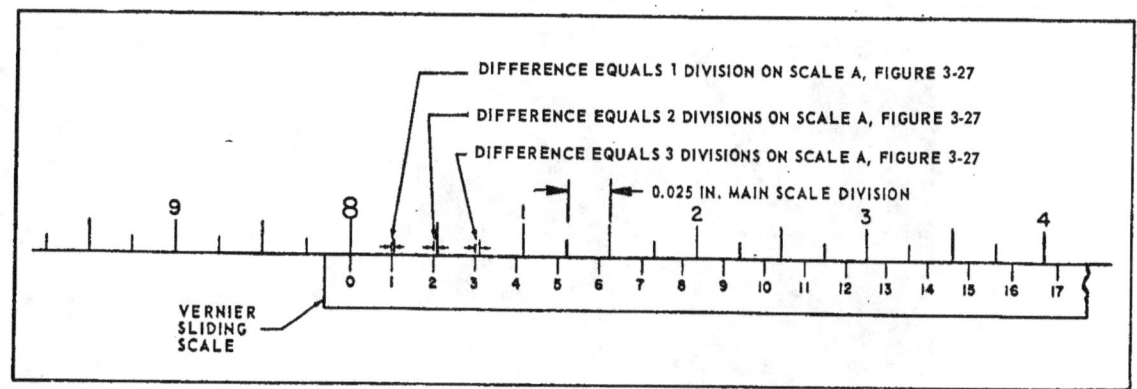

Figure 28.—Expanded view of the vernier scale.

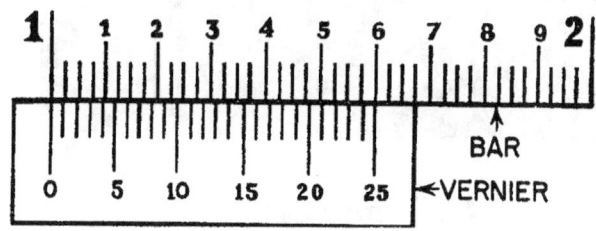

Figure 29.—English-measure vernier scale.

graduations are not significant in this position. But when the zero graduation does not align with a graduation on the main scale, it can be readily determined how many thousandths the zero missed the 0.025 inch graduation by counting the misaligned graduation at either end of the small scale. When the zero or index line on the sliding scale does not quite reach the graduation, the amount of misalignment must be subtracted, but when it passes the 0.025 graduation from which the reading is made, it must be added. This illustrates the simple arrangement to increase the accuracy of a common scale. Unfortunately, the 0.001 inch graduations are not too legible and so the system is not practical. A vernier arrangement overcomes this problem.

VERNIER SCALE ARRANGEMENT

The main difference between the vernier scale and the arrangement shown in fig. -27 is the spacing of the 25 divisions. Instead of 25 graduations crowded within the space of one main scale division, the vernier graduations are arranged at intervals exactly 0.001 inch less than the main scale graduations, as shown in fig. 28. This arrangement results in an accumulation of misalignments starting with the first vernier graduation past the zero so that each may be marked as shown with a number representing the space in thousandths to the next upper scale graduation. For example, if the zero index line would be moved past the 8 inch graduation until the vernier graduation number 5 aligned with the next main scale graduation, the exact reading would be 8 inches plus 0.005 or 8.005 inches.

READING A VERNIER CALIPER

Figure 29 shows a bar 1 inch long divided by graduations into 40 parts so that each graduation indicates one-fortieth of an inch (0.025 inch). Every fourth graduation is numbered; each number indicates tenths of an inch (4 x 0.025 inch). The vernier, which slides along the bar, is graduated into 25 divisions which together, are as long as 24 divisions on the bar. Each division of the vernier is 0.001 inch smaller than each division on the bar. Verniers that are calibrated as just explained are known as English-measure verniers. The metric-measure vernier is read the same, except that the units of measurement are in millimeters.

In figure 30, insert A illustrates the English measure vernier caliper. Insert B shows an enlarged view of the vernier section. As you can see in this figure, when the zero on the vernier coincides with the 1-inch mark, no other lines coincide until the 25th mark on the vernier.

MEASURING TOOLS AND TECHNIQUES

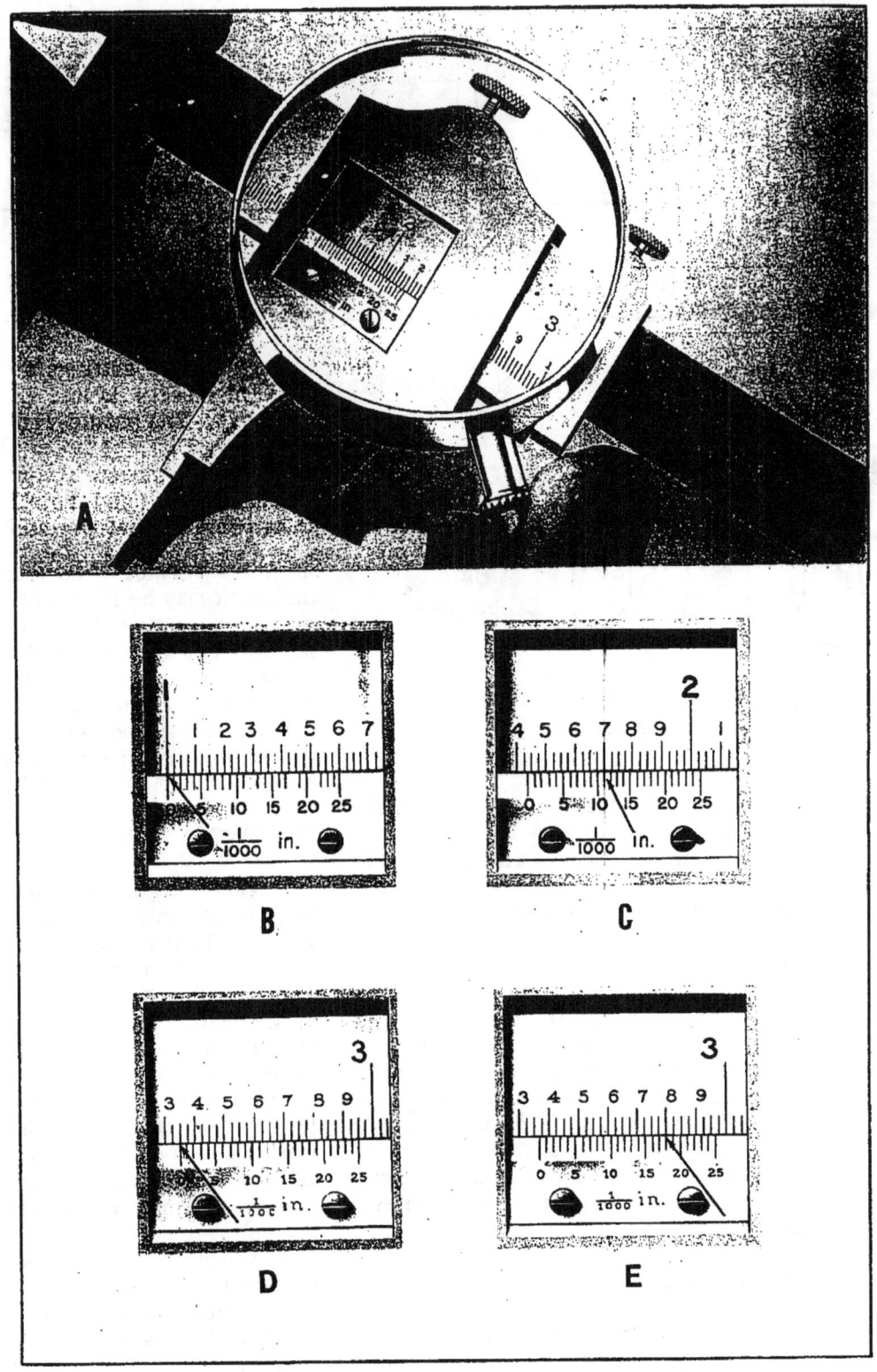

Figure -30.—Vernier caliper.

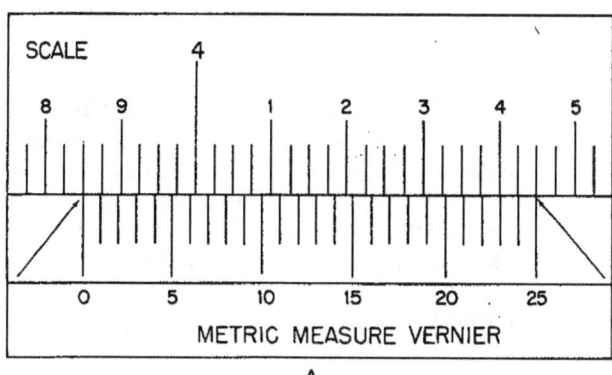

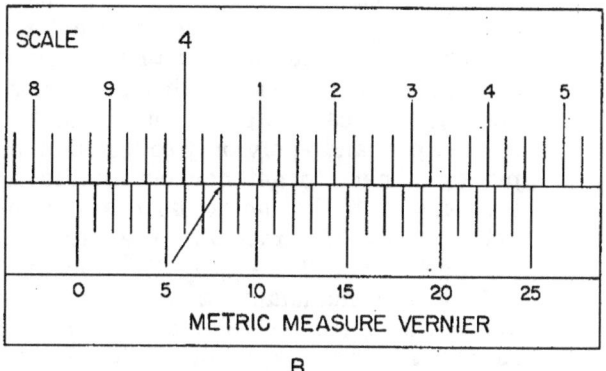

Figure 31.—Metric-measure vernier scales.

To read the caliper in insert C, write down in a column the number of inches (1.000 in.), of tenths of an inch (0.400 in.), and of thousandths of an inch that the zero mark on the vernier is from the zero mark on the rule. Because the zero mark on the vernier is a little past a 0.025 in. mark, write down the 0.025 in. and then note the highest number on the vernier where a line on the vernier coincides with one on the rule. In this case it is at the 0.011 in. line on the vernier, so you also write the 0.011 in. in the column which will then look like this:

    1.000 in.
     .400 in.
     .025 in.
     .011 in.
    1.436 in.

The reading on the caliper shown in insert C is 1.436 in. and was obtained by adding four separate "readings." After a little practice you will be able to make these calculations mentally.

Table 1.—Measuring Point Allowances
44.216

Size of Caliper	English Measure	Metric Measure
6" or 150 mm .	Add 0.250"...	Add 6.35 mm.
12" or 300 mm .	.300"...	7.62 mm.
24" or 600 mm .	.300"...	7.62 mm.
36" or 600 mm .	.500"...	12.70 mm.

Now try to read the settings of the two verniers shown in inserts D and E. Follow the above procedure. You should read 2.350 in. on D and 2.368 in. on E.

To read a metric-measure vernier, note the number of millimeters, and the 0.25 millimeter if the setting permits, that the zero on the vernier has moved from the zero on the scale. Then add the number of hundredths of a millimeter indicated by the line on the vernier that coincides with a line on the scale.

For example, figure 31A shows the zero graduation on the vernier coinciding with a 0.5-mm graduation on the scale resulting in a 38.50 mm reading. The reading in figure 31B indicates that 0.08 mm should be added to the scale reading and results in 38.00 mm + 0.50 mm + 0.08 mm = 38.58 mm.

If a vernier caliper is calibrated in either English measure or in metric measure, usually one side will be calibrated to take outside measurements and the other to take inside measurements directly. The vernier plate for inside measurements is set to compensate for the thickness of the measuring points of the tools. But if a vernier caliper is calibrated for both English and metric measure, one of the scales will appear on one side and one on the other. Then it will be necessary, when taking inside measurements over the measuring points, to add certain amounts to allow for their thickness. For example, table 1 shows the amounts to be added for various sizes of vernier calipers.

Outside Surface Measurements

To measure the distance between outside surfaces or the outside diameter of round stock with a vernier caliper, steady the stock with one hand and hold the caliper in the other as shown in figure 32. In the figure, the clamping

MEASURING TOOLS AND TECHNIQUES

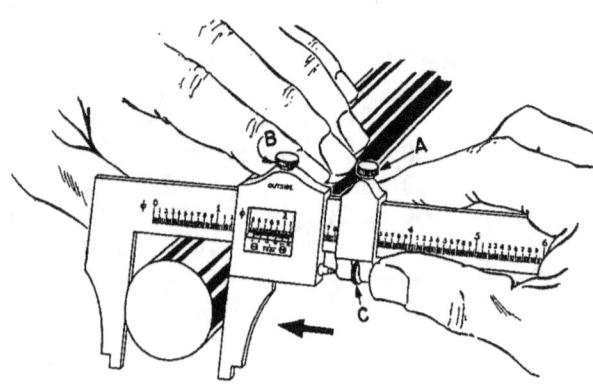

Figure 32.—Measuring an outside diameter with a vernier caliper.

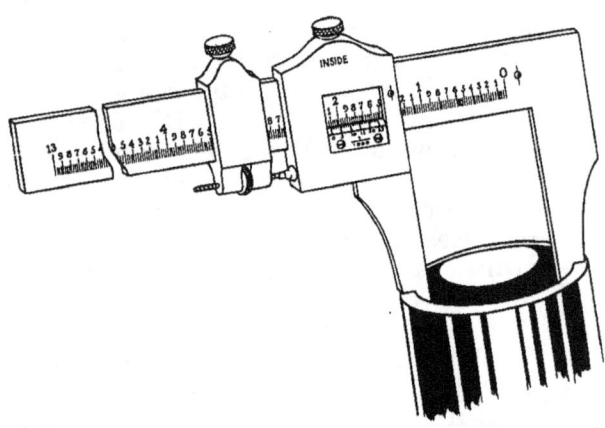

Figure 33.—Measuring an inside diameter with a vernier caliper.

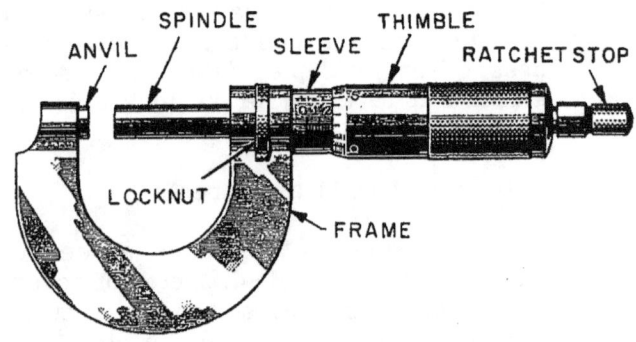

Figure 34.—Nomenclature of an outside micrometer caliper.

screws are at A and B; the horizontal adjusting screw nut is at C. With A and B loose, slide the movable jaw toward the piece being measured until it is almost in contact. Then tighten A to make C operative. With C, adjust the movable jaw to the proper feel and secure the setting with B. The reading can then be taken as explained previously.

Inside Surface Measurements

To measure the distance between inside surfaces, or the inside diameter of a hole, with a vernier caliper, use the scale marked "inside." Figure 33 shows the measuring points in place. Remember that if you are using a vernier caliper with both metric and English scales, the scales appear on opposite sides of the caliper and apply only to outside measurements. Then, to get correct inside measurements, you add to the actual reading the measuring point allowance for the size of caliper you are using. Take this allowance from table 1 or the manufacturer's instructions. The actual measurement in this case is made in the same manner as taking an outside measurement.

CARE OF THE VERNIER CALIPER

The inside faces of the jaws and the outside of the tips must be treated with great care. If they become worn, or the jaws bent, the tool will no longer give accurate readings. The accuracy of vernier calipers should be checked periodically by measuring an object of known dimension. Vernier calipers can be adjusted when they are not accurate, but the manufacturer's recommendations for this adjustment must be followed. Keep vernier calipers lightly oiled to prevent rust and keep them stored away from heavy tools.

IV. MICROMETER

In much wider use than the vernier caliper is the micrometer commonly called the "mike." It is important that a person who is working with machinery or in a machine shop thoroughly understand the mechanical principles, construction, use, and care of the micrometer. Figure 34 shows an outside micrometer caliper with the various parts clearly indicated. Micrometers are used to measure distances to the nearest one thousandth of an inch. The measurement is usually expressed or written as a

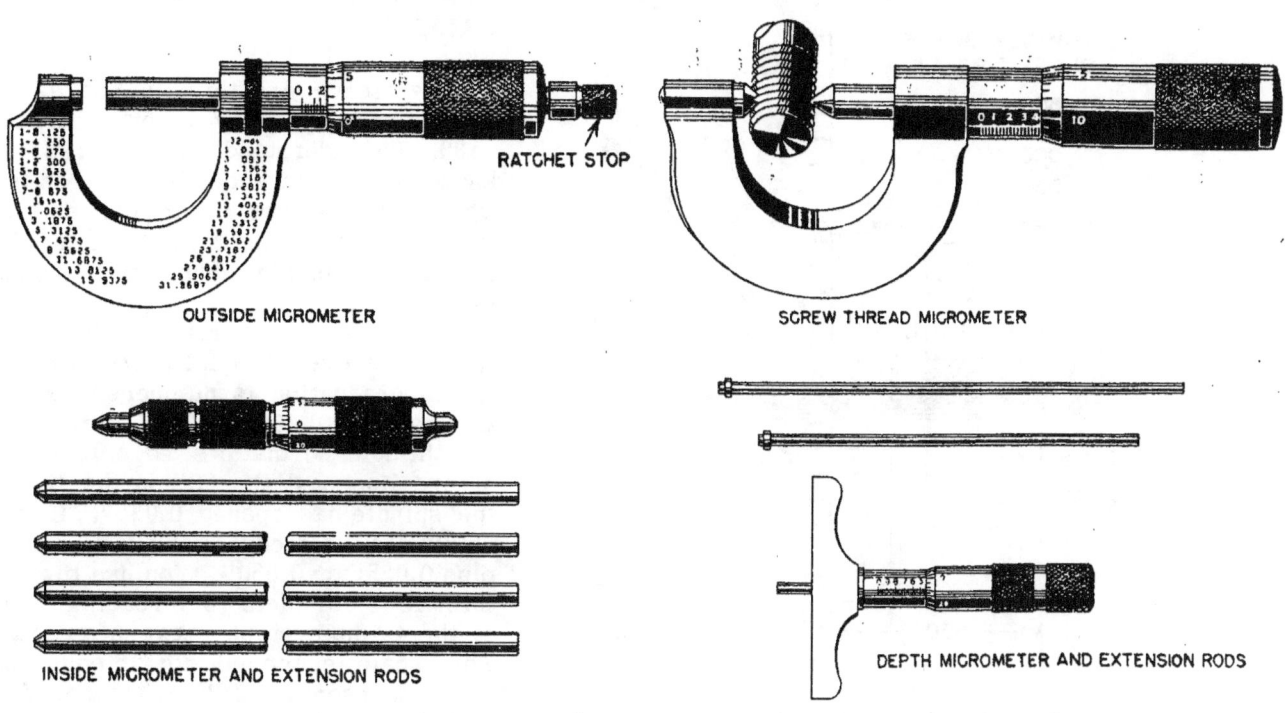

Figure 35.—Common types of micrometers.

decimal; so you must know the method of writing and reading decimals.

TYPES

There are three types of micrometers that are most commonly used:
the outside micrometer caliper (including the screw thread micrometer), the inside micrometer, and the depth micrometer. (See fig. 35.) The outside micrometer is used for measuring outside dimensions, such as the diameter of a piece of round stock. The screw thread micrometer is used to determine the pitch diameter of screws. The inside micrometer is used for measuring inside dimensions, as for example, the inside diameter of a tube or hole, the bore of a cylinder, or the width of a recess. The depth micrometer is used for measuring the depth of holes or recesses.

SELECTING THE PROPER MICROMETER

The types of micrometers commonly used are made so that the longest movement possible between the spindle and the anvil is 1 inch. This movement is called the "range." The frames of micrometers, however, are available in a wide variety of sizes, from 1 inch up to as large as 24 inches. The range of a 1-inch micrometer is from 0 to 1 inch; in other words, it can be used on work where the part to be measured is 1 inch or less. A 2-inch micrometer has a range from 1 inch to 2 inches, and will measure only work between 1 and 2 inches thick; a 6-inch micrometer has a range from 5 to 6 inches, and will measure only work between 5 and 6 inches thick. It is necessary, therefore, that the mechanic in selecting a micrometer first find the approximate size of the work to the nearest inch, and then select a micrometer that will fit it. For example, to find the exact diameter of a piece of round stock; use a rule and find the approximate diameter of the stock. If it is found to be approximately 3 1/4 inches, a micrometer with a 3- to 4-inch range would be required to measure the exact diameter. Similarly, with inside and depth micrometers, rods of suitable lengths must be fitted into the tool to get the approximate dimension within an inch, after which the exact measurement is read by turning the thimble. The size of a micrometer indicates the size of the largest work it will measure.

MEASURING TOOLS AND TECHNIQUES

READING A MICROMETER CALIPER

The sleeve and thimble scales of the micrometer caliper have been enlarged in figure 36. To understand these scales, you need to know that the threaded section on the spindle, which revolves, has 40 threads per inch. Therefore, every time the thimble completes a revolution, the spindle advances or recedes 1/40" (0.025").

Notice that the horizontal line on the sleeve is divided into 40 equal parts per inch. Every fourth graduation is numbered 1, 2, 3, 4, etc., representing 0.100", 0.200", etc. When you turn the thimble so that its edge is over the first sleeve line past the "0" on the thimble scale, the spindle has opened 0.025". If you turn the spindle to the second mark, it has moved 0.025" plus 0.025" or 0.050". You use the scale on the thimble to complete your reading when the edge of the thimble stops between graduated lines. This scale is divided into 25 equal parts, each part representing 1/25 of a turn. And 1/25 of 0.025" is 0.001". As you can see, every fifth line on the thimble scale is marked 5, 10, 15,

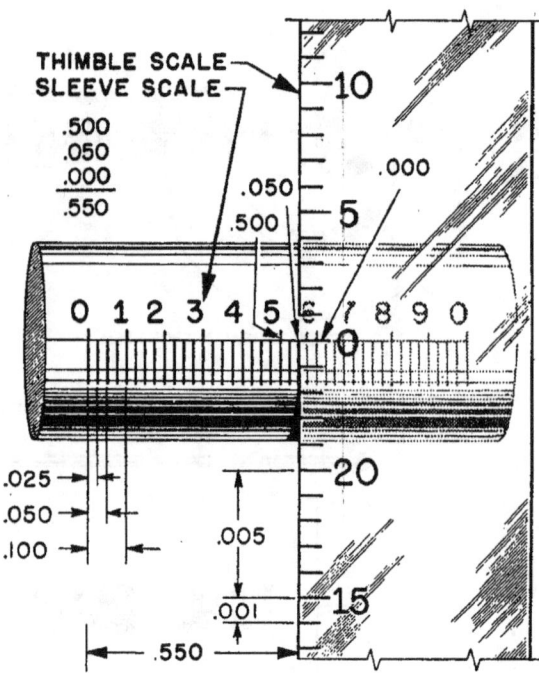

Figure 36.—Sleeve and thimble scales of a micrometer (enlarged).

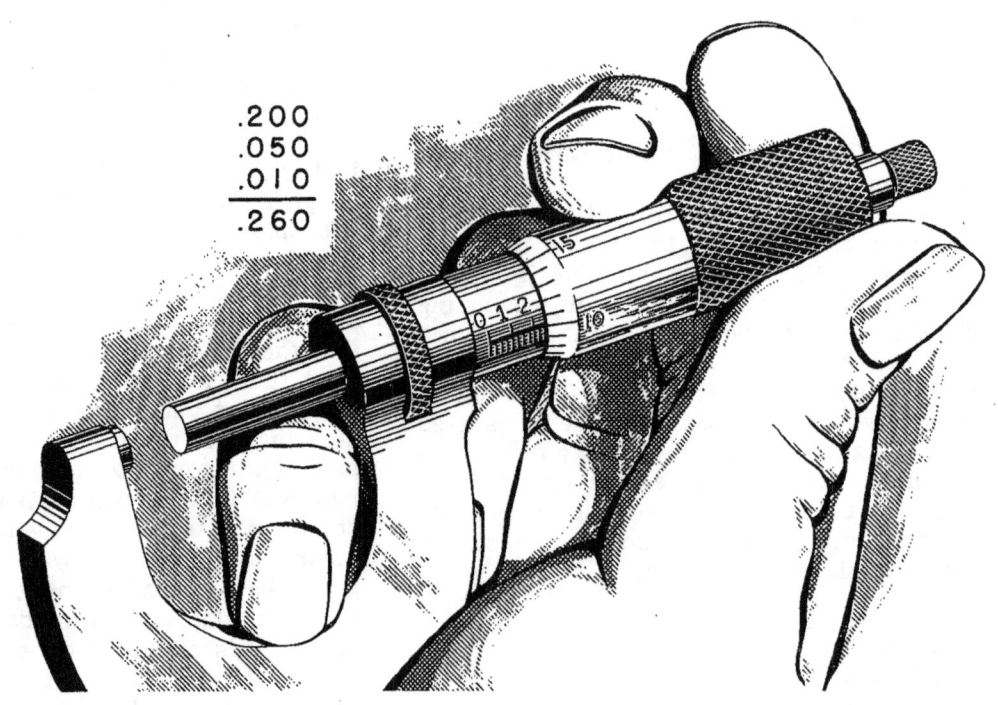

Figure 37.—Read a micrometer caliper.

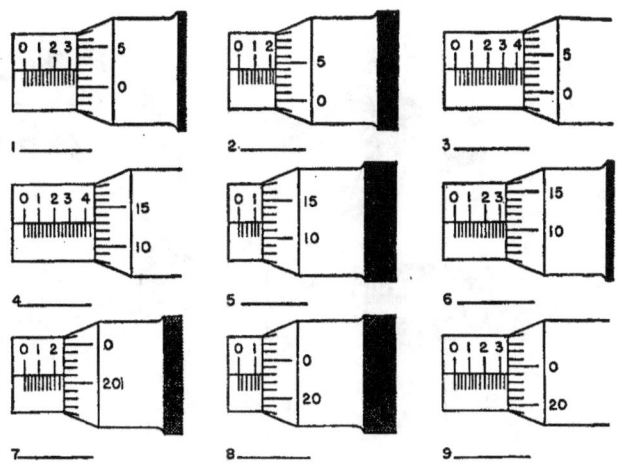

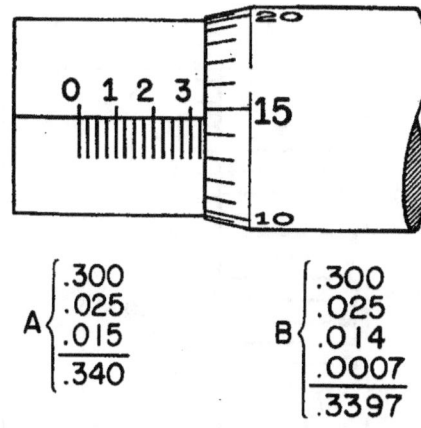

Figure 39.—Interpolating a micrometer reading.

Answers for checking—

1. = 0.327   4. = 0.438   7. = 0.246
2. = 0.229   5. = 0.137   8. = 0.148
3. = 0.428   6. = 0.336   9. = 0.349

Figure 38.—Micrometer-reading exercises.

etc. The thimble scale, therefore, permits you to take very accurate readings to the thousandths of an inch, and, since you can estimate between the divisions on the thimble scale, fairly accurate readings to the ten thousandth of an inch are possible.

The closeup in figure 37 will help you understand how to take a complete micrometer reading. Count the units on the thimble scale and add them to the reading on the sleeve scale. The reading in the figure shows a sleeve reading of 0.250" (the thimble having stopped slightly more than halfway between 2 and 3 on the sleeve) with the 10th line on the thimble scale coinciding with the horizontal sleeve line. Number 10 on this scale means that the spindle has moved away from the anvil an additional 10 x 0.001" or 0.010". Add this amount to the 0.250" sleeve reading, and the total distance is 0.260".

Read each of the micrometer settings in figure 38 so that you can be sure of yourself when you begin to use this tool on the job. The correct readings are given following the figure so that you can check yourself.

Figure 39 shows a reading in which the horizontal line falls between two graduations on the thimble scale and is closer to the 15 graduation than it is to the 14. To read this to THREE decimal places, refer to figure 39 and calculation A. To read it to FOUR decimal places, estimate the number of tenths of the distance between thimble-scale graduations the horizontal line has fallen. Each tenth of this distance equals one ten-thousandth (0.0001) of an inch. Add the ten-thousandths to the reading as shown in the calculations of figure 39B.

READING A VERNIER MICROMETER CALIPER

Many times you will be required to work to exceptionally precise dimensions. Under these conditions it is better to use a micrometer that is accurate to ten-thousandths of an inch. This degree of accuracy is obtained by the addition of a vernier scale. This scale, shown in figure 40, furnishes the fine readings between the lines on the thimble rather than making you estimate. The 10 spaces on the vernier are equivalent to 9 spaces on the thimble. Therefore, each unit on the vernier scale is equal to 0.0009" and the difference between the sizes of the units on each scale is 0.0001".

When a line on the thimble scale does not coincide with the horizontal sleeve line, you can determine the additional space beyond the readable thimble mark by finding which vernier mark coincides with a line on the thimble scale. Add this number, as that many ten-thousandths of an inch, to the original reading. In figure 41 see how the second line on the vernier scale coincides with a line on the thimble scale.

MEASURING TOOLS AND TECHNIQUES

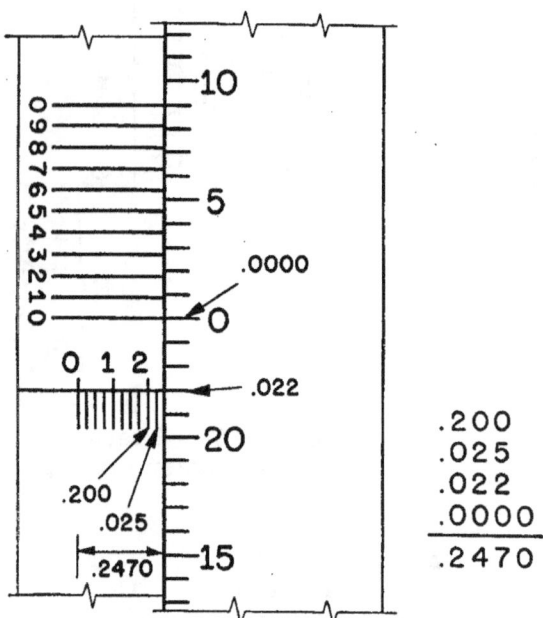

Figure 40.—Vernier scale on a micrometer.

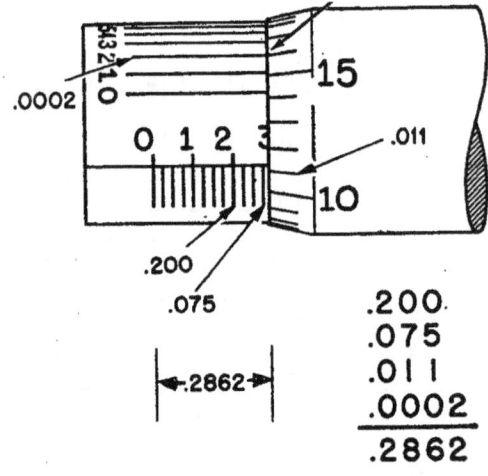

Figure 41.—Read a vernier micrometer caliper.

This means that the 0.011 mark on the thimble scale has been advanced an additional 0.0002" beyond the horizontal sleeve line. When you add this to the other readings, the reading will be 0.200 + 0.075 + 0.011 + 0.0002 or 0.2862", as shown.

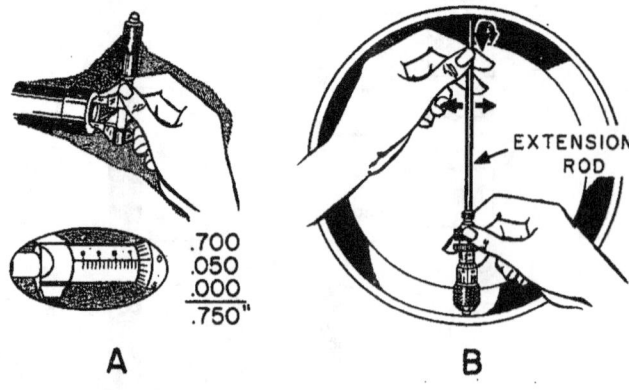

Figure 42.—Measuring an inside diameter with an inside caliper.

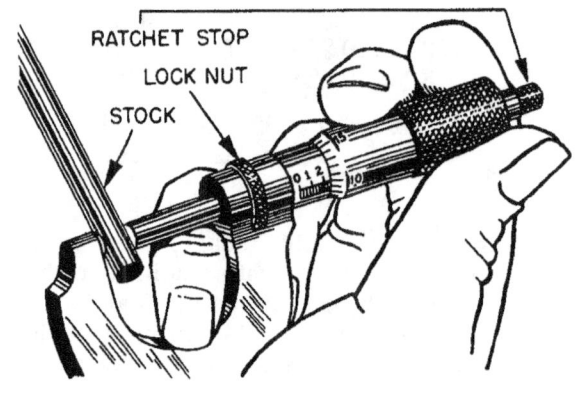

Figure 43.—Measuring round stock with a micrometer caliper.

MEASURING HOLE DIAMETERS WITH AN INSIDE MICROMETER CALIPER

To measure the diameter of small holes from 0.2" to 1" in diameter, an inside micrometer caliper of the jaw type as shown in figure 42A may be used. Note that the figures on both the thimble and the barrel are reversed, increasing in the opposite direction from those on an outside micrometer caliper. This is because this micrometer reads inside measurements. Thus as you turn the thimble clockwise on this micrometer, the measuring surfaces move farther apart and the reading increases. (On an outside micrometer caliper, as you turn the thimble clockwise, the measuring surfaces move closer together and the reading decreases.)

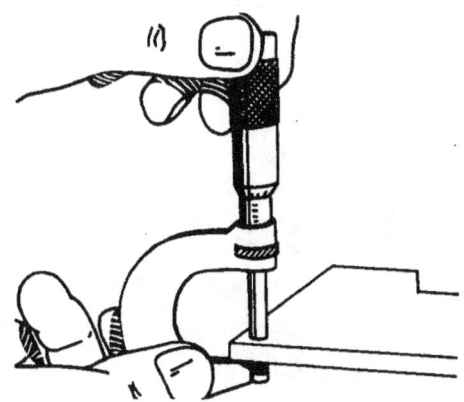

Figure 44.—Measuring flat stock with a micrometer caliper.

For holes from 2" up to several feet in diameter, select the inside micrometer having extension rods whose range includes the required dimension. The extension rod marked "6-7," for example, when inserted into the head of the micrometer, will measure inside diameters from 6" to 7". The shoulder on the rod must seat properly to ensure a correct reading. Figure 42B shows that, for large measurements, both hands are used to set the micrometer for checking a diameter. Hole one end in place with one hand as you "feel" for the maximum possible setting by moving the other end from left to right, and in and out of the hole with the other hand. When no left-to-right movement is possible, and a slight drag is noticed on the in-and-out swing, take the reading.

MEASURING ROUND STOCK

When measuring the diameter of a small piece of round stock, hold the stock to be measured in one hand. Hold the micrometer in the other hand so that the thimble rests between the thumb and the forefinger. (See fig. 43.) The third finger is then in a position to hold the frame against the palm of the hand. The frame is supported in this manner and makes it easy to guide the work over the anvil. The thumb and forefinger are in position to turn the thimble either directly or through the ratchet and bring the spindle over against the surface being measured.

Turn the spindle down to contact by "feel," or else use the ratchet stop. Your feel should produce the same contact pressure and therefore the same reading as that produced when the ratchet stop is used. Develop your "feel" by measuring a certain dimension both with and without the aid of the ratchet stop. When you have the correct feel, you will get the same readings by both methods.

In measuring round stock the feel must be very light because there is only a line contact between the spindle and the stock and the anvil and the stock. Therefore the contact area is exceptionally small, causing a proportionally high contact pressure per unit of area. This tends to give a reading smaller than the true reading unless the light feel is used. Moreover, in measuring a ball from a ball bearing, the contact is at only two points, so the contact area is again very small, which results in a tremendous pressure per unit of area. This condition requires only the lightest possible contact pressure to give a true reading.

Hold the micrometer lightly and for only as long as is necessary to make the measurement. Wrapping the hand around it or holding it for too long a time will cause expansion of the metal and will introduce errors in measurement. Read the setting on the thimble scale (if the object is small) without removing the micrometer caliper from the object.

MEASURING A FLAT SURFACE

When measuring a flat surface with a micrometer caliper, the entire area of both the anvil and the spindle is in contact with the surface being measured. This causes a proportionally low contact pressure per unit of area. Therefore the "feel" should be slightly heavier than when measuring round stock.

On large flat work, it is necessary to have the work stationary and positioned to permit access for the micrometer. The proper method of holding a micrometer when checking a part too large to be held in one hand is shown in figure 44. The frame is held by one hand to position it and to locate it square to the measured surface. The other hand operates the thimble either directly or through the ratchet. A large flat surface should be measured in several places to determine the amount of variation. It is good practice to lock the spindle in place with the locknut before removing the micrometer from the part being measured. After removal of the micrometer the measurement indicated on the thimble scale can then be read.

MEASURING TOOLS AND TECHNIQUES

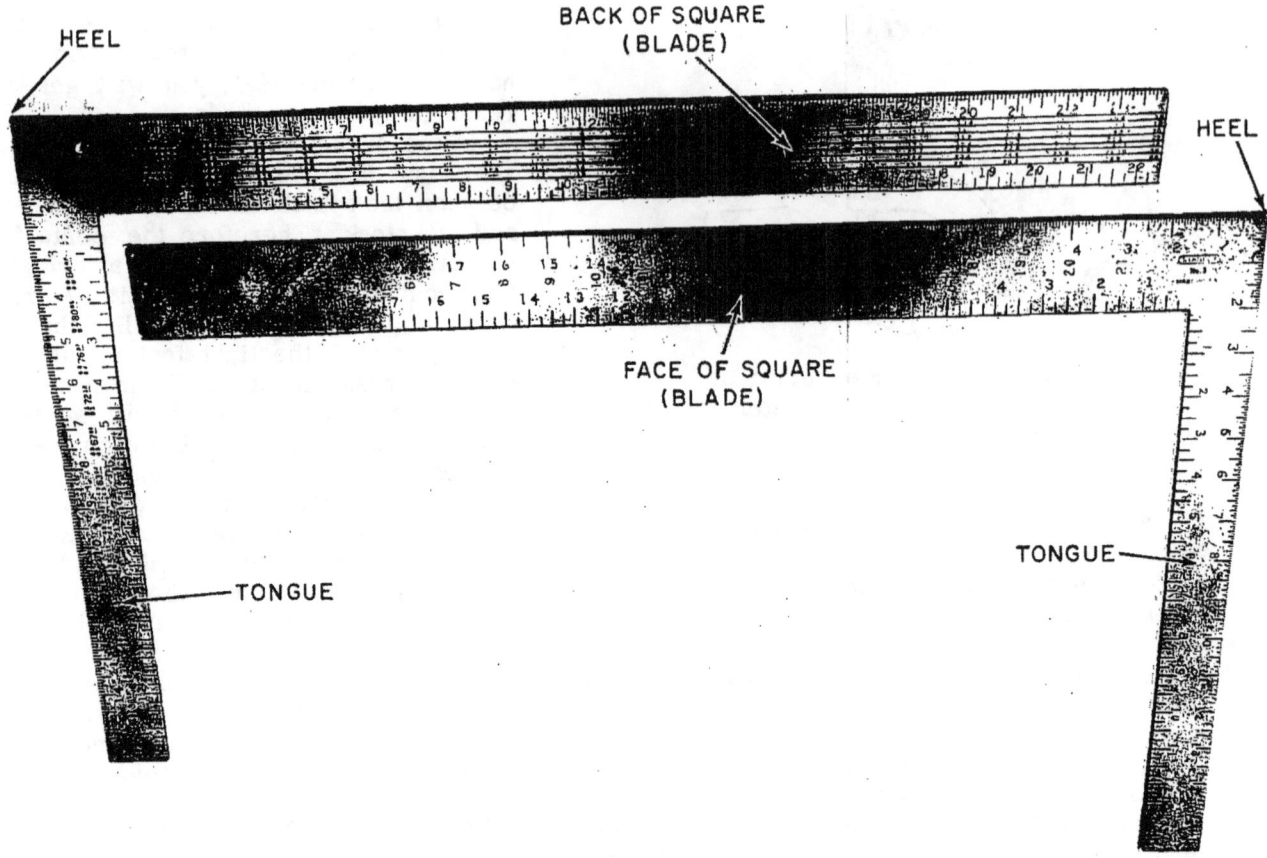

Figure 45.—Carpenter's square.

To retain a particular setting, in cases where several pieces are to be gaged, lock the spindle in place with the locknut. When a piece is "gaged" with a micrometer whose spindle is locked to a particular setting, the piece can quickly be identified as oversize, correct size, or undersize.

CARE OF MICROMETERS

Keep micrometers clean and lightly oiled. Make sure they are placed in a case or box when they are not in use. Anvil faces must be protected from damage and must not be cleaned with emery cloth or other abrasive.

V. SQUARES

Squares are primarily used for testing and checking trueness of an angle or for laying out lines on materials. Most squares have a rule marked on their edge. As a result they may also be used for measuring. There are several types of squares commonly used.

CARPENTER'S SQUARE

The size of a carpenter's steel square (fig. 45) is usually 12 inches x 8 inches, 24 inches x 16 inches, or 24 inches x 18 inches. The flat sides of the blade and the tongue are graduated in inches and fractions of an inch. (The square also contains information that helps to simplify or eliminate the need for computations in many woodworking tasks.) The most common uses for this square are laying out and squaring up large patterns, and for testing the flatness and squareness of large surfaces. Squaring is accomplished by placing the square at right angles to adjacent surfaces and observing if light shows between the work and the square.

One type of carpenter's square (framing) has additional tables engraved on the square. With

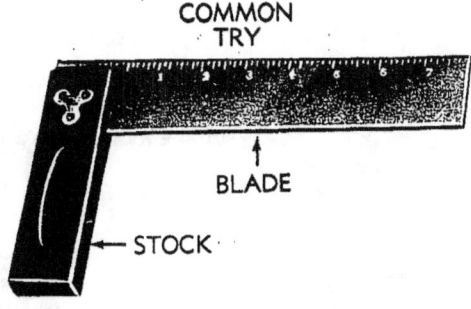

Figure 46.—Common try square.

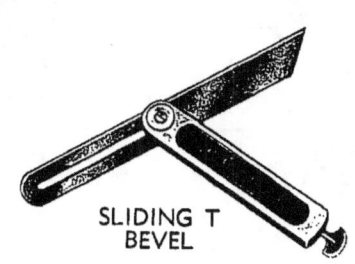

Figure 47.—Sliding T-bevel.

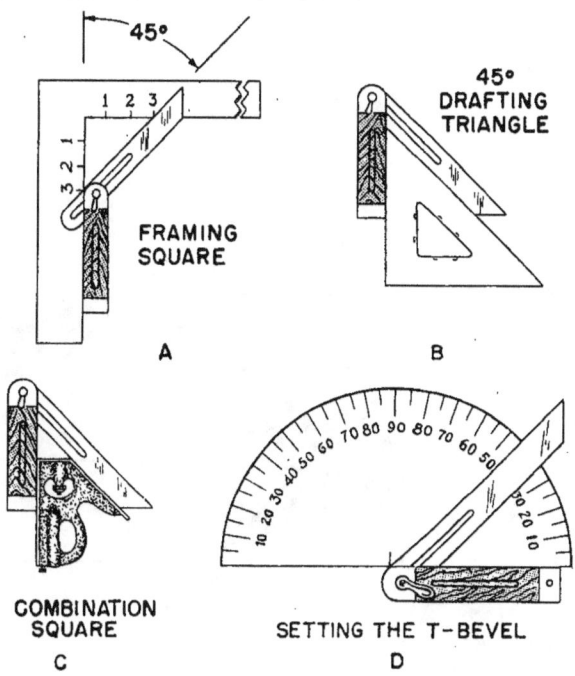

Figure 48.—Adjusting a sliding T-bevel to a desired setting.

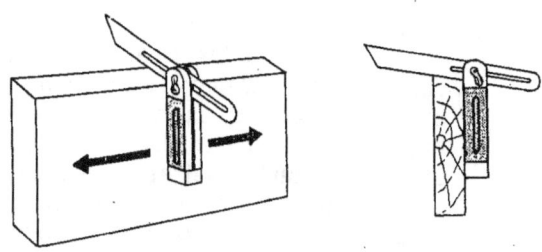

Figure 49.—Testing the trueness of a bevel.

the framing square, the craftsman can perform calculations rapidly and layout rafters, oblique joints and stairs.

TRY SQUARE

The try square (fig. 46) consists of two parts at right angles to each other; a thick wood or iron stock and a thin, steel blade. Most try squares are made with the blades graduated in inches and fractions of an inch. The blade length varies from 2 inches to 12 inches. This square is used for setting or checking lines or surfaces which have to be at right angles to each other.

SLIDING T BEVEL

The sliding T-bevel (fig. 47) is an adjustable try square with a slotted beveled blade. Blades are normally 6 or 8 inches long. The sliding T-bevel is used for laying out angles other than right angles, and for testing constructed angles such as bevels. These squares are made with either wood or metal handles.

Adjustments

To adjust a sliding T-bevel to a desired setting, loosen the blade screw, at the round end of the handle, just enough to permit the blade to slide along its slot and to rotate with slight friction.

To set the blade at a 45° angle, hold the handle against a framing square, as shown in figure 48A, with the blade intersecting equal graduations on the tongue and blade of the square. Or: hold the bevel against the edges of

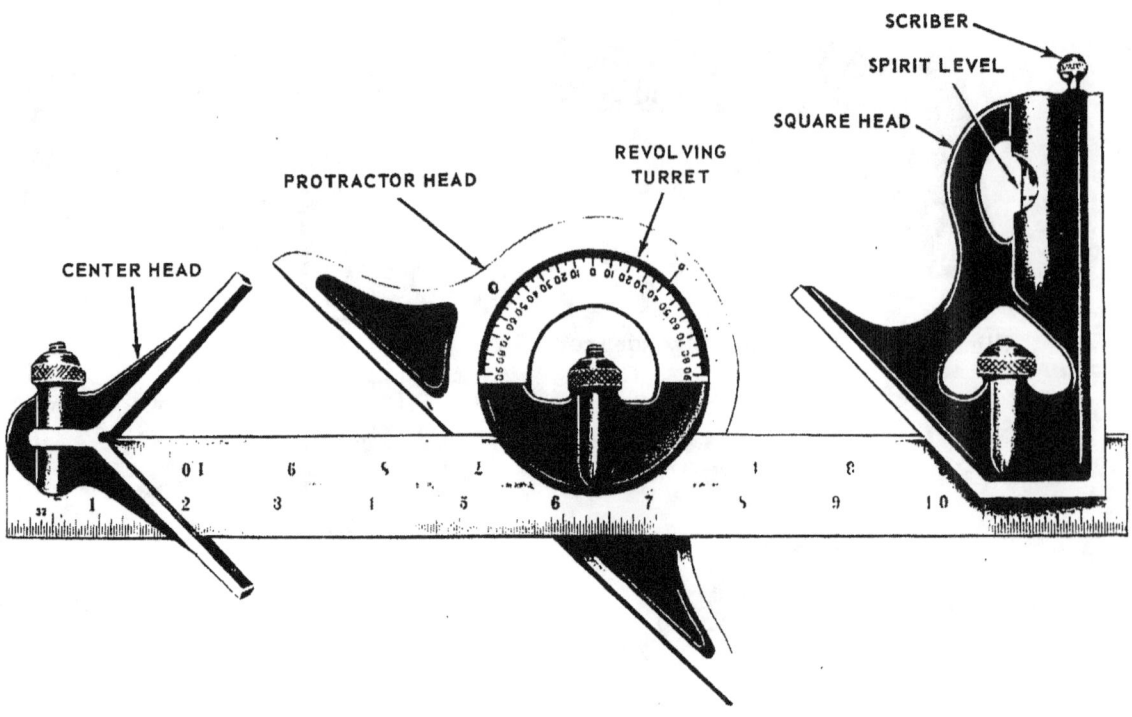

Figure 50.—Combination square set.

a 45° drafting triangle as shown in figure 48B. When using drafting triangles for setting a sliding T-bevel, different size triangles must be used for each different setting. A 45° angle can also be set by using the squaring head of a combination set as shown in figure 48C.

A sliding T-bevel can be set to any desired angle by using a protractor. Loosen the blade screw as before, and hold the bevel with its blade passing through the graduation selected, and the center of the protractor as shown at (D) in figure 48.

Constructed Angle Verification

To test a chamfer or bevel for trueness, set the T-bevel to the required angle, and hold the handle to the working face of the stock being tested. Face a source of light, and with the blade brought into contact with the surface to be tested, pass the blade along the length of the surface. (See fig. 49.) The appearance of light between the blade and the surface of the stock indicates where the angle is not correct. Figure 49 indicates the checking of a bevel, but testing the trueness of a chamfer is accomplished in the same way.

COMBINATION SQUARE

A combination square is equipped with movable heads called a SQUARE HEAD, PROTRACTOR HEAD, and a CENTER HEAD. These combine the functions of several tools, and serve a wide variety of purposes. (See figs. 50 and 51.) Normally, only one head is used at a time.

The SQUARE HEAD may be adjusted to any position along the scale and clamped securely in place. The combination square can thus serve as a depth gage, height gage, or scribing gage. Two of the faces of the head are ground at right angles to each other, and a third face at 45 degrees. A small spirit level is built into the head for checking whether surfaces are plumb, and a small scriber is housed in a hole in the end of the head for marking layout lines.

The CENTER HEAD can be slid on to the blade in place of the square head. This is a V-shaped member so designed that the center of the 90 degree V will lie exactly along one edge of the blade. This attachment is useful when locating the exact center of round stock.

The PROTRACTOR HEAD, commonly called a bevel protractor, can be attached to the scale,

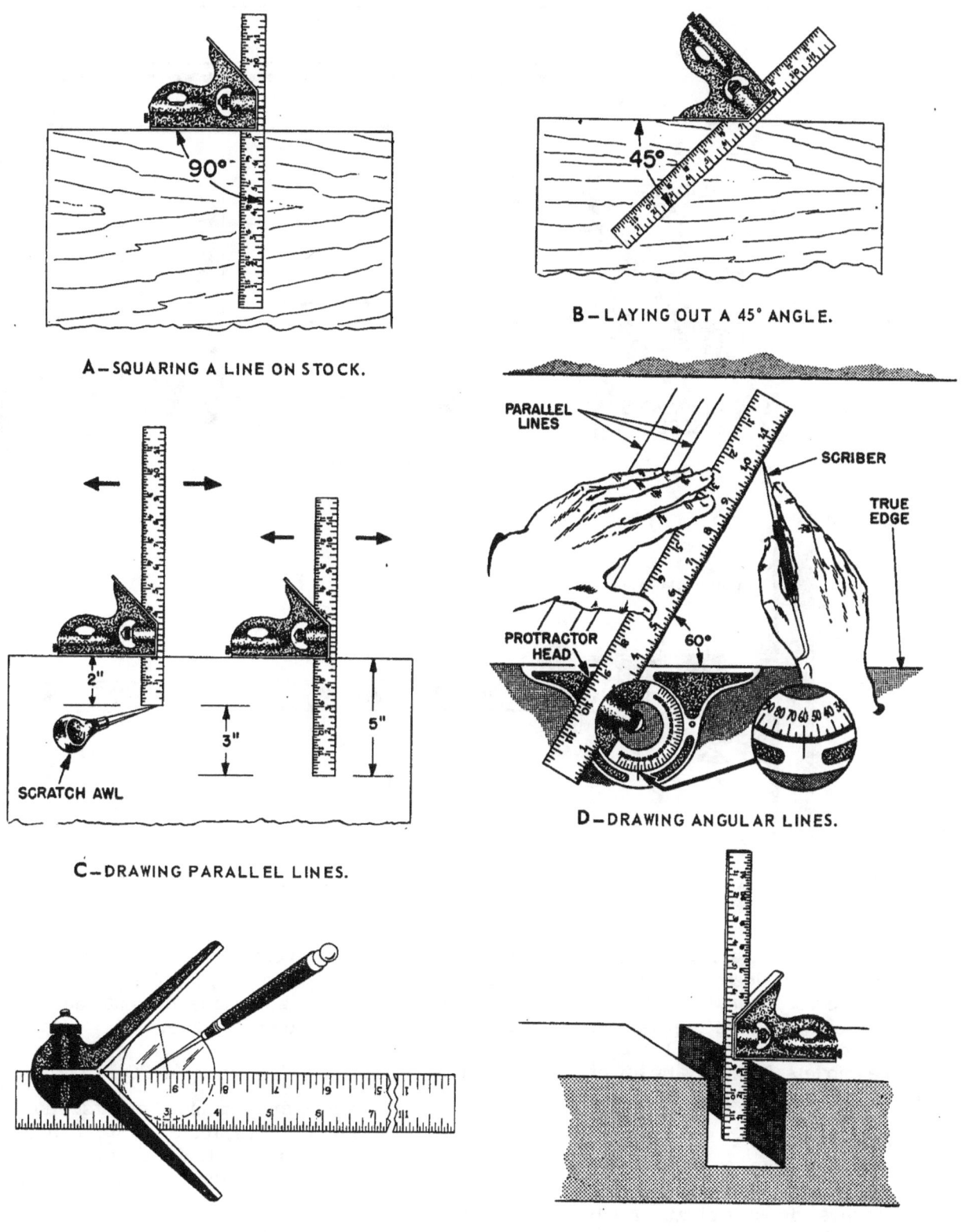

Figure 51.—Combination square applications.

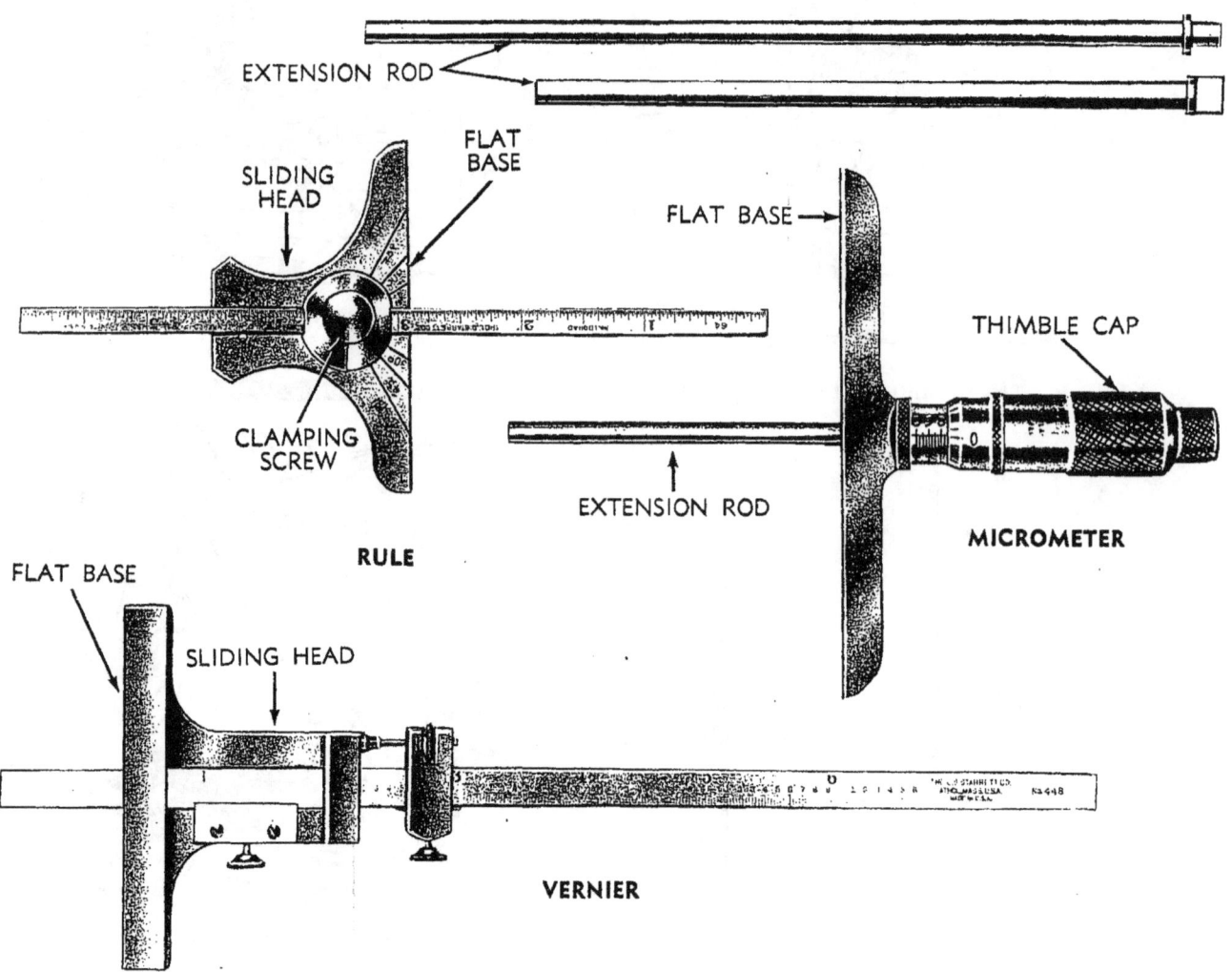

Figure 52.—Types of depth gages.

adjusted to any position on it, and turned and locked at any desired angle. Angular graduations usually read from 0 to 180 degrees both ways, permitting the supplement of the angle to be read. A spirit level may be included on some models forming, in effect, an adjustable level to show any required degree.

Care of Squares

Make certain the blades, heads, dials, and all accessories are clean. Apply a light coat of oil on all metal surfaces to prevent rusting when not in use. Do not use squares for purposes other than those intended. When storing squares or bevels for long periods of time, apply a liberal amount of oil or rust-preventive compound to all surfaces, wrap in oiled paper or cloth, and place in containers or on racks away from other tools.

VI. MISCELLANEOUS GAGES

There are a number of miscellaneous gages. The depth gage, feeler gage, thread gage, telescoping gage, dividers, and plumb bob are among some of the gages that will be discussed here.

DEPTH GAGE

A depth gage is an instrument for measuring the depth of holes, slots, counterbores, recesses,

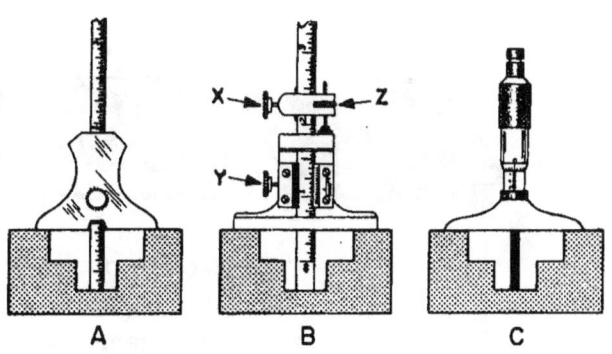

Figure 53.—Using depth gages.

and the distance from a surface to some recessed part. The RULE DEPTH GAGE and the MICROMETER DEPTH GAGE are the most commonly used. (See fig. 52.)

The rule depth gage is a graduated rule with a sliding head designed to bridge a hole or slot, and to hold the rule perpendicular to the surface on which the measurement is taken. This type has a measuring range of 0 to 5 inches. The sliding head has a clamping screw so that it may be clamped in any position. The sliding head has a flat base which is perpendicular to the axis of the rule and ranges in size from 2 to 2 5/8 inches in width and from 1/8 to 1/4 inch in thickness.

The micrometer depth gage consists of a flat base attached to the barrel (sleeve) of a micrometer head. These gages have a range from 0 to 9 inches, depending on the length of extension rod used. The hollow micrometer screw (the threads on which the thimble rotates) itself has a range of either 1/2 or 1 inch. Some are provided with a ratchet stop. The flat base ranges in size from 2 to 6 inches. Several extension rods are normally supplied with this type of gage.

To measure the depth of a hole or slot with reasonable accuracy, use a depth gage as shown in figure 53A. Hold the body of the depth gage against the surface from which the depth is to be measured and extend the scale into the hole or slot. Tighten the setscrew to maintain the setting. Withdraw the tool from the work and read the depth on the scale.

To measure the depth of a hole or slot with more accuracy than is possible with an ordinary depth gage, place a vernier depth gage over the slot as shown in figure 53B. Notice

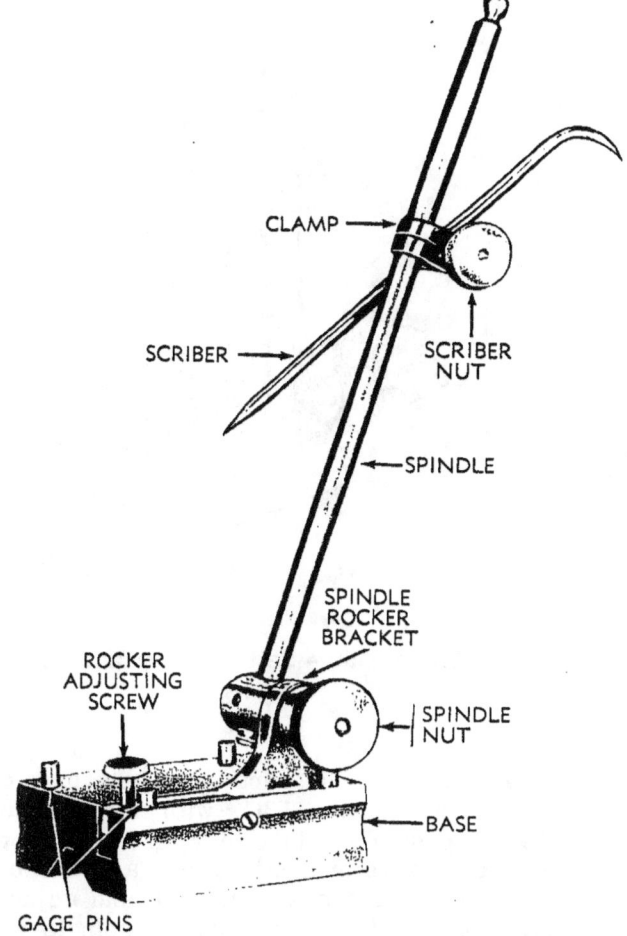

Figure 54.—Surface gage.

the clamping screws are at X and Y; the horizontal adjusting screw nut is at Z. With X and Y loose, slide the scale down into the slot being measured until it is almost in contact. Then tighten X to make Z operative. With Z, adjust the scale to the "proper feel" and secure the setting with Y. By proper feel we mean the adjustment at which you first notice contact between the end of the scale and the bottom of the slot. Then read the setting as described under "Reading a vernier scale."

To set the vernier depth gage to a particular setting, loosen both setscrews at X and at Y and slide the scale through the gage to the approximate setting. Tighten the setscrew at X, turn the knurled nut at Z until the desired setting is made, and tighten the setscrew at Y to hold the setting.

MEASURING TOOLS AND TECHNIQUES

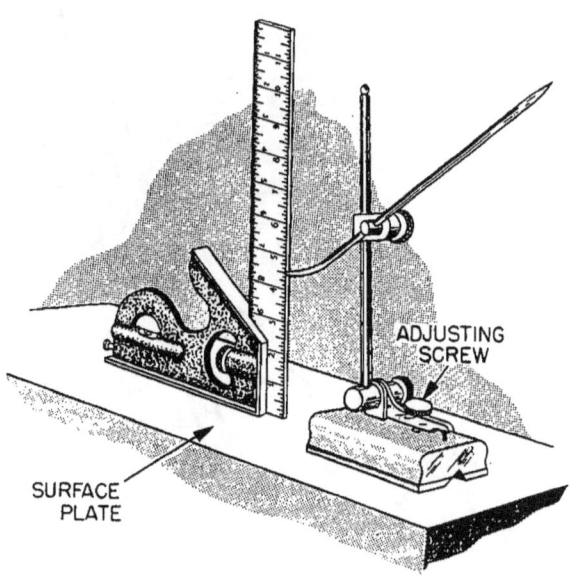

Figure 55.—Setting a surface gage to height.

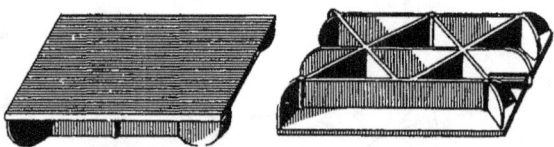

Figure 56.—Surface plate.

To measure the depth of a hole or slot, as shown in figure 53C, with more accuracy than is possible with either an ordinary depth gage or a vernier depth gage, place a micrometer depth gage over the slot and adjust the thimble until the contact of the spindle causes the ratchet stop to slip. Remove the micrometer from the work and read the micrometer. Remember, if extension rods are used, the total depth reading will be the sum of the length of the rods plus the reading on the micrometer.

SURFACE GAGE

A surface gage is a measuring tool generally used to transfer measurements to work by scribing a line, and to indicate the accuracy or parallelism of surfaces.

The surface gage (fig. 54) consists of a base with an adjustable spindle to which may be clamped a scriber or an indicator. Surface gages are made in several sizes and are classified by the length of the spindle, the smallest spindle being 4 inches long, the average 9 or 12 inches long and the largest 18 inches. The scriber is fastened to the spindle with a clamp. The bottom and the front end of the base of the surface gage have deep V-grooves cut in them, which allow the gage to be seated on a cylindrical surface.

The spindle of a surface gage may be adjusted to any position with respect to the base and tightened in place with the spindle nut. The rocket adjusting screw provides for the finer adjustment of the spindle by pivoting the spindle rocker bracket. The scriber can be positioned at any height and in any desired direction on the spindle by tightening the scriber nut. The scriber may also be mounted directly in the spindle nut mounting, in place of the spindle, and used where the working space is limited and the height of the work is within range of the scriber.

To set a surface gage for height, first wipe off the top of a layout table or surface plate and the bottom of the surface gage. Use either a combination square or a rule with rule holder to get the measurement. A rule alone cannot be held securely without wobbling and consequently an error in setting generally results. Because a combination square is generally available, its use for setting a surface gage is explained in this section.

Place the squaring head of a combination square on a flat surface as shown in figure 55, and secure the scale so that the end is in contact with the surface. Move the surface gage into position and set the scriber to the approximate height required, using the adjusting clamp that holds the scriber onto the spindle. Make the final adjustment for the exact height required (4 1/2 inches in this case) with the adjusting screw on the base of the gage.

SURFACE PLATE

A surface plate provides a true, smooth, plane surface. It is a flat-topped steel or cast iron plate that is heavily ribbed and reinforced on the under side. (See fig. 56.) It is often used in conjunction with a surface gage as a level base on which the gage and part to be measured are placed to obtain accurate measurements. The surface plate can also be used for testing parts that must have flat surfaces.

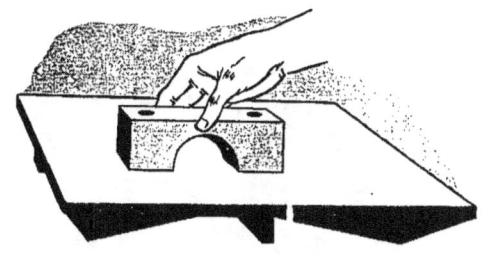

Figure 57.—Testing a surface for flatness.

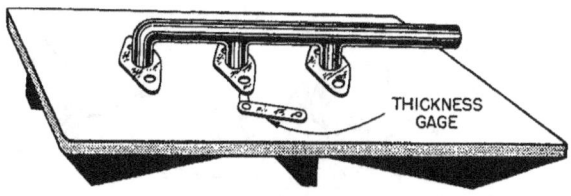

Figure 59.—Checking the conformity of a flat surface.

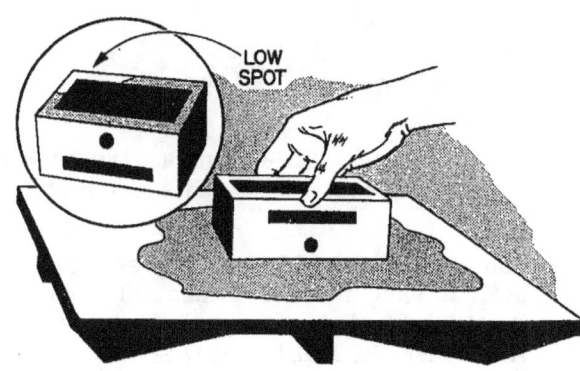

Figure 58.—Using prussian blue to aid in testing a flat surface.

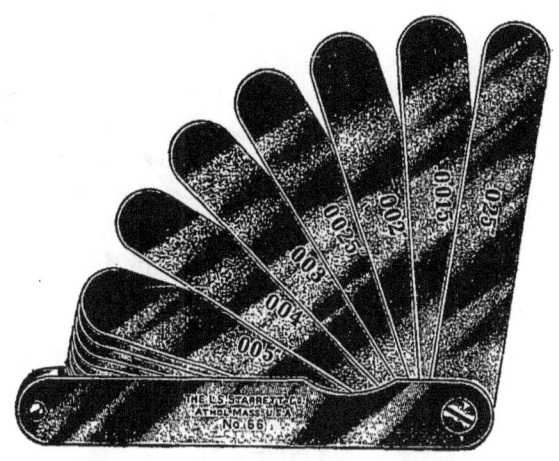

Figure 60.—Thickness gages.

To test a surface for flatness, carefully clean it and remove all burrs. Then place the surface of the object on a flat area such as the surface plate in figure 57. Any rocking motion that is apparent will indicate a variance from flatness of the piece being tested.

For very fine work, lightly coat the surface plate with prussian blue (bearing blue) and move the piece being tested across the blue surface. (See fig. 58.) The low spots on the surface being tested will not take the blue; the high spots will. See insert in figure 58.

To determine how much variation there is from flatness—and where it is—you can insert leaves of a thickness gage to determine the amount of variation of flatness. Remember to add the thickness of all leaves together to get the total variation. (See fig. 59.)

A surface also may be tested for flatness with a straightedge. To do this, clean the surface thoroughly and hold the straightedge on the surface in several places as you look toward a source of light. The light showing between the surface being tested and the straightedge will reveal the low spots.

Care of Surface Plates

The surface plate should be covered when not in use to prevent scratching, nicking, and denting. It must be handled carefully to prevent warping (twisting). Never use the surface plate as an anvil or workbench—except for precision layout work (marking and measuring).

THICKNESS (FEELER) GAGE

Thickness (feeler) gages are used for checking and measuring small openings such as contact point clearances, narrow slots, etc. These gages are made in many shapes and sizes and, as shown in figure 60, thickness gages can be made with multiple blades (usually 2 to 26). Each blade is a specific number of thousandths of an inch thick. This enables the application of one tool to the measurement of a variety of

MEASURING TOOLS AND TECHNIQUES

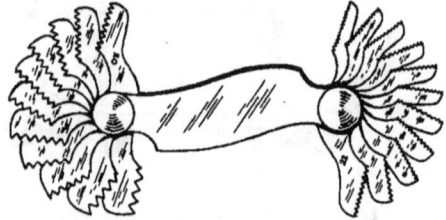

Figure 61.—Screw pitch gage.

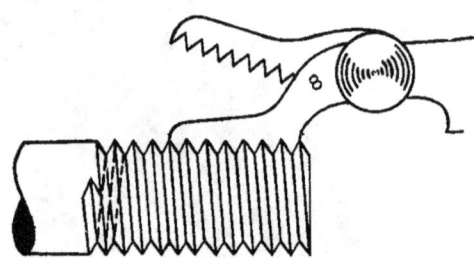

GAGING SINGLE PITCH EXTERNAL THREAD

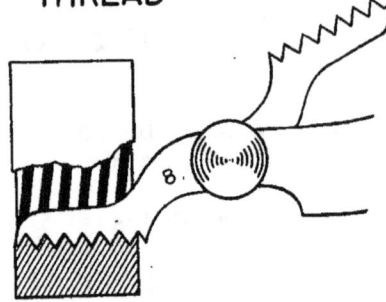

GAGING INTERNAL THREAD

Figure 62.—Using a screw pitch gage.

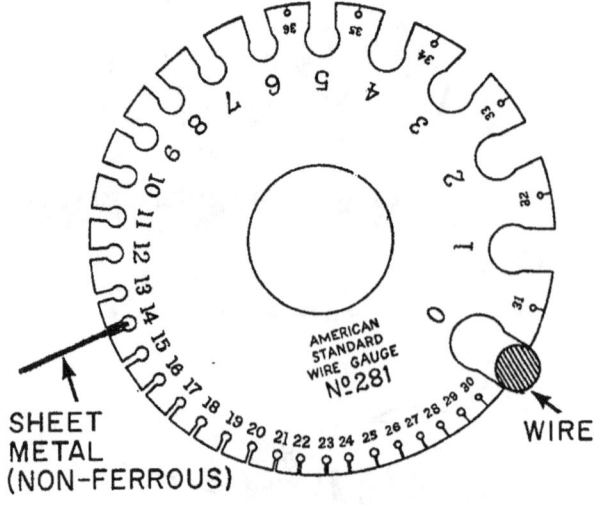

Figure 63.—Using a wire gage to measure wire and sheet metal.

thicknesses. Some thickness gage blades are straight, while others are bent at 45 and 90 degree angles at the end. Thickness gages can also be grouped so that there are several short and several long blades together. Before using a feeler gage, remove any foreign matter from the blades. You cannot get a correct measurement unless the blades are clean.

When using a feeler gage consisting of a number of blades, insert various blades or combinations of blades between two surfaces until a snug fit is obtained. The thickness of the individual blade or the total thickness of ALL THE BLADES USED is the measurement between the surfaces.

Care of Thickness Gages

Handle the blades with care at all times. Keep from forcing the blades into openings that are too small for them. Some blades are very thin and can be bent or kinked easily. Blade edges and polished surfaces are also easy to damage. When not using a thickness gage, keep it closed.

THREAD GAGE

Thread gages (screw-pitch gages) are used to determine the pitch and number of threads per inch of threaded fasteners. (See fig. 61.) They consist of thin leaves whose edges are toothed to correspond to standard thread sections.

To measure the unknown pitch of a thread, compare it with the standards of the screw pitch gage. Hold a gage leaf to the thread being measured (fig. 62), substituting various sizes until you find an exact fit. Look at the fit toward a source of light for best results.

The number of threads per inch is indicated by the numerical value on the blade which is found to fit the unknown threads. Using this

Table 2.—Wire and Sheet Metal Gages

Gage No.	Birmingham wire gage (B.W.G.) or Stubs iron wire gage, for iron wires, hot and cold rolled sheet steel	American wire gage, or Brown & Sharpe (for non-ferrous sheet and wire)	U.S. Standard gage for sheet and plate iron and steel	Steel wire gage, or the W & M (Washburn & Moen) for steel wire
0	.340	.3249	.3125	.3065
1	.300	.2893	.2812	.2830
2	.284	.2576	.2656	.2625
3	.259	.2294	.2500	.2437
4	.238	.2043	.2343	.2253
5	.220	.1819	.2187	.2070
6	.203	.1620	.2031	.1920
7	.180	.1443	.1876	.1770
8	.165	.1285	.1718	.1620
9	.148	.1144	.1562	.1483
10	.134	.1019	.1406	.1350
11	.120	.0907	.1250	.1205
12	.109	.0808	.1093	.1055
13	.095	.0719	.0937	.0915
14	.083	.0640	.0781	.0800
15	.072	.0570	.0703	.0720
16	.065	.0508	.0625	.0625
17	.058	.0452	.0562	.0540
18	.049	.0403	.0500	.0475
19	.042	.0359	.0437	.0410
20	.035	.0319	.0375	.0348
21	.032	.0284	.0343	.0317
22	.028	.0253	.0312	.0286
23	.025	.0225	.0281	.0258
24	.022	.0201	.0250	.0230
25	.020	.0179	.0218	.0204
26	.018	.0159	.0187	.0181
27	.016	.0142	.0171	.0173
28	.014	.0126	.0156	.0162
29	.013	.0112	.0140	.0150
30	.012	.0100	.0125	.0140
31	.010	.0089	.0109	.0132
32	.009	.0079	.0101	.0128
33	.008	.0071	.0093	.0118
34	.007	.0063	.0085	.0104
35	.005	.0056	.0078	.0095
36	.004	.0050	.0070	.0090

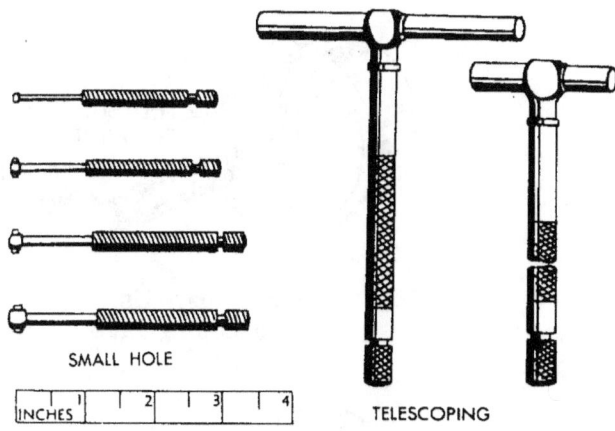

Figure 64.—Small hole and telescoping gages.

wires and sheet metals. The names of some common standard wire gages and their uses are given in the column headings of table 2. The body of this table contains gage numbers and their corresponding equivalents in decimal fractions of an inch.

Wire diameters may also be expressed in mils as well as by gage numbers. One mil equals one thousandth of an inch. Each decimal equivalent in table 2 can be converted to mils by multiplying by 1,000. For example, the circled decimal in the table is equivalent to .0640 x 1000 or 64 mils.

To use table 2, you select from the four gages listed in the table the one that applies to the sheet of metal or wire you want to gage. For instance, column 2 of the table tells you that the American Wire Gage shown in figure 63 is the one to use for nonferrous sheet or wire. Notice that each of the four gages has its own decimal equivalent for a particular gage number.

To measure wire size, apply the gage to the wire as shown in figure 63. Do not force the wire into the slot. Find the slot that refuses to pass the wire without forcing. Then, try the next larger slot until one is found that passes the wire. This is the correct size. Remember, your measurements are taken at the slot portion of the cutout rather than the inner portion of the gage. Now that you have the gage number turn your gage over and read the decimal equivalent for that number.

To measure the gage of a piece of metal, first remove any burr from the place where you

value as a basis, correct sizes of nuts, bolts, tap cutters, and die cutters are selected for use.

WIRE GAGE

The wire gage shown in fig. 63, is used for measuring the diameters of wires or the thickness of sheet metal. This gage is circular in shape with cutouts in the outer perimeter. Each cutout gages a different size from No. 0 to No. 36. Examination of the gage will show that the larger the gage number, the smaller the diameter or thickness.

Gages similar to the one shown in figure 63 are available for measuring a variety of

MEASURING TOOLS AND TECHNIQUES

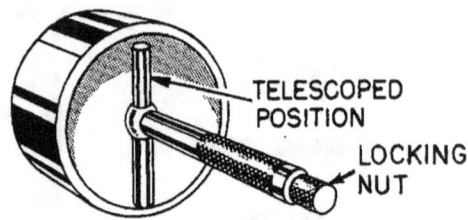

Figure 65.—Using a telescoping gage.

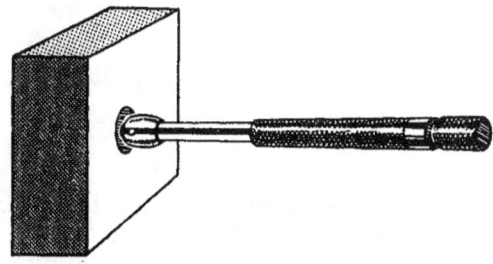

Figure 66.—Measuring the diameter of a hole with a small hole gage.

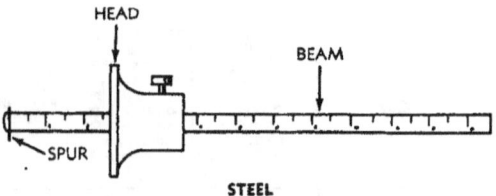

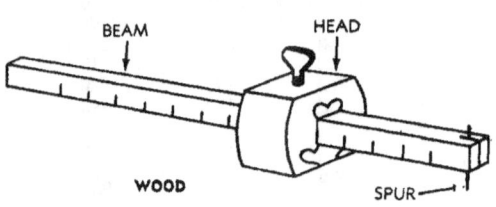

Figure 67.—Marking gages.

intend to apply the gage. Then select the appropriate gage for the metal to be measured.

After the right gage has been selected, apply the gage to the wire, or to the edge of the sheet as shown in figure 63. The number opposite the slot that fits the wire or sheet is its gage number. The decimal equivalent is stamped on the opposite face of the gage.

TELESCOPING GAGE

Telescoping gages are used for measuring the inside size of slots or holes up to 6 inches in width or diameter. They are T-shaped tools in which the shaft of the T is used as a handle, and the crossarm used for measuring. (See fig. 64.) The crossarms telescope into each other and are held out by a light spring. To use the gage the arms are compressed, placed in the hole to be measured, and allowed to expand. A twist of the locknut on top of the handle locks the arms. The tool may then be withdrawn and the distance across the arms measured.

These tools are commonly furnished in sets, the smallest gage for measuring the distances from 5/16 to 1/2 inch, and the largest for distances from 3 1/2 to 6 inches.

To measure the diameter of a hole from 1/2" to 6" in diameter, select from a set of telescoping gages the one whose range includes the size you need. Loosen the knurled nut at the end of the handle, and telescope the adjustable end of the gage to a size slightly smaller than the hole and retighten the nut. Insert the gage into the hole as shown in figure 65, loosen the nut to permit the spring-loaded adjustable end to expand to the hole diameter, and tighten the nut. The spring loaded contact of the adjustable end will assure proper contact. Make sure, however, that the gage is held with the telescoping end at right angles to the axis of the hole to measure the true, maximum diameter. Remove the gage and measure the setting with an outside micrometer caliper.

SMALL HOLE GAGE

For measuring smaller slots or holes than the telescoping gages will measure, small hole gages can be used. These gages come in sets of four or more and will measure distances of approximately 1/8 to 1/2 inch.

The small hole gage (fig. 64) consists of a small, split, ball-shaped member mounted on the end of a handle. The ball is expanded by turning a knurled knob on the handle until the proper feel is obtained (the slight drag of the ball end on the sides of the hole). The gage is then withdrawn (fig. 66) and the size of the ball-shaped member on the end of the gage can be measured with an outside micrometer caliper. On some types of small hole gages, the

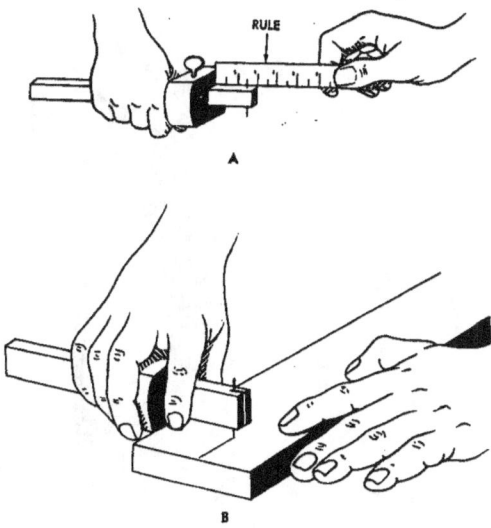

Figure 68.—Using the marking gage.

Figure 70.—Scribing a circle with a divider.

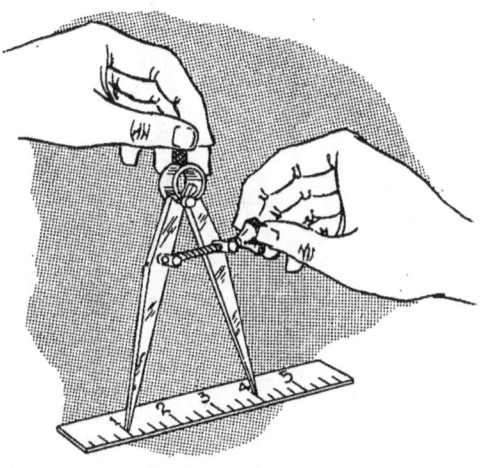

Figure 69.—Setting a divider to a desired radius.

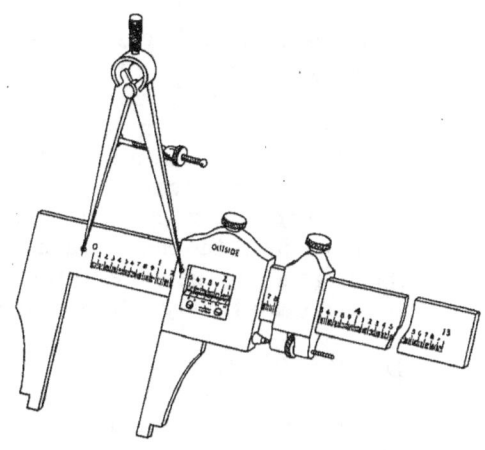

Figure 71.—Setting a divider with a vernier caliper.

the ball is flattened at the bottom near the centerline to permit use in shallow holes and recesses.

MARKING GAGES

A marking gage is used to mark off guidelines parallel to an edge, end, or surface of a piece of wood or metal. It has a sharp spur or pin that does the marking.

Marking gages (fig. 67) are made of wood or steel. They consist of a graduated beam about 8 inches long on which a head slides. The head can be fastened at any point on the beam by means of a thumbscrew. The thumbscrew presses a brass shoe tightly against the beam and locks it firmly in position. The steel pin or spur that does the marking projects from the beam about 1/16 inch.

To draw a line parallel to an edge with a marking gage, first determine the distance the line must be from the edge of the stock. Adjust the marking gage by setting the head the desired distance from the spur. Although the bar of a marking gage is graduated in inches, the spur may work loose or bend. If this occurs, accurate measurement should be made with a

MEASURING TOOLS AND TECHNIQUES

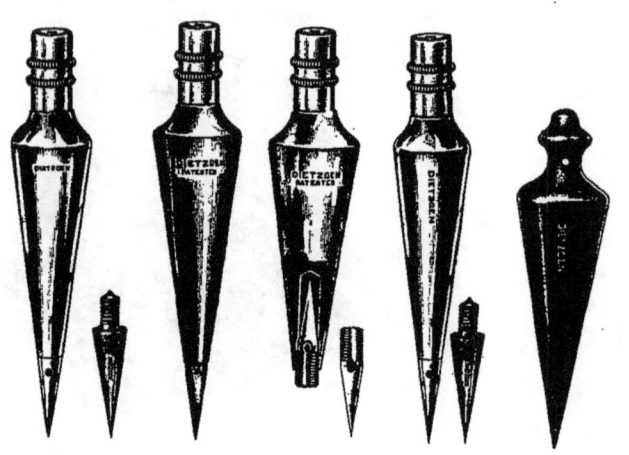

Figure 72.—Plumb bobs.

rule between the head and spur. (See fig. 68A.) To draw a line after setting the gage, grasp the head of the gage with the palm and fingers as shown in figure 68B; extend the thumb along the beam towards the spur. Press the head firmly against the edge of the work to be marked, and with a wrist motion tip the gage forward until the spur touches the work. Push the gage along the edge to mark the work, keeping the head firmly against the edge of the work.

DIVIDERS

Dividers are useful instruments for transferring measurements and are frequently used in scribing arcs and circles in layout work.

To lay out a circle with a divider, set the divider at the desired radius, using a rule as shown in figure 69. Note that the 3-inch radius being set here is being taken at a central portion rather than at the end of the rule. This reduces the chance of error, as each point of the dividers can be set on a graduation.

Place one leg of the divider at the center of the proposed circle, lean the tool in the direction it will be rotated, and rotate it by rolling the knurled handle between your thumb and index finger (fig. 70).

Vernier calipers, which have two center points similar to prick punchmarks are particularly useful in setting a divider to exact dimensions. One center point will be found near the zero end of the scale on the rule. The other point is in line with the first and to the left of the zero on the vernier scale. (See fig. 71.)

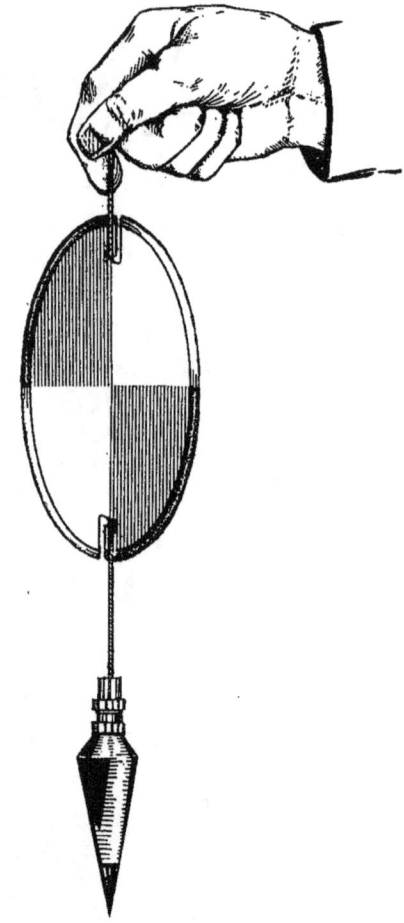

Figure 73.—Plumb bob, cord, and target.

Set and secure the desired setting on the vernier caliper and adjust the divider until both points readily enter the center points on the vernier caliper as shown in figure 71.

PLUMB BOB

A plumb bob (fig. 72) is a pointed, tapered brass or bronze weight which is suspended from a cord for determining the vertical or plumb line to or from a point on the ground. Common weights for plumb bobs are 6, 8, 10, 12, 14, 16, 18, and 24 oz.

A plumb bob is a precision instrument and must be cared for as such. If the tip becomes bent, the cord from which the bob is suspended will not occupy the true plumb line over the point indicated by the tip. A plumb bob usually has a detachable tip, as shown in figure 72, so that if the tip should become damaged it can

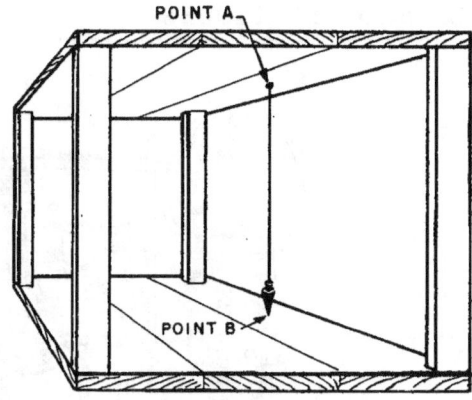

Figure 74.—Locating a point with a plumb bob.

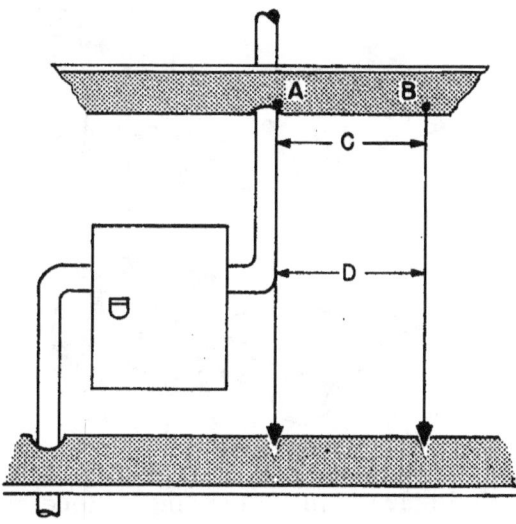

Figure 75.—Plumbing a structural member with a plumb bob.

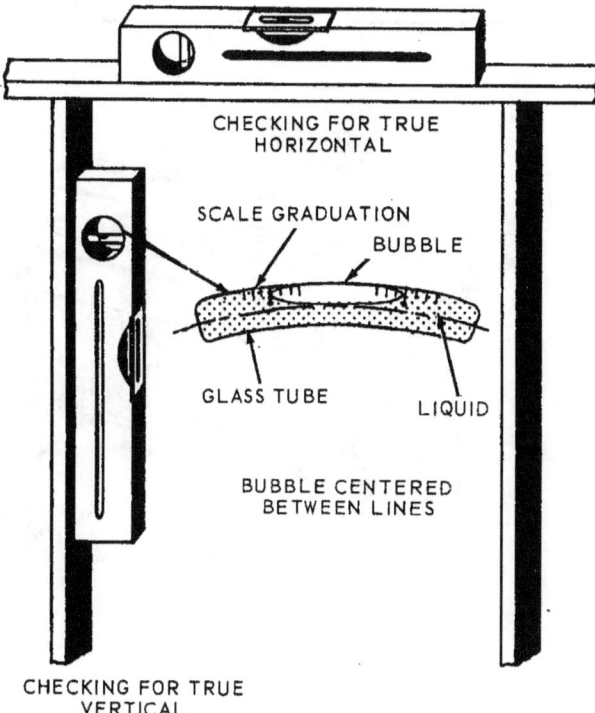

Figure 76.—Horizontal and vertical use of level.

be renewed without replacing the entire instrument.

The cord from a plumb bob can be made more conspicuous, for observation purposes, by attachment of a red-and-white target as shown in figure 73.

The plumb bob is used in carpentry to determine true verticality when erecting vertical uprights and corner posts of framework. Surveyors use it for transferring and lining up points.

To locate a point which is exactly below a particular point in space, when working ashore or on a ship in drydock, secure the plumb bob string to the upper point, such as A in figure

74. When the plumb stops swinging, the point as indicated at B in the illustration, will be exactly below A.

To plumb a structural member, or an electrical conduit, as shown by figure 75, secure the plumb line A so that you can look at both the line and piece behind the line. Then, by sighting, line up the member or conduit with the plumb line.

If this cannot be done, it may be necessary to secure the plumb line at some point such as B, and then measure the offset from the line to the piece at two places so that, for example, C and D in figure 75 are equal. If the distances between C and D are not equal, adjust the structural member or conduit until they are.

LEVELS

Levels are tools designed to prove whether a plane or surface is true horizontal or true vertical. Some precision levels are calibrated so that they will indicate in degrees, minutes, and seconds, the angle inclination of a surface in relation to a horizontal or vertical surface.

MEASURING TOOLS AND TECHNIQUES

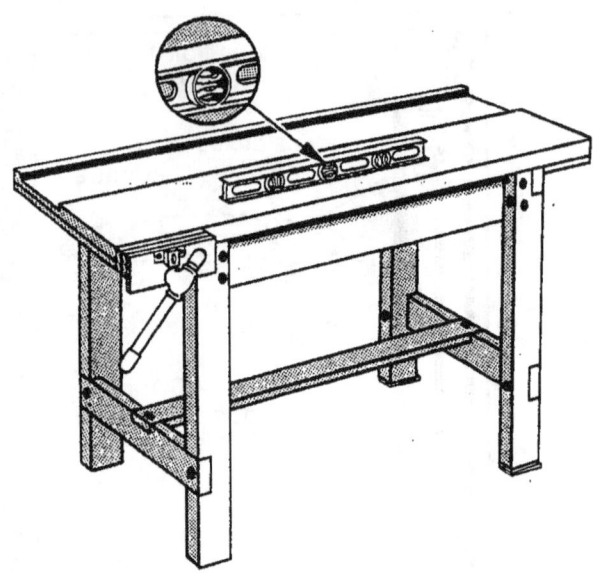

Figure 77.—Leveling a bench.

The level is a simple instrument consisting of a liquid, such as alcohol or chloroform, partially filling a glass vial or tube so that a bubble remains. The tube is mounted in a frame which may be aluminum, wood, or iron. Levels are equipped with one, two, or more tubes. One tube is built in the frame at right angles to another (fig. 76). The tube indicated in figure 76 is slightly curved, causing the bubble to seek always the highest point in the tube. On the outside of the tube are two sets of graduation lines separated by a space. Leveling is accomplished when the air bubble is centered between the graduation lines.

To level a piece of equipment, such as the workbench in figure 77, with a carpenter's level, set the level on the bench top parallel to the front edge of the bench. Notice that the level has several pairs of glass vials. Regardless of the position of the level, always watch the bubble in the bottom vial of a horizontal pair. Shim or wedge up the end of the bench that will return that bubble to the center of its vial. Recheck the first position of the level before securing the shims or wedges.

To plumb a piece of equipment, such as the drill press shown in figure 78, place the level

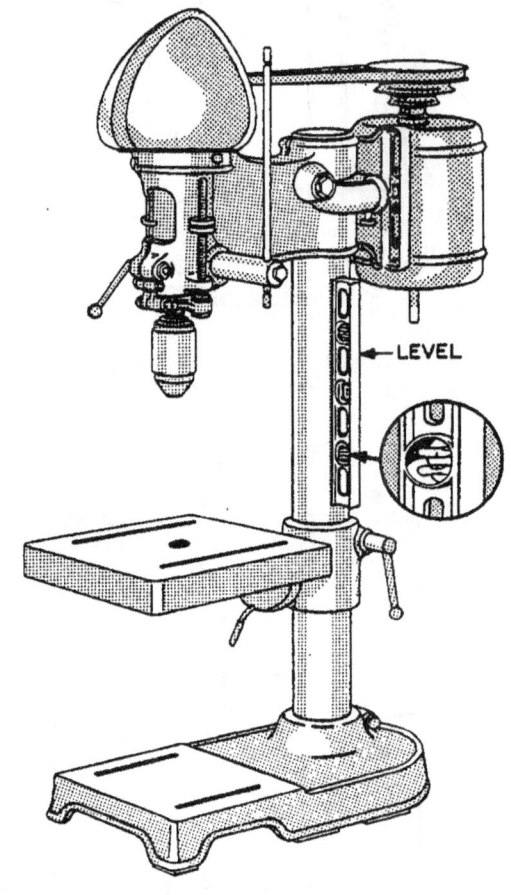

Figure 78.—Plumbing a piece of equipment with a level.

on the side and on the front of the main column of the press. Figure 78 shows the level on the side. Use shims as necessary to bring the bubble in the lower vial of either pair of the horizontal vials to the center in each case.

Levels must be checked for accuracy. This is readily accomplished by placing the level on a true horizontal surface and noting the vial indication. Reverse the level end for end. If the bubble appears on one side of the graduations with reference to the operator on the first reading and on the other side for the second reading, the level is out of true and must be adjusted.

Do not drop or handle a level roughly. To prevent damage, store it in a rack or other suitable place when not in use.

BASIC FUNDAMENTALS OF COMMON POWER TOOLS

CONTENTS

	Page
I. SAFETY	1
II. PORTABLE ELECTRIC POWER TOOLS	3
III. PORTABLE PNEUMATIC POWER TOOLS	9
IV. COMMON POWER MACHINE TOOLS	12

BASIC FUNDAMENTALS OF COMMON POWER TOOLS

Power tools are so commonplace in the shop that many workers use some power" tools at one time or another. This section will be devoted to the more common types of electric and air-driven power tools and equipment. Upon completion, you should be able to identify them, discuss applicable safety measures, and describe the general operating prattices and care of these tools.

I. SAFETY

Safe practices in the use of power tools cannot be overemphasized. There are several general safety measures to observe in operating or maintaining power equipment.

• First of all, never operate power equipment unless you are thoroughly familiar with its controls and operating procedures. When in doubt, consult the appropriate operating instruction or ask someone who knows.
• All portable tools should be inspected before use to see that they are clean and in a proper state of repair.
• Have ample illumination. If extension lights are required, ensure that a light guard is provided (fig.   1).
• Before a power tool is connected to a source of power (electricity, air, etc.), BE SURE that the switch on the tool is in the "OFF" position.
• When operating a power tool, give it your FULL and UNDIVIDED ATTENTION.
• Keep all safety guards in position and use safety shields or goggles when necessary.
• Fasten all loose sleeves and aprons.
• DO NOT DISTRACT OR IN ANY WAY DISTURB another man while he is operating a power tool.
• Never try to clear jammed machinery unless you remove the source of power first.
• After using a power tool, turn off the power, remove the power source, wait for all rotation of the tool to stop, and then clean the tool. Remove all waste and scraps from the work area and stow the tool in its assigned location.
• Never plug the power cord of a portable electric tool into an electrical power source before ensuring that the source has the voltage and type of current (alternating or direct) called for on the nameplate of the tool.
• If an extension cord is required, always connect the cord of a portable electric power tool into the extension cord before the extension code is inserted into a convenience outlet (fig. 2). Always unplug the extension cord from the receptacle before the cord of the portable power tool is unplugged from the extension cord. (The extension cord and the power cord can each be no longer than 25 feet in length. Extra extension cords should be limited, wherever possible, to maintain allowable resistance to ground.)

Figure 1.—Safety poster.

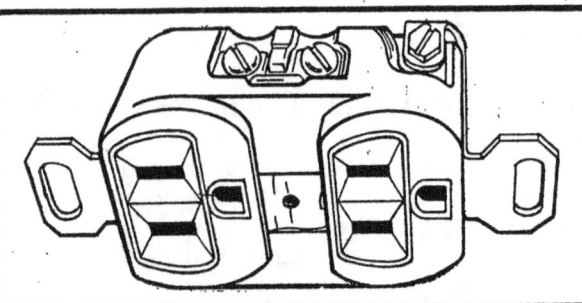

USE THE CORRECT PLUG!

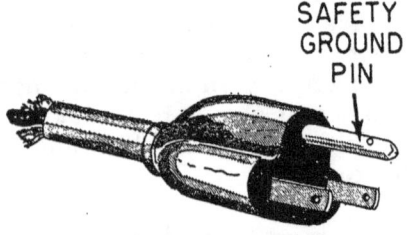

SAFETY GROUND PIN

MAKE CERTAIN THAT THE TOOLS YOU USE HAVE A SAFETY PLUG AND CORD WITH INTEGRAL GROUNDING CONDUCTOR.

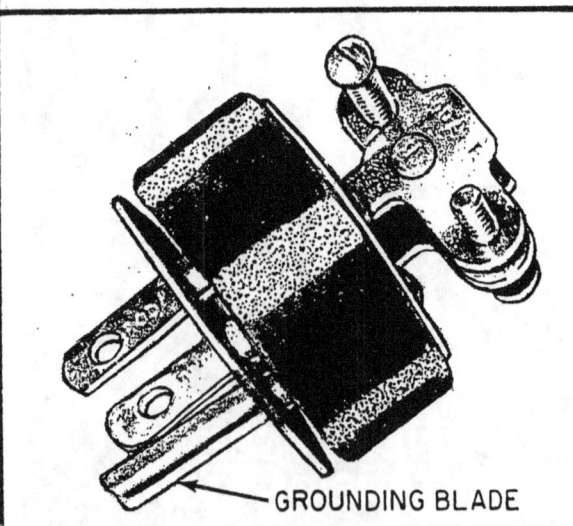

GROUNDING BLADE

Figure 2.—Grounding plugs and convenience outlet.

• Be sure to use a grounded plug and 3-conductor cord. Figure 2 shows a permanently molded type of grounded plug and also one used for replacement purposes.

The purpose of the properly grounded conductor in the 3-conductor cord is to minimize the possibility of electrical shock. The end of the grounding conductor within the tool or equipment is connected to the metal housing by the manufacturer, and the other end is connected to the grounding blade or pin of the grounded plug. In this manner, the grounding conductor simulates the mounting bolts of permanent equipment; namely, it joins the metal case of portable electric equipment to the metal of the ship's hull.

One exception to the use of 3-conductor grounded cord concerns plastic-cased tools (drills, sanders, grinders, etc.) that have been developed to eliminate the risk of electric shock. In these tools the shafts and chucks are isolated electrically from the drive motors. DO NOT replace the two-conductor cable on plastic-cased tools with 3-conductor cable IF the plastic-cased tool has an information plate on it stating that "grounding is not required"!

• Be sure that power cords do not come in contact with sharp objects. The cords should not be allowed to kink, nor should they be allowed to come in contact with oil, grease, hot surfaces, or chemicals.

• When cords are damaged, they should be replaced.

• Portable cables should be of sufficient length that they will not be subjected to longitudinal stresses or need to be pulled taut to make connections.

• Electrical portable cables should be checked frequently while in service to detect unusual heating. Any cable which feels more than comfortably warm to the bare hand placed outside the insulation should be checked immediately for overloading by competent electrical personnel.

• See that all cables are positioned so that they will not constitute tripping hazards.

• Electricity must be treated with respect and handled properly (fig. 3). If water exists anywhere in the vicinity of energized equipment—be especially cautious, and wherever possible, deenergize the equipment.

• Always remember:

1. ELECTRICITY strikes without warning.
2. Every electrical circuit is a POTENTIAL SOURCE OF DANGER and MUST BE TREATED AS SUCH.
3. Make no electrical repairs yourself unless you are qualified to do so.

COMMON POWER TOOLS

Figure 3.—Know what you are doing.

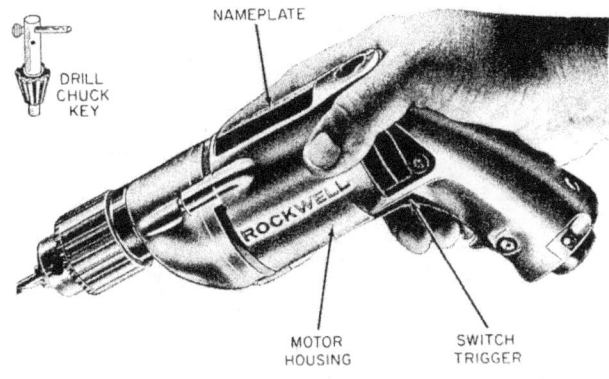

Figure 4.—1/4-inch portable electric drill.

4. Sparking electric tools should never be used in places where flammable gases or liquids or exposed explosives are present. Pneumatic tools are used in these areas.

5. The power should always be disconnected before accessories on tools are changed.

• Shipboard conditions are particularly conducive to electric shock possibilities because the body may contact the ship's metal structure. Extra care is therefore needed, especially when body resistance may be low because of perspiration or damp clothing. Insulate yourself from ground by means of insulating material covering any adjacent grounded metal with which you might come into contact. Suitable materials include dry wood, dry canvas, dry phenolic material, several thicknesses of dry paper, or rubber mats. ALWAYS REPORT ANY SHOCK RECEIVED from electrical equipment. Minor shocks often lead to fatal shocks later on.

III. PORTABLE ELECTRIC POWER TOOLS

Portable power tools are tools that can be moved from place to place. Some of the most common portable power tools that you will use are electrically powered and include drills, sanders, grinders and saws.

DRILLS

The portable electric drill (fig. 4) is probably the most frequently used power tool in the Navy. Although it is especially designed for drilling holes, by adding various accessories you can adapt it for different jobs. Sanding, sawing, buffing, polishing, screw-driving, wire brushing, and paint mixing are examples of possible uses.

Portable electric drills commonly used have capacities for drilling holes in steel from 1/16 inch up to 1 inch in diameter. The sizes of portable electric drills are classified by the maximum size straight shank drill it will hold. That is, a 1/4 inch electric drill will hold a straight shank drill up to and including 1/4 inch.

The revolutions per minute (rpm) and power the drill will deliver are most important when choosing a drill for a job. You will find that the speed of the drill motor decreases with an increase in size, primarily because the larger units are designed to turn larger cutting tools or to drill in heavy materials, and both these factors require slower speed.

If you are going to do heavy work, such as drilling in masonry or steel, then you would probably need to use a drill with a 3/8 or 1/2 inch capacity. If most of your drilling will be forming holes in wood or small holes in sheet metal, then a 1/4-inch drill will probably be adequate.

The chuck is the clamping device into which the drill is inserted. Nearly all electric drills

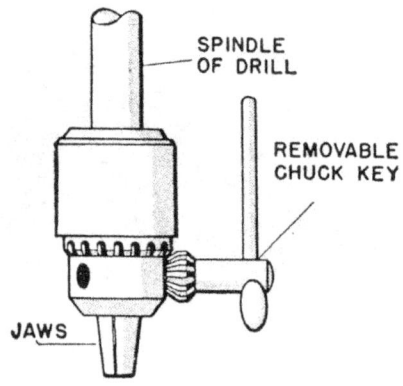

Figure 2-5.—Three jaw chuck and chuck key.

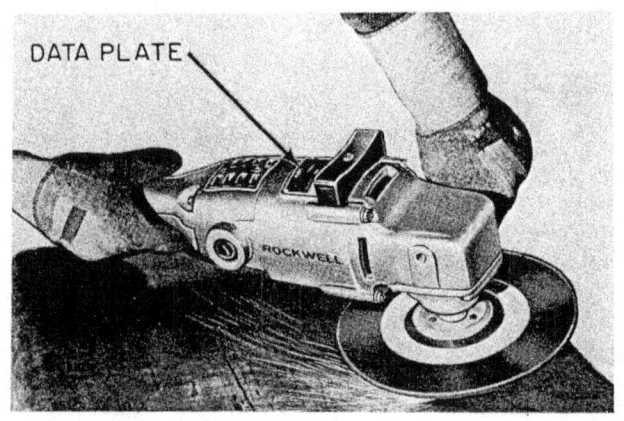

Figure 6.—Portable electric sander.

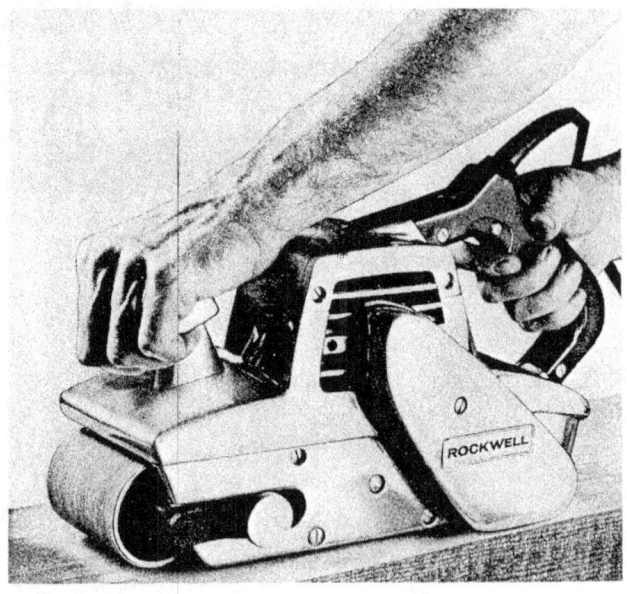

Figure 7.—Portable belt sander.

1/4-inch drill in figure 4. This drill has a momentary contact trigger switch located in the handle. The switch is squeezed to start the electric drill and released to stop it.

The trigger latch is a button in the bottom of the drill handle. It is pushed in, while the switch trigger is held down, to lock the trigger switch in the "ON" position. The trigger latch is released by squeezing and then releasing the switch trigger.

SANDERS

Portable sanders are tools designed to hold and operate abrasives for sanding wood, plastics and metals. The most common types found in the Navy are the DISK, BELT, and RECIPROCATING ORBITAL sanders.

Disk Sander

Electric disk sanders (fig. 6) are especially useful on work where a large amount of material is to be removed quickly such as scaling surfaces in preparation for painting. This machine, however, must not be used where a mirror smooth finish is required.

The disk should be moved smoothly and lightly over the surface. Never allow the disk to stay in one place too long because it will cut into the metal and leave a large depression.

are equipped with a three-jaw chuck. Some of the drill motors have a hand-type chuck that you tighten or loosen by hand but most of the drills used in the shop have gear-type, three-jaw chucks which are tightened and loosened by means of a chuck key, shown in figure 5. Do not apply further pressure with pliers or wrenches after you hand tighten the chuck with the chuck key.

Always remove the key IMMEDIATELY after you use it. Otherwise the key will fly loose when the drill motor is started and may cause serious injury to you or one of your shipmates. The chuck key is generally taped on the cord of the drill; but if it is not, make sure you put it in a safe place where it will not get lost.

All portable electric drills used in the shop have controls similar to the ones shown on the

COMMON POWER TOOLS

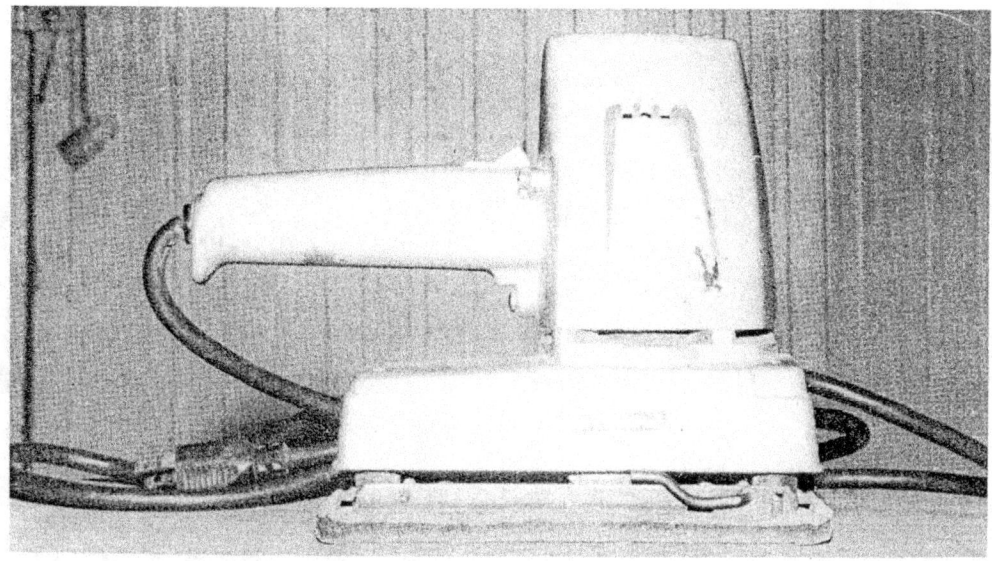

Figure 8.—Orbital sander.

Belt Sander

The belt sander (fig. 7) is commonly used for surfacing lumber used for interior trim, furniture, or cabinets. Wood floors are almost always made ready for final finishing by using a belt sander. Whereas these types of sanding operations were once laborious and time-consuming, it is now possible to perform the operations quickly and accurately with less effort.

The portable belt sanders use endless sanding belts that can be obtained in many different grades (grits). The belts are usually 2, 3, or 4 inches wide and can be easily changed when they become worn or when you want to use a different grade of sanding paper.

The first thing to do when preparing to use the sander is to be sure that the object to be sanded is firmly secured. Then, after the motor has been started verify that the belt is tracking on center. Any adjustment to make it track centrally is usually made by aligning screws.

The moving belt is then placed on the surface of the object to be sanded with the rear part of the belt touching first. The machine is then leveled as it is moved forward. When you use the sander, don't press down or "ride" it, because the weight of the machine exerts enough pressure for proper cutting. (Excessive pressure also causes the abrasive belt to clog and the motor to overheat). Adjust the machine over the surface with overlapping strokes, always in a direction parallel to the grain.

By working over a fairly wide area, and avoiding any machine tilting or pausing in any one spot, an even surface will result. Upon completion of the sanding process, lift the machine off the work and then stop the motor.

Some types of sanders are provided with a bag that takes up the dust that is produced. Use it if available.

Orbital Sander

The orbital sander (fig. 8) is so named because of the action of the sanding pad. The pad moves in a tiny orbit, with a motion that is hardly discernible, so that it actually sands in all directions. This motion is so small and so fast that, with fine paper mounted on the pad, it is nearly impossible to see any scratches on the finished surface.

The pad, around which the abrasive sheet is wrapped, usually extends beyond the frame of the machine so it is possible to work in tight corners and against vertical surfaces.

Some models of the orbital sanders have a bag attached to catch all dust that is made from the sanding operation. Orbital sanders (pad sanders) do not remove as much material as

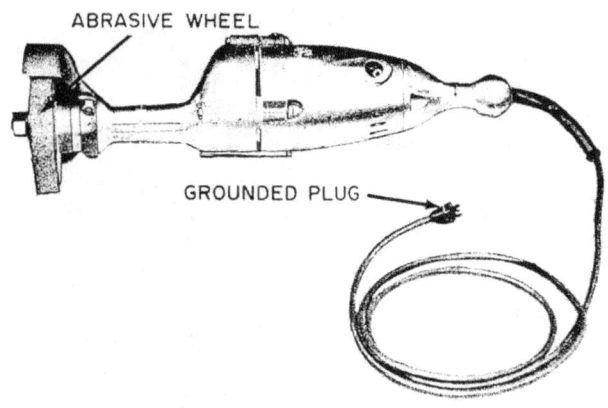

Figure 9.—Portable grinder.

fast as the belt sander or disk sander but do a better job on smoothing a surface for finishing. If both a belt or disk sander and an orbital sander are available you should use the belt or disk sander for rough, preliminary work and the orbital sander for finishing. The sandpaper used on the sander may be cut to size from a bulk sheet of paper or may be available in the correct size for the sander you have. The paper is wrapped around a pad on the sander and is fastened to the pad by means of levers on the front and rear of the sander. The lever action fasteners make changing the paper easy and quick.

PORTABLE GRINDERS

Portable grinders are power tools that are used for rough grinding and finishing of metallic surfaces. They are made in several sizes; however, the one used most in the Navy uses a grinding wheel with a maximum diameter of 6 inches. (See fig. 9.)

The abrasive wheels are easily replaceable so that different grain size and grades of abrasives can be used for the varying types of surfaces to be ground and the different degrees of finish desired.

A flexible shaft attachment is available for most portable grinders. This shaft is attached by removing the grinding wheel then attaching the shaft to the grinding wheel drive spindle. The grinding wheel can then be attached to the end of the flexible shaft. This attachment is invaluable for grinding surfaces in hard to reach places.

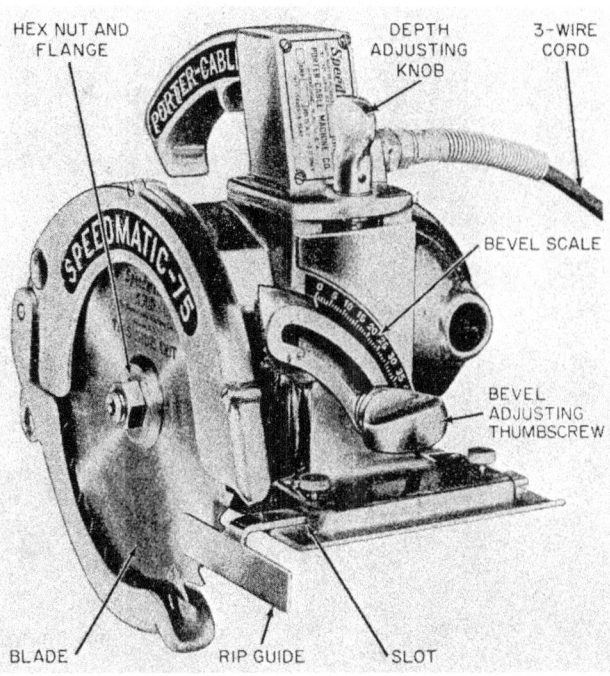

Figure 10.—Portable electric circular saw.

The wheel guard on the grinder should be positioned so that abrasive dust and metal particles will be deflected away from your face.

Before you turn the grinder on, make sure the abrasive grinding wheel is properly secured to the grinder spindle and not cracked or damaged.

PORTABLE CIRCULAR SAW

The portable circular saw is becoming more and more popular as a woodworking tool because of the time and labor it saves, the precision with which it works, and its ease of handling and maneuverability.

Because of the many types of portable circular saws in the Navy supply system, and the changes being made in the design of these saws, only general information will be given in this section. Information concerning a particular saw can be found by checking the manufacturer's manual.

The sizes of portable electric saws range from one-sixth horsepower with a 4-inch blade to one-and-one half horsepower with a 14-inch blade. They are so constructed that they may be used as a carpenter's handsaw, both at the job site or on a bench in the woodworking shop.

The portable electric saw (fig. 10) is started by pressing a trigger inserted in the handle and stopped by releasing it. The saw will run only when the trigger is held.

Most saws may be adjusted for crosscutting or for ripping. The ripsaw guide shown in figure 10 is adjusted by the two small knurled nuts at the base of the saw. When the guide is inserted in the rip guide slot to the desired dimensions, the nuts are then tightened to hold it firmly in place.

In crosscutting, a guideline is generally marked across the board to be cut. Place the front of the saw base on the work so that the guide mark on the front plate and the guide line on the work are aligned. Be sure the blade is clear of the work. Start the saw and allow the cutting blade to attain full speed. Then advance the saw, keeping the guide mark and guide line aligned. If the saw stalls, back the saw out. DO NOT RELEASE the starting trigger. When the saw resumes cutting speed, start cutting again.

Additional adjustments include a depth knob and a bevel thumbscrew. The depth of the cut is regulated by adjusting the depth knob. The bevel adjusting thumbscrew is used for adjusting the angle of the cut. This permits the base to be tilted in relation to the saw. The graduated scale marked in degrees on the quadrant (fig. 10) enables the operator to measure his adjustments and angles of cut.

The bottom plate of the saw is wide enough to provide the saw with a firm support on the lumber being cut. The blade of the saw is protected by a spring guard which opens when lumber is being cut but snaps back into place when the cut is finished. Many different saw blades may be placed on the machine for special kinds of sawing. By changing blades almost any building material from slate and corrugated metal sheets to fiberglass can be cut.

To change saw blades, first disconnect the power. Remove the blade by taking off the saw clamp screw and flange, using the wrench provided for this purpose. Attach the new saw blade making certain the teeth are in the proper cutting direction (pointing upward toward the front of the saw) and tighten the flange and clamp screw with the wrench.

CAUTION: Do not put the saw blade on backwards; most blades have instructions stamped on them with the words "This Side Out."

THE PORTABLE ELECTRIC SAW IS ONE OF THE MOST DANGEROUS POWER TOOLS IN EXISTENCE WHEN IT IS NOT PROPERLY USED. Make sure the board you are sawing is properly secured so it will not slip or turn. After making a cut be sure the saw blade has come to a standstill before laying the saw down.

When using an electric saw remember that all the blade you can normally see is covered; the portion of the blade that projects under the board being cut is not covered. The exposed teeth under the work are dangerous and can cause serious injury if any part of your body should come into contact with them.

Make sure the blade of a portable circular saw is kept sharp at all times. The saw blade will function most efficiently when the rate of feed matches the blade's capacity to cut. You will not have to figure this out—you will be able to feel it. With a little practice you will know when the cut is smooth and you will know when you are forcing it. Let the blade do its own cutting. The tool will last longer and you will work easier because it is less fatiguing.

Figure 11.—Saber or bayonet saw operations.

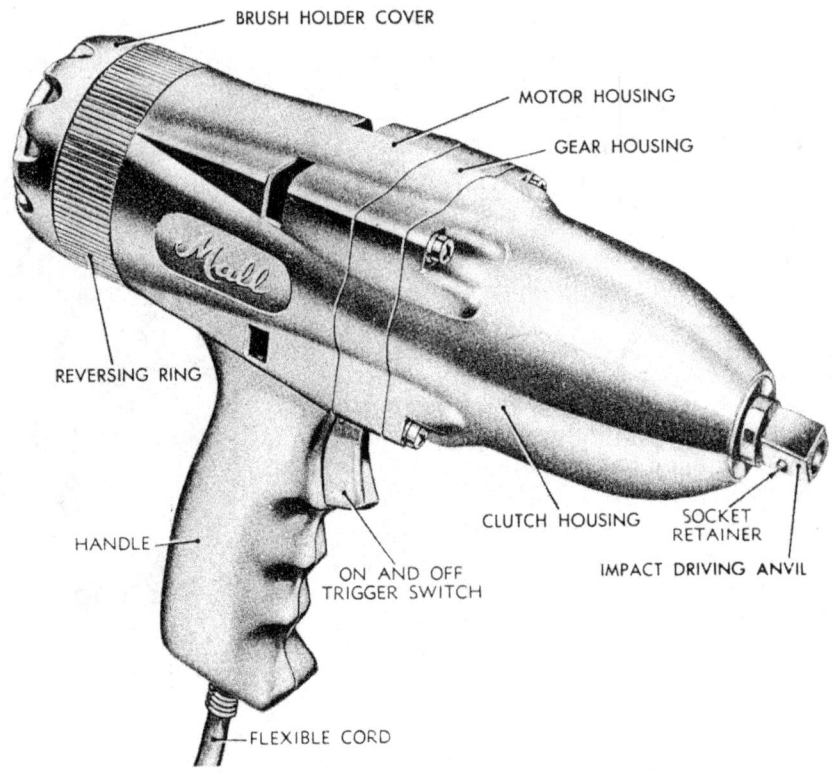

Figure 12.—Reversible electric impact wrench.

SABER SAW

The saber saw (fig. 11) is a power driven jigsaw that will let you cut smooth and decorative curves in wood and light metal. Most saber saws are light duty machines and are not designed for extremely fast cutting.

There are several different blades designed to operate in the saber saw and they are easily interchangeable. For fast cutting of wood, a blade with coarse teeth may be used. A blade with fine teeth is designed for cutting metal.

The best way to learn how to handle this type of tool is to use it. Before trying to do a finished job with the saber saw, clamp down a piece of scrap plywood and draw some curved as well as straight lines to follow. You will develop your own way of gripping the tool, and this will be affected somewhat by the particular tool you are using. On some tools, for example, you will find guiding easier if you apply some downward pressure on the tool as you move it forward. If you are not firm with your grip, the tool will tend to vibrate excessively and this will roughen the cut. Do not force the cutting faster than the design of the blade allows or you will break the blade.

ELECTRIC IMPACT WRENCH

The electric impact wrench (fig. 12) is a portable hand-type reversible wrench. The one shown has a 1/2-inch square impact driving anvil over which 1/2-inch square drive sockets can be fitted. Wrenches also can be obtained that have impact driving anvils ranging from 3/8 inch to 1 inch. The driving anvils are not interchangeable, however, from one wrench to another.

The electric wrench with its accompanying equipment is primarily intended for applying and removing nuts, bolts, and screws. It may also be used to drill and tap metal, wood, plastics, etc., and drive and remove socket-head, Phillips-head, or slotted-head wood, machine, or self-tapping screws.

Before you use an electric impact wrench depress the on-and-off trigger switch and allow the electric wrench to operate a few seconds, noting carefully the direction of rotation.

COMMON POWER TOOLS

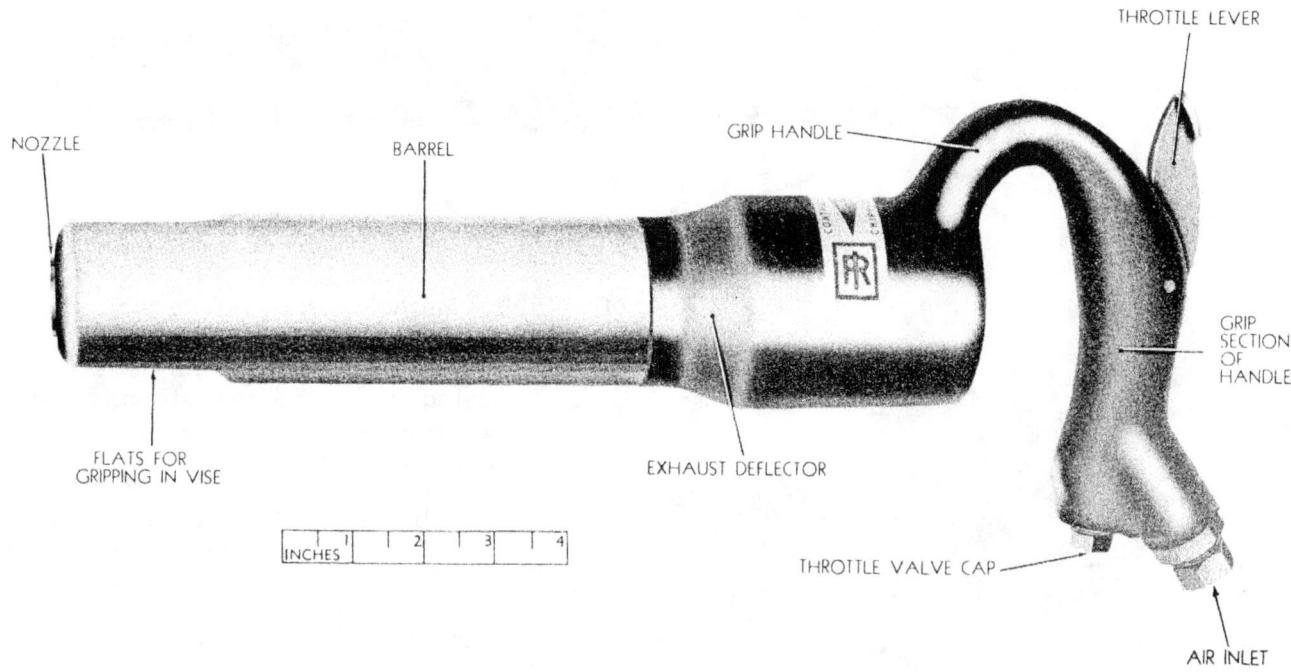

Figure 13.—Pneumatic chipping hammer.

Release the trigger switch to stop the wrench. Turn the reversing ring located at the rear of the tool; it should move easily in one direction (which is determined by the current direction of rotation). Depress the on-and-off trigger again to start the electric wrench. The direction of rotation should now be reversed. Continue to operate for a few seconds in each direction to be sure that the wrench and its reversible features are functioning correctly. When you are sure the wrench operates properly, place the suitable equipment on the impact driving anvil and go ahead with the job at hand.

III. PORTABLE PNEUMATIC POWER TOOLS

Portable pneumatic power tools are tools that look much the same as electric power tools but use the energy of compressed air instead of electricity. Because of the limited outlets for compressed air aboard ship and shore stations, the use of pneumatic power tools is not as widespread as electric tools. Portable pneumatic tools are used most around a shop where compressed air outlets are readily accessible.

SAFETY

In operating or maintaining air-driven tools, take the following precautionary measures to protect yourself and others from the damaging effects of compressed air.

● Inspect the air hose for cracks or other defects; replace the hose if found defective.

● Before connecting an air hose to the compressed air outlet, open the control valve momentarily. Then, make sure the hose is clear of water and other foreign material by connecting it to the outlet and again opening the valve momentarily.

CAUTION: Before opening the control valve, see that nearby personnel are not in the path of the air flow. Never point the hose at another person.

● Stop the flow of air to a pneumatic tool by closing the control valve at the compressed air outlet before connecting, disconnecting, adjusting, or repairing a pneumatic tool.

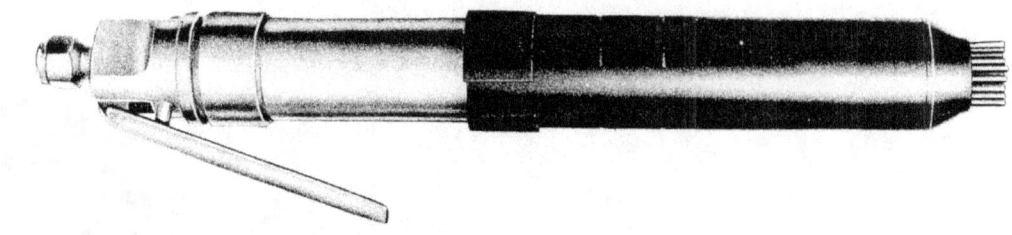

Figure 14.—Needle impact scaler.

Figure 15.—Rotary impact scaler.

PNEUMATIC CHIPPING HAMMER

The pneumatic chipping hammer (fig. 13) consists basically of a steel piston which is reciprocated (moved backward and forward alternately) in a steel barrel by compressed air. On its forward stroke the piston strikes the end of the chisel, which is a sliding fit in a nozzle pressed into the barrel. The rearward stroke is cushioned by compressed air to prevent any metal-to-metal contact. Reciprocation of the piston is automatically controlled by a valve located on the rear end of the barrel. Located on the rear end of the barrel is a grip handle, containing a throttle valve.

The throttle valve is actuated by a throttle lever which protrudes from the upper rear of the grip handle for thumb operation. Projecting from the butt of the handle is an air inlet. The handle is threaded onto the barrel and is prevented from unscrewing by a locking ring. Surrounding and retaining the locking ring is an exhaust deflector. This deflector may be located in any of four positions around the barrel in order to throw the stream of exhaust air in the desired direction.

The pneumatic hammer may be used for beveling, calking or beading operations, and for drilling in brick, concrete, and other masonry.

Chipping hammers should not be operated without safety goggles and all other persons in the immediate vicinity of the work should wear goggles.

While working never point the chipping hammer in such a direction that other personnel might be struck by an accidentally ejected tool. When chipping alloy steel or doing other heavy work, it is helpful to dip the tool in engine lubricating oil about every 6 inches of the cut and make sure the cutting edge of the tool is sharp and clean. This will allow faster and easier cutting and will reduce the possibility of the tool breaking.

When nearing the end of a cut, ease off on the throttle lever to reduce the intensity of the blows. This will avoid any possibility of the chip or tool flying.

If for any reason you have to lay the chipping hammer down, always remove the attachment tool from the nozzle. Should the chipping hammer be accidentally started when the tool is free, the blow of the piston will drive the tool out of the nozzle with great force and may damage equipment or injure personnel.

NEEDLE AND ROTARY IMPACT SCALERS

Needle and rotary scalers (figs. 14 and 15) are used to remove rust, scale, and old paint from metallic and masonry surfaces. You must be especially careful when using these tools since they will "chew" up anything in their path. Avoid getting the power line or any part of your body in their way.

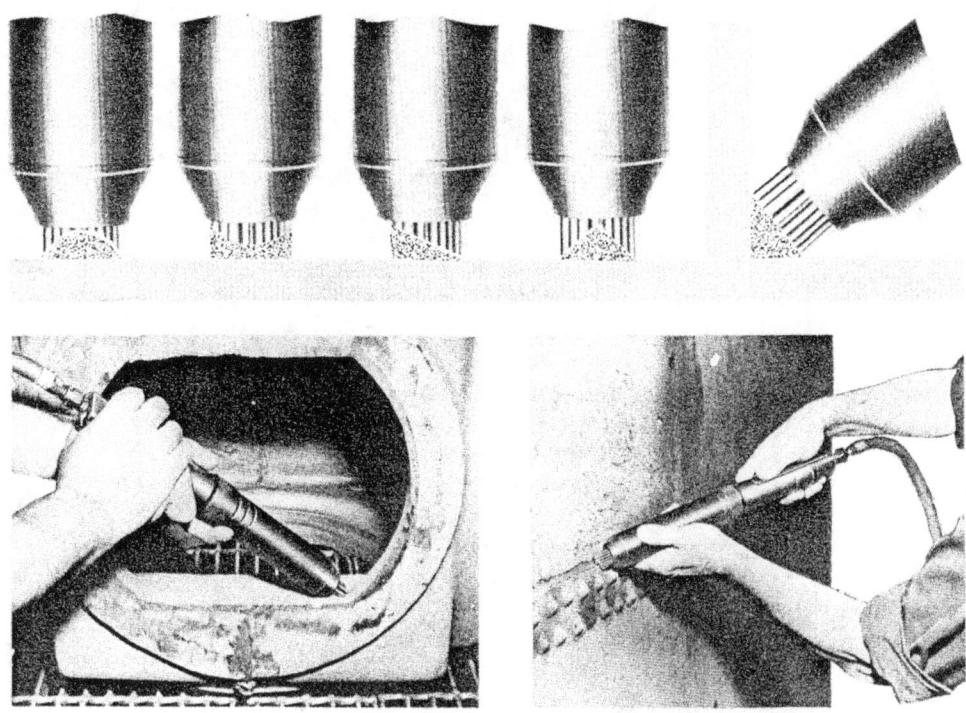

Figure 16.—Needle scaler operations.

Needle scalers accomplish their task with an assembly of individual needles impacting on a surface hundreds of times a minute. The advantage of using individual needles is that irregular surfaces can be cleaned readily. See the operations and how the needle scaler self-adjusts to the contour of various surfaces in figure 16.

The rotary scaling and chipping tool, sometimes called a "jitterbug," has a bundle of cutters or chippers for scaling or chipping (fig. 15). In use, the tool is pushed along the surface to be scaled and the rotating chippers do the work. Replacement bundles of cutters are available when the old ones are worn.

BE SURE YOU ARE NOT DAYDREAMING when you use the rotary scaler.

PORTABLE PNEUMATIC
IMPACT WRENCH

The portable pneumatic impact wrench (fig. 17) is designed for installing or removing nuts and bolts. The wrench comes in different sizes and is classified by the size of the square anvil on the drive end. The anvil is equipped with a socket lock which provides positive locking of the socket wrenches or attachments. The wrench has a built-in oil reservoir and an adjustable air valve regulator which adjusts the torque output of the wrench. The torque regulator reduces the possibility of shearing or damaging threads when installing nuts and bolts to their required tension.

Nearly all pneumatic wrenches operate most efficiently on an air pressure range of 80 to 90 psi. A variation in excess of plus or minus 5 pounds is serious. Lower pressure causes a decrease in the driving speeds while higher pressure causes the wrench to overspeed with subsequent abnormal wear of the motor impact mechanisms.

The throttle lever located at the rear of the pneumatic wrench provides the means for starting and stopping the wrench. Depressing the throttle lever starts the wrench in operation. Upon release, the lever raises to its original position stopping the wrench.

The valve stem is seated beneath the pivot end of the throttle lever. Most wrenches have a window cut in the throttle lever so that the markings on the upper surface of the valve stem will be visible. Two letters, "F" and "R," have been engraved on the head of the

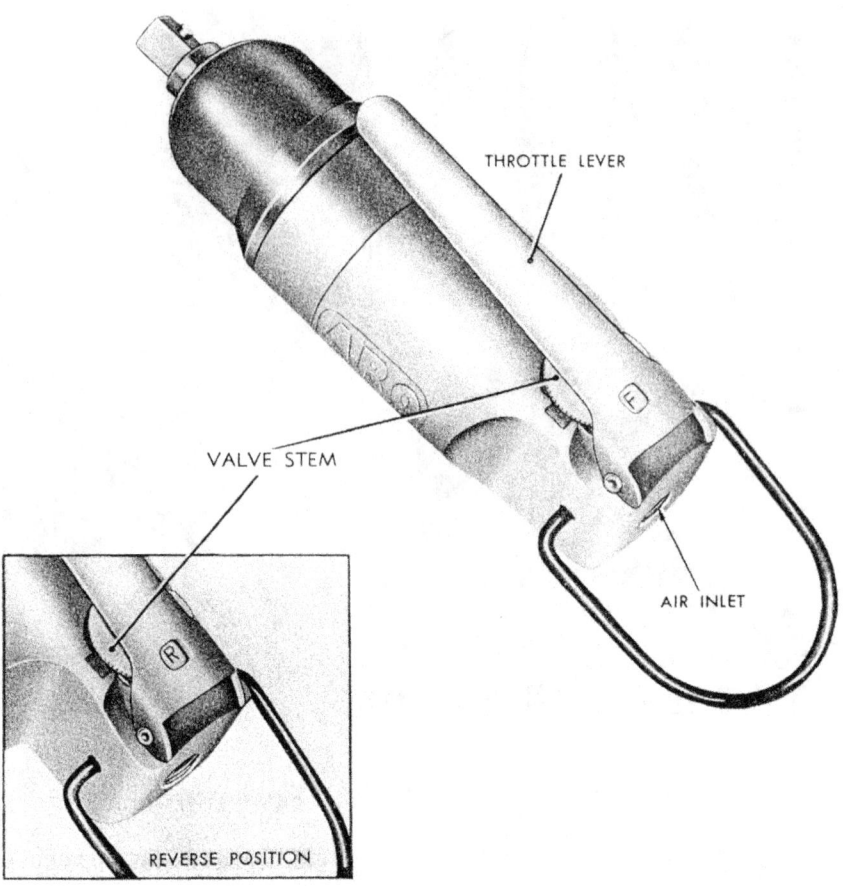

Figure 17.—Portable pneumatic impact wrench.

valve stem to indicate the forward (clockwise) and reverse (counterclockwise) rotation of the anvil. To change from forward to reverse rotation, or vice versa, turn the valve stem 180° until the desired marking is visible through the window in the throttle lever. When the valve stem is in proper position, the valve stem pin engages a recess on the under side of the valve stem, preventing accidental turning of the stem.

The air valve regulator is located at the bottom and towards the rear of the wrench. Using a screwdriver and altering the setting of the air regulator up to 90°, either to the right or left, reduces the torque from full power to zero power.

Before operating the pneumatic impact wrench make sure the socket or other attachment you are using is properly secured to the anvil. It is always a good idea to operate the wrench free of load in both forward and reverse directions to see that it operates properly. Check the installation of the air hose to make sure it is in accordance with the manufacturer's recommendation.

IV. COMMON POWER MACHINE TOOLS

Small power machine tools are, generally speaking, not portable. All work that is to be done must be brought to the shop where the machine is set up. Only the most common types of power machine tools will be discussed in this chapter. The drill press and the bench grinder may be found in several shops aboard ship or on shore stations. They are tools that are not confined to operation by men of any one particular rating but may be used by men of several ratings.

DRILL PRESS

The drill press (fig. 18) is an electrically operated power machine that was originally designed as a metal-working tool. Available

COMMON POWER TOOLS

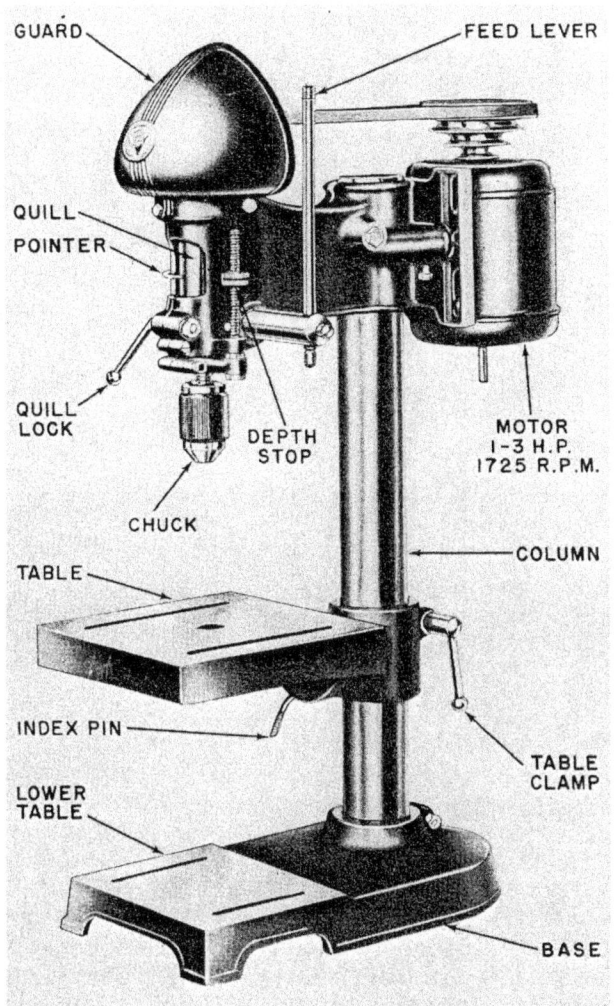

Figure 18.—Drill press.

diameter. The driving motors range in size from 1/3 hp to 3 hp.

The motor is mounted to a bracket at the rear of the head assembly and designed to permit V-belt changing for desired spindle speed without removing the motor from its mounting bracket. Four spindle speeds are obtained by locating the V-belt on any one of the four steps of the spindle-driven and motor-driven pulleys.

The controls of drill presses are all similar. The terms "right" and "left" are relative to the operator's position standing in front of and facing the drill press. Forward applies to movement toward the operator. Rearward applies to movement away from the operator.

The power switch (fig. 19) is located on the right side of the head assembly. The power cord is placed in the power receptacle and the motor started by placing the switch in the "ON" position.

The spindle and quill feed handle (fig. 19) is located on the lower right-front side of the head assembly. Pulling forward and down on any one of the three spindle and quill feed handles, which point upward at the time, moves the spindle and quill assembly downward. Release the feed handle and the spindle and quill assembly will return to the retracted or upper position by spring action.

The quill lock handle (fig. 20) enables the drill press to be used as a milling tool and is located at the lower left-front side of the head assembly. Turn the quill lock handle clockwise to lock the quill at a desired operating position. Release the quill by turning the quill lock handle counterclockwise. However, in most cases, the quill lock handle will be in the released position.

The head lock handle (fig. 20) is located at the left-rear side of the head assembly. Turn the head lock handle clockwise to lock the head assembly at a desired vertical height on the bench column. Turn the headlock handle counterclockwise to release the head assembly. When operating the drill press, the head lock handle must be tight at all times.

The head collar support lock handle (fig. 19) is located at the right side of the head collar support and below the head assembly. The handle locks the head collar support, which secures the head vertically on the bench column, and prevents the head from dropping when the head lock handle is released. Turn the head

accessories, plus jigs and special techniques, now make it a versatile wood-working tool as well.

There are two basic types of drill presses used in the shop; the bench-type and the upright-type. These are basically the same, the difference being in the mounting. As the names suggest, the bench-type drill press is mounted on a work bench and the upright-type drill press is mounted on a pedestal on the floor.

Drill presses are manufactured in a number of sizes. Only the small size drill press will be discussed in this text. The drill presses most commonly found in shops in the Navy have a capacity to drill holes in metal up to 1 inch in

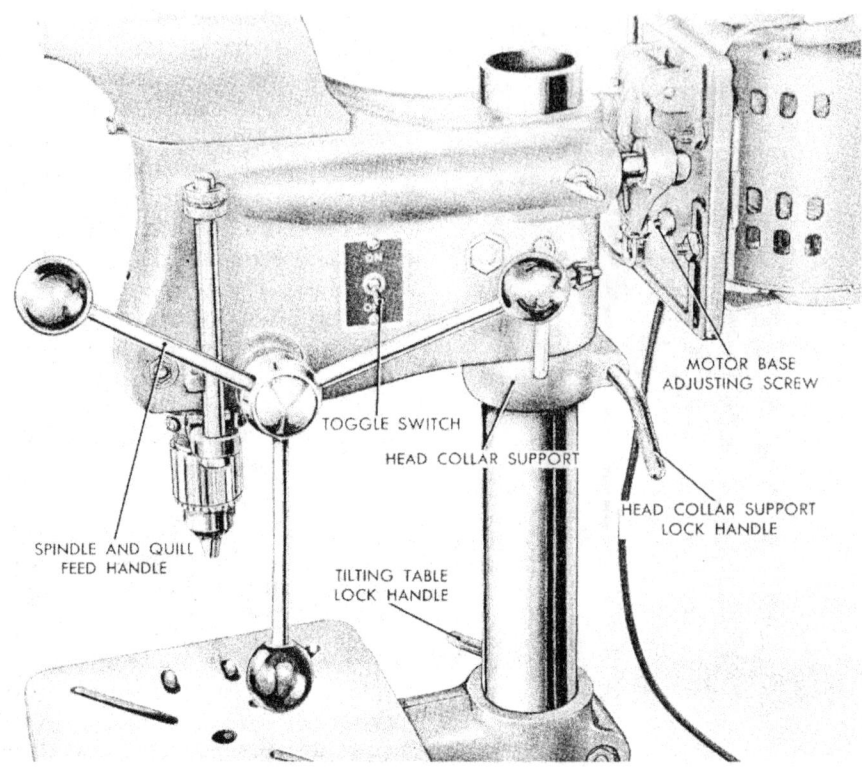

Figure 19.—Drill press controls—right side view.

collar support lock handle clockwise to lock the support to the bench column and counterclockwise to release the support. When operating the drill press, the head collar support lock handle must be tight at all times.

The tilting table lock handle (fig. 19) is located at the left-rear side of the tilting table bracket. Turn the tilting table lock handle counterclockwise to release the tilting table bracket so it can be moved up and down or around the bench column. Lock the tilting table assembly at desired height by turning the lock handle clockwise. When operating the drill press, the tilting table lock handle must be tight at all times.

The tilting table lockpin (S, fig. 21) is located below the tilting table assembly (T, fig. 21). The lockpin secures the table at a horizontal or 45° left or right from the horizontal position. To tilt the table left or right from its horizontal position, remove the lockpin and turn the table to align the lockpin holes. Insert the lockpin through the table and bracket holes after desired position is obtained.

The depth gage rod adjusting and locknuts (BB and CC, fig. 21) are located on the depth gage rod (Z, fig. 21). The purpose of the adjusting and locknuts is to regulate depth drilling. Turn the adjusting and locknut clockwise to decrease the downward travel of the spindle. The locknut must be secured against the adjusting nut when operating the drill press.

When operating a drill press make sure the drill is properly secured in the chuck and that the work you are drilling is properly secured in position. Do not remove the work from the tilting table or mounting device until the drill press has stopped.

Operate the spindle and quill and feed handles with a slow, steady pressure. If too much pressure is applied, the V-belt may slip in the pulleys, the twist drill may break, or the starting switch in the motor may open and stop the drill press. If the motor should stop because of overheating, the contacts of the starting switch will remain open long enough for the motor to cool, then automatically close to resume normal operation. Always turn the toggle switch to "OFF" position while the motor is cooling.

COMMON POWER TOOLS

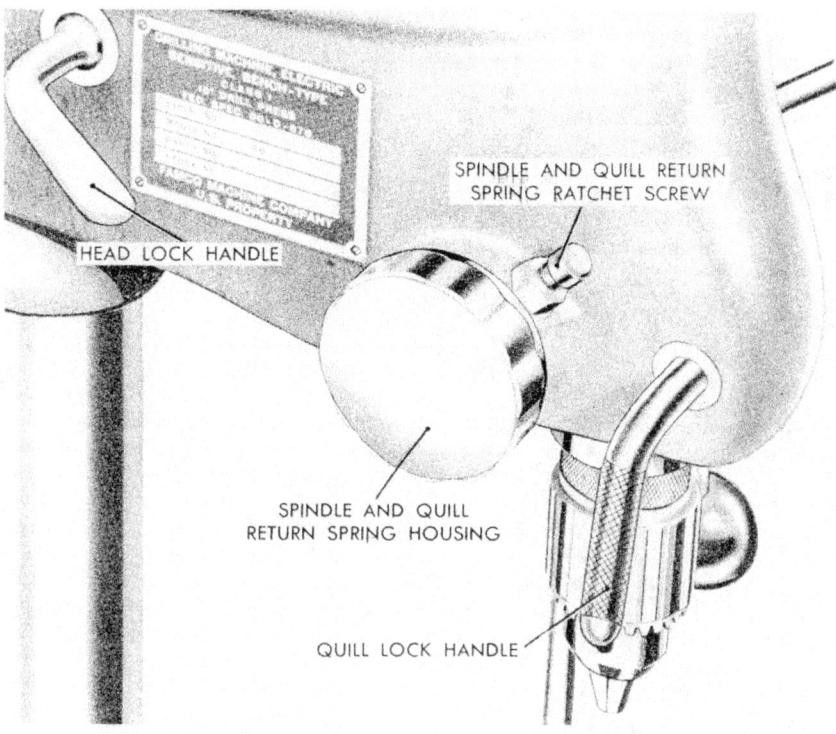

Figure 20.—Drill press controls—left side view.

Check occasionally to make sure all locking handles are tight, and that the V-belt is not slipping and adjust as necessary in accordance with the manufacturer's manual.

Before operating any drill press, visually inspect the drill press to determine if all parts are in the proper place, secure, and in good operating condition. Check all assemblies, such as the motor, head, pulleys, and bench for loose mountings.

While the drill press is operating, be alert for any sounds that may be signs of trouble, such as squeaks or unusual noise. Report any unusual or unsatisfactory performance to the petty officer in charge of the shop.

After operating a drill press, wipe off all dirt, oil, and metal particles. Inspect the V-belt to make sure no metal chips are imbedded in the driving surfaces.

BENCH GRINDER

The electric bench grinder (fig. 22) is designed for hand grinding operations, such as sharpening chisels or screw drivers, grinding drills, removing excess metal from work, and smoothing metal surfaces. It is usually fitted with both a medium grain and fine grain abrasive wheel; the medium wheel is satisfactory for rough grinding where a considerable quantity of metal has to be removed, or where a smooth finish is not important. For sharpening tools or grinding to close limits of size, the fine wheel should be used as it removes metal slower, gives the work a smooth finish and does not generate enough heat to anneal the cutting edges.

When a deep cut is to be taken on work or a considerable quantity of metal removed, it is often practical to grind with the medium wheel first and finish up with the fine wheel. Most bench grinders are so made that wire brushes, polishing wheels, or buffing wheels can be substituted for the removable grinding wheels.

To protect the operator during the grinding operation, an eye shield and wheel guard are provided for each grinding wheel. A tool rest is provided in front of each wheel to rest and

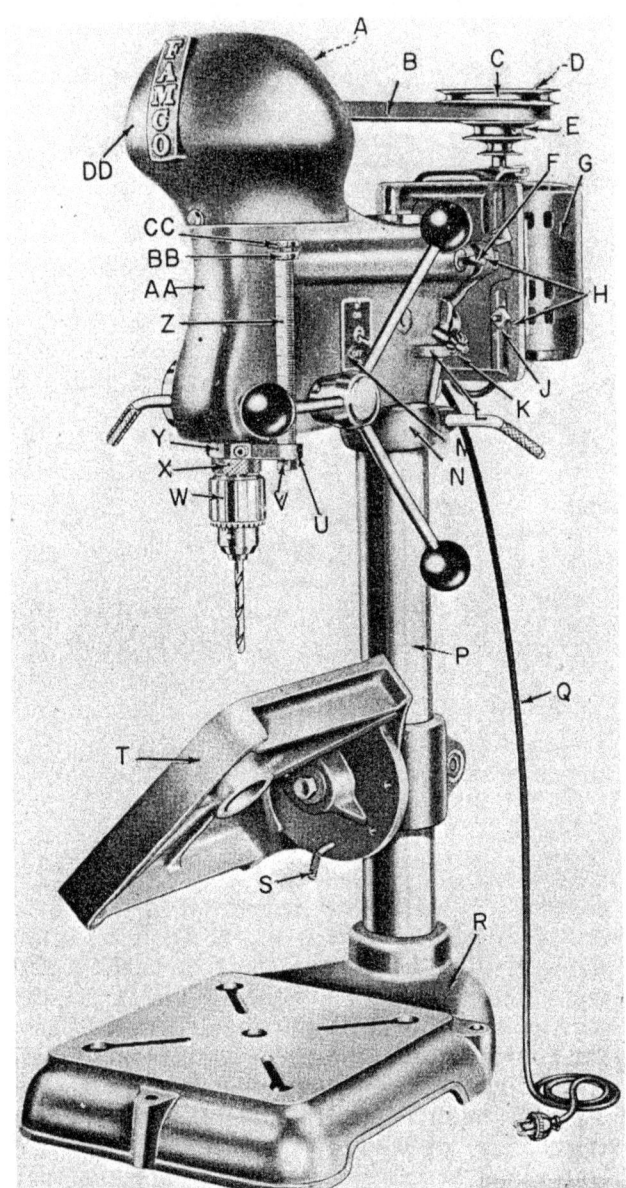

A	SPINDLE DRIVEN PULLEY
B	V-BELT
C	MOTOR DRIVE PULLEY
D	1/8 SQ x 1 SQ-END KEY
E	NO 10-24 x 5/8 HDLS SET SCREW
F	MOTOR BRACKET STUD THUMBSCREW
G	MOTOR
H	MOTOR BASE AND BRACKET ASSEMBLY
J	1/4-20NC 2 x 1 SQ-NECK RD-HD CARRIAGE BOLT AND 1/4-20NC-2 SQ NUT
K	DRILL CHUCK KEY
L	DRILL CHUCK KEY BRACKET
M	TOGGLE SWITCH PLATE
N	HEAD COLLAR SUPPORT
P	BENCH COLUMN
Q	CORD
R	BENCH BASE
S	TILTING TABLE LOCKPIN
T	TILTING TABLE ASSEMBLY
U	DEPTH GAGE ROD BRACKET
V	HEX NUT
W	DRILL CHUCK
X	CHUCK KNOCKOUT COLLAR
Y	SPINDLE AND QUILL ASSEMBLY
Z	DEPTH GAGE ROD
AA	HEAD ASSEMBLY
BB	DEPTH GAGE ROD ADJUSTING NUT
CC	DEPTH GAGE ROD LOCKNUT
DD	SPINDLE DRIVEN PULLEY GUARD

Figure 21.—Drill press nomenclature.

guide the work during the grinding procedure. The rests are removable, if necessary, for grinding odd-shaped or large work.

When starting a grinder, turn it on and stand to one side until the machine comes up to full speed. There is always a possibility that a wheel may fly to pieces when coming up to full speed. Never force work against a cold wheel; apply work gradually to give the wheel an opportunity to warm. You thereby minimize the possibility of breakage.

Handle grinding wheels carefully. Before replacing a wheel always check it for cracks. Make sure that a fiber or rubber gasket is in place between each side of the wheel and its retaining washer. Tighten the spindle nut just enough to hold the wheel firmly; if the nut is tightened too much the clamping strain may

COMMON POWER TOOLS

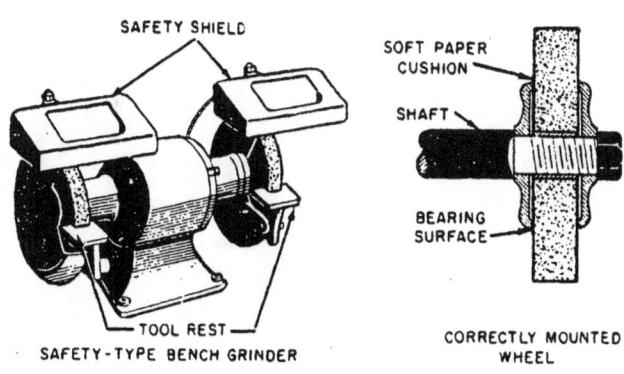

Figure 22.—Bench grinder and wheel.

damage the wheel. When selecting a replacement wheel, ascertain that the grinder will not exceed the manufacturer's recommended speed for the wheel.

When grinding, always keep the work moving across the face of the wheel; grinding against the same spot on the wheel will cause grooves to be worn into the face of the wheel. Keep all wheel guards tight and in place. Always keep the tool rest adjusted so that it just clears the wheel and is at or just below the center line of the wheel, to prevent accidental jamming of work between tool rest and wheel.

Wear goggles, even if eye shields are attached to the grinder. Keep your thumbs and fingers out of the wheel.